"BIGOTRY!"

RECENT TITLES IN
CONTRIBUTIONS IN POLITICAL SCIENCE
Series Editor: Bernard K. Johnpoll

Morris Hillquit: A Political History of an American Jewish Socialist
Norma Fain Pratt

The Establishment in Texas Politics: The Primitive Years, 1938-1957
George Norris Green

When Europe Speaks with One Voice: The External Relations of the European Community
Phillip Taylor

Project SEARCH: The Struggle for Control of Criminal Information in America
Gordon Karl Zenk

Unequal Americans: Practices and Politics of Intergroup Relations
John Slawson

The Constitution of Silence: Essays on Generational Themes
Marvin Rintala

International Conflict in an American City: Boston's Irish, Italians, and Jews, 1935-1944
John F. Stack, Jr.

The Fall and Rise of the Pentagon: American Defense Policies in the 1970s
Lawrence J. Korb

Calling a Truce to Terror: The American Response to International Terrorism
Ernest Evans

Spain in the Twentieth Century World: Essays on Spanish Diplomacy, 1898-1978
James W. Cortada

From Rationality to Liberation: The Evolution of Feminist Ideology
Judith A. Sabrosky

Truman's Crises: A Political Biography of Harry S. Truman
Harold F. Gosnell

To the
Seventh Sister

Contents

Preface

As INDICATED IN the acknowledgments, this study was originally researched and written in 1964-65, but it was then extended to include the results of the 1968 election and rewritten in 1970. The original focus was upon the growing importance of ethnic politics and the declining role of political parties, especially urban "machines," in determining electoral outcomes in the United States. Since that time another force has come to be recognized as a latent but nevertheless dominant one in American politics and social life—that of sexism. With that recognition, or perhaps because of it, the role of women in society and in politics has begun to shift, and this study was revised in 1978 in order to take account of that changing role.

This case, therefore, might be considered a classic in at least one sense: three of the most important factors in pre- and post-Vietnam politics in the United States were all prominent, and tested themselves against each other, in the preliminary battles that occurred on the rather tiny stage of this 1964 senatorial campaign in Pennsylvania. Somewhat like the way in which the Spanish Civil War served as the dress rehearsal for World War II, this election gave witness to the continuing decline of the urban political machine, foreshadowed the rise of ethnic politics in the later 1960s and 1970s, and was one of the early indicators of some of the obstacles that women in the 1970s would face in their renewed battle for political equality.

The details of this campaign are tawdry in parts, as is much of American politics all too frequently. But the forces they demonstrate and the patterns of interactions they reveal are all too powerful and real. They show, for example, the interaction of class and ideology—the cleavages that exist between the blue-collar ethnic and the upper-class liberal—as well as the all too frequent readiness of the male politician to sacrifice the political aspirations of a staunch party loyalist who happens to be female to the "realities" of political life. The study of this campaign also reveals that a machine, even one in decline or one that has only a peripheral hold upon the allegiance of its adherents, may, nevertheless, have a considerable impact upon the political events of its locale—through its negative actions or strategic inactions, if not through positive design.

The protagonists within the Democratic party—the party whose machine we here examine—consisted of an Italian-American judge (Justice Michael A. Musmanno) chosen by that party's hierarchy to satisfy the power proclivities of a particular city branch (Philadelphia), a woman (Miss Genevieve Blatt)[1] selected by the liberal-reform elements of the party to stand against that branch, and a patrician leader of the liberal reformers (Senator Joseph S. Clark) who appeared to understand little of the cultural and socioeconomic forces that held his own party together.

This case details how gaps in understanding and communication can exist among people who are presumed to have the same goals, but who cannot, because of the differences in their interests and their circumstances, comprehend that those goals may be interpreted and operationalized in totally different ways by each differing individual and interest group; in other words, goals are abstract, but the actions and words and deeds into which they are translated and from which they were abstracted are not. This case also shows how one woman came close to becoming the *first* woman senator of the United States to be elected to a full term of office without having stepped into the shoes of a dead husband on the way.[2] She didn't make it—and in the fourteen years since, with one questionable exception,[3] no one else has either.

There is one other sense in which this case can be considered a classic: it chronicles one of the longest primary battles in the history of American politics. This was a primary that began with the filing by the second of the two major contenders for the Democratic nomination of February 18, 1964, and did not end until the United States Supreme Court refused to hear the final appeal on the outcome—October 12—a total of 236 days! Had the Court not refused, there is every reason to believe that the senatorial election could not possibly have been held that year, and that it might have had to be delayed by at least one, and maybe as much as two years. As it was, the events of this primary led to the rather staggering result that the Democratic candidate for the United States Senate in Pennyslvania (Miss Blatt) lost that election to her Republican opponent (Senator Hugh Scott) by 70,000 votes, while Lyndon Johnson was winning the presidency statewide by 1.4 million votes.

The facts of this campaign, no matter how depicted, or how much one may want to understate them, border on the bizarre. The reader will probably find it difficult to believe some of the things he or she will read here; despite the fact that the author witnessed many of them first hand, she too had difficulty believing them. So heated were the emotions aroused by this primary, that its impact continued to be felt to the end of the decade. The statewide party organization, established by the western Allegheny County segment of the party, never completely recovered from the blow; and the Philadelphia city organization, which precipitated the conflict, staggered into the next decade a somewhat altered entity.

Attitudes change, but very slowly. The American political party is even more enfeebled today than it was in 1964.[4] The number of Independents continues to climb—having already left the Republicans in third place while creeping rapidly up behind the Democrats. And the blue-collar ethnic continues to struggle with the intellectual liberal for control of the Democratic party. In some areas the liberal has been replaced by the black as the dominant element for reform, and the conflict has tended to look like a race war. Where blacks have won, however, they have succeeded in setting up their own organization—this time with the blue-collar white ethnic in the minority (as in Newark, New Jersey).

But women have an even longer way to go. Their concerns have always been subordinated to the "larger" social and economic issues of their times. Their battle may have become a bit more vocal than that of the white ethnics in recent years—perhaps as much because of the fading of the personal career of George Wallace as because of the rise in the Women's Movement. And blacks—now beginning to enter the middle class—still seek to find their own true homeland in American politics. But all that is required to demonstrate how viable and potentially explosive all these factors remain, is for a particular issue or a strong personality to come along and galvanize the opinions and mobilize the troops for action. Today it may be the Equal Rights Amendment—but tomorrow a black or a Jewish president?

In revising this manuscript a second time, I have used the advantage of hindsight to increase certain emphases while decreasing others. I have also added a few observations here and there to make the piece more reflective of the third of the three political elements than had originally been elaborated upon—that of sexism. This was necessary, because at that time the term had not even been coined. Betty Friedan had just published her book *The Feminine Mystique,* which furnished the rallying cry for the revival of feminism in political life. But women had to wait for the combined forces of the Civil Rights Movement and the anti-Vietnam War mobilization, to give them the courage to face the prospect of radical action in behalf of their own rights.

The "end of ideology" passivist of the 1950s required a great deal of "consciousness-raising" and "frustration-awareness" to be able, once again, to take to the streets in political protest. The tradition was not dead in this country—just stifled by the McCarthy era and the postwar struggle for economic affluence. When reawakened, political protest exploded with such a force that two presidents were toppled by it and the entire country was reoriented in its goals and self-image. It was a wiser and sadder electorate that chose Jimmy Carter as its leader in 1976—but one that in so doing also demonstrated its desire to recover its innocence and the harmony of a peaceful, perhaps earlier, time.

Nostalgia for our revolutionary beginnings combined, in 1976, with a strong desire to believe in ourselves, once again, as a "good" people. It may be that this is the reason why the unfinished business of the radical late 1960s and early 1970s still remains basically unfinished at this writing, and why, once again, an end of ideology passivism appears to have crept back into our thoughts and actions, and the pursuit of economic affluence to be uppermost in our aspirations. We do not like to be reminded of our continuing inequities — and so the blacks continue to have the highest unemployment rates of all the American people, and the Equal Rights Amendment remains unadopted. But waves, as every ocean-goer has observed, are always followed by troughs — and then by other waves. If the need is great enough, and articulated clearly and persistently, it will in time be met when the conditions, presumably, are right. But if it continues to be suppressed, one can only await a larger, and perhaps more destructive, wave.

NOTES

1. Miss Genevieve Blatt will be referred to as "Miss Blatt" throughout this study because this was the title she preferred and by which she was known throughout the campaign. The term "Ms" had not yet been coined.

2. Margaret Chase Smith was then the only woman to have been elected to a full term in the Senate on her own, but she first succeeded her husband in the House of Representatives after his death. Maureen Neuberger was also elected to a full term, but to succeed her husband as a member of the Senate. Other women have been elected and/or appointed to fill out the terms of others (in most cases their own husbands) who died in office. But *none* can be said to have won a full term to the Upper House after having built up a political base *exclusively* on her own. See Hope Chamberlin's *A Minority of Members: Women in the U. S. Congress* (New York: New American Library, 1973).

3. In 1978 one woman, Ms. Nancy Landon Kassebaum, did win election to the Senate without succeeding a dead husband; but even here one must wonder whether or not she could have done so had her father not been the very popular (in Kansas) nonagenarian, and former 1936 Republican candidate for the presidency, Alf Landon.

4. Editorial opinion following the 1978 congressional and gubernatorial elections appeared to be virtually unanimous on this point. See especially Lance Morrow, "The Decline of the Parties," *Time* 112 (November 20, 1978): 42.

Acknowledgments

THE ASSISTANCE AND encourage-
ment of a considerable number of people went into the writing
of this book. The author was privileged to be a recipient of a
Faculty Fellowship in State and Local Politics awarded by the
National Center for Education in Politics in 1964-65. Part of her
assignment was to serve as a member of the campaign staff of
Miss Genevieve Blatt, one of the principals in this study, from
June of 1964 until the election. She then spent the rest of her
fellowship year conducting the research that made this study
possible. The sixty-one people who granted her lengthy interviews
and supplied her with many unpublished documents are to be
thanked and are all listed alphabetically in Appendix 2. An additional twenty-eight respondents to a questionnaire mailed to a
select number of campaign volunteers helped shed some light on
certain attitudes and events in the 1964 senatorial campaign;
their responses are analyzed in Appendix 1. Professors Bernard
C. Hennessy,[1] Executive Director of the National Center for Education in Politics, and Sidney Wise,[2] Director of the Pennsylvania
Center for Education in Politics, plus several professors at Yale
where she later enjoyed an appointment as a postdoctoral research
fellow—Robert Dahl, Russell Murphy, and others—all offered
suggestions on the treatment of several aspects of the piece.
Legal implications of the reporting of some of the incidents were
reviewed by John T. Mulligan, Esq., of Media, Pennsylvania. At
the time this piece was completed, case studies were falling into
disuse as a method of scientific study for the purpose of theory

building. Their value has since been reaffirmed and more widely accepted by members of the social science community[3]—hence this new and updated version. For this final outcome, Professor Bernard K. Johnpoll,[4] Political Science Editor of Greenwood Press, must be thanked. And for their assistance in securing the funds and personnel to type this final version, the Research Office of the University of Tulsa and Dr. Allen Soltow must be thanked as well.

One more observation before commencing the study: despite the position of the author as a participant-observer in many of the events recorded, all efforts were made to provide as objective an account as was humanly possible. Nevertheless, human failings being what they are, there are bound to be some people who will disagree with certain aspects of the work. To them the author can only reply *"Pace!"* If, however, there are any factual errors in the narrative, then truly the author must be held accountable, but only she and no one else.

NOTES

1. Now with the University of California, Hayward.
2. Franklin and Marshall College, Lancaster, Pa.
3. See Harry Eckstein, "Case Study and Theory in Political Science," in *Strategies of Inquiry, Handbook of Political Science,* vol. 7, ed. Fred I. Greenstein and Nelson W. Polsby (Reading, Mass.: Addison-Wesley, 1975), pp. 79-137.
4. S.U.N.Y., Albany.

"BIGOTRY!"

1

Introduction

ASSUMPTIONS

As POLITICAL SCIENTISTS, reporters, and everyday political observers have been telling us for quite some time now, big city political machines are slowly on their way out in this country. They no longer serve the function they once did, of assisting in the assimilation of immigrants, providing jobs and welfare for the poor, and acting as vehicles of upward mobility for the status-deprived.[1] Schools and welfare bureaucracies now perform the latter two functions on a far broader scale.

Nevertheless, habit, inherited political loyalties and political socialization, plus the increasing concentration of large segments of the population in urban areas, did serve in the 1950s and 1960s to perpetuate the image of the parties as powerful political organizations capable of swinging huge numbers of votes in the direction of their especially favored candidates. The persistence of New Deal issues, and of lower income and ethnic group identification with the Democratic party throughout the Eisenhower administration, also helped to maintain some of the strength of political machines in the cities. Thus, even though the nation was experiencing increasing affluence and the suburbs rather than the cities were fast becoming the major beneficiaries of a new migration, awe of big city political machines by both the candidates and the voters continued to be a psychological fact of political life in those areas that had traditionally been the breeding grounds for such organizations. Pennsylvania was one such area, and the cities of Philadelphia and Pittsburgh were the sites of the two largest and the most powerful machines in the state.

During the 1960s, however, the old New Deal Democratic coalition began to unravel under the stress of this growing affluence and the subsequent weakening of economic ties to the party. A reawakening and intensification of ethnic and racial consciousness and separatism occurred. The old liberal establishment gradually began to move away from its former allies, the blue-collar workers (who in the cities were largely composed of white ethnic groups), and toward the new lower class, the poor blacks.[2] Later, the growing radicalization of college students and young adults as a result of the Civil Rights Movement and the Vietnam War led to an even greater alienation between the blue-collar "hardhats" and the intellectual liberals. Inevitably, such strains not only weakened the Democratic party but the big city machines to which it had fallen heir.

In Pennsylvania the first signs of such a breakup occurred in the 1964 Democratic primary when Genevieve Blatt challenged the party's "endorsed" candidate, Justice Michael Angelo Musmanno, for the nomination to the United States Senate. Immediately thereafter one primary battle followed upon another, as the liberal "reform" groups throughout the state, bit by bit, challenged and defeated each segment of the party in the cities and in the state, again and again, until little remained of the state organization. By 1970 Pittsburgh's machine was in its death-throes, and the city of Philadelphia was being temporarily held together by a quasi-reform, quasi-machine alliance, soon to be replaced by a new coalition of white ethnic elements under the leadership of Mayor Frank Rizzo.

In itself the 1964 primary and its election aftermath were fought on an issue that divided the party on two political dimensions. Initially, the machine and its evils were the main target of the dissenters. However, because the machine at that moment was apparently espousing the cause of one of its traditional clients— an urban immigrant minority—its candidate, the self-opted spokesman for that minority, was able to switch the focus of the debate away from the machine and toward an incident of alleged bigotry. This switch did not occur in time to win the primary for the machine, but it did, to a great extent, cause the "perpetrators" of the "injustice," otherwise known as "reformers," to lose their untarnished images and eventually their political careers in the elections that followed.

The subject of this book is that primary campaign and its aftermath—both for the individuals who figured prominently in the battle and for the party that suffered the consequences. Its purpose is to illuminate three disparate but related phenomena in American political life: the awakening of ethnic political consciousness and the increasing demands of such hitherto inarticulate minority groups for greater recognition in the political arena; the ongoing decline of previously all-powerful city-based political machines; and the then rarely acknowledged fact of political bias against the female sex.

The treatment of these phenomena is based on a series of assumptions and observations. First, that when a minority group feels insecure in the society it is striving to enter, substantial numbers of that group will tend to join together and form protective/fraternal organizations. Given the right stimuli, these organizations will occasionally act as political blocs giving support to those institutions, parties, factions, or individuals that promise to help them attain their goals.

Second, that as people become more affluent and better educated they also tend to become more independent politically and less willing to submit to paternalistic treatment by machines or parties or governments in general. Improvement in economic and social status is correlated with a greater desire for self-determination and participation in political decisionmaking. Thus, while party identification may remain fairly constant throughout life, the tendency to split one's ticket or to vote for selected candidates on criteria other than party affiliation increases as one's economic status and self-esteem rise.

Third, that the old Democratic coalition of upper-middle-class liberals, intellectuals, workers, and mainly white ethnic groups was perhaps temporarily being replaced by a new coalition of upper-middle-class liberals, intellectuals, and blacks, as the white ethnic groups and workers began to move into the ranks of the middle classes. These social and economic changes, plus the political events of the 1960s (Civil Rights, Vietnam), are probably what caused the decline of the big city machines, just as they are very likely responsible for the split in the national Democratic party which occurred in 1968.[3]

Fourth, that the rapid changes in the social and economic order in this country are having their effect upon the structure of the political parties as well as upon the groups that compose them. Not only are the machines gradually dying out, but parallel independent political organizations are cropping up all over the country — some calling themselves parties (but most not). Practically all are attempting to propose candidates for political office within, or independently of, the traditional parties. They raise money, conduct campaigns, and construct platforms of broad or limited ideological scope — in short, performing functions that in almost every instance were once the exclusive right of legitimate (i.e., legally recognized) political parties. Some of these organizations are nationwide (the American Independent party), some regional (the New Democratic Coalition), and some are nonpartisan and purely issue-oriented (the Common Cause); but practically all hover in a kind of limbo, sometimes cooperating with, but often competing against, the established parties and their candidates. Most of these organizations exist on the opposite ends of the ideological spectrum, thus indicating not only a proliferation of groups and an increase in the percentage of the population that is gradually becoming politically active, but also indicating a tendency toward polarization among the active segment of the American people.

Fifth, that the rank and file of the American people, while becoming more independent of the traditional political parties, are developing a new consensus around political goals such that the older ideological issue clusters, which used to characterize the New Deal era and the coalitions that it engendered, no longer hold their appeal for the American voter. Not only does a larger proportion of the population today consider itself conservative rather than liberal, but the overwhelming percentage of conservative identifiers hold such traditionally nonconservative beliefs as "government ought to see to it that everybody who wants a job can get one," and "government ought to help people get medical care at low cost."[4] For the parties and future political candidates the consequences of these trends will be, in all likelihood, an increase in the degree of nonpartisan appeals in electoral campaigns, and if not the demise of the parties altogether, then certainly a change in their ideological constitutions and/or coalitions; the outlines of such a change are only dimly perceptible today. Not radical left versus radical right perhaps, but some new realignment of ideological issue clusters or interest groups, nevertheless.[5]

Sixth, that the decline of the political party is also being induced by the very reforms that have been put into effect in the past few decades; for example, the freeing of candidates from control by the party hierarchies through the development of alternative sources of funds (Political Action Committees and so on), the increasing use of primaries as a method of nomination to public office, and the increasing reliance upon television and professional campaign managers and polls, even for local elections, thereby reducing the need for party workers in canvassing, getting out the vote, and so forth.

Seventh, that far more powerful than racism is the prejudice that all races appear to have concerning the proper role of women in society. This prejudice manifests itself in virtually every aspect of male-female interaction, but is perhaps most powerful in the political arena. The Women's Movement has made some headway in the past few years in attempting to change the situation, but full equality of the sexes in politics, as well as in all aspects of employment and social life, is still, unfortunately, a long way off.[6]

Finally, that people in power try to remain in power — certainly a truism by anyone's reading of political history. This particular case is no different. When factions exist they invariably battle for supremacy. Occasionally their battles threaten the body politic. This one did not, but the perceptions of those involved without doubt caused them to conclude that some of their individual and collective interests were being threatened — and in some instances those interests were projected as being of vital importance to the health of the body politic. That some people have a tendency to project their private interests into the political arena is a cliche in modern political science, thanks to the much revered work of Harold Lasswell. This study may well be considered one more detailing a series of such projections by many of the persons involved — by the leadership of the Italian-American community, by Miss Blatt perhaps, by Senator Clark, by Senator Hugh Scott, by Justice Musmanno certainly, and perhaps even by the Philadelphia political machine. What the voters themselves thought is, at this moment, still unknown.

These theories are only assumptions. They will not be proved by this study, but they are critical to the treatment of the topic, nevertheless. The events described will trace the reactions of the active segment of one emerging minority group to a perceived deprivation of dignity at a time when its own sensors told it that such deprivations could no longer be tolerated by reason of its present status and power in the total society. The study will also link the impact of this main break in the machine's control of the party's political life to the many challenges that followed. It will attempt to shed some light on the shape of the political party to come, as revealed by the history of the Pennsylvania Democratic party in the 1960s, and will illuminate certain aspects of the type of opposition a woman running for a major political office in this country is bound to encounter.

This study will not attempt to prove that bigotry of any variety caused any candidate to lose the 1964 election or any subsequent election, although a survey of election statistics is attempted in Appendix 1. It will only recount the events as they occurred and the reactions the candidates and certain leadership groups displayed as those events unfolded. As behavioral research of recent years has only too well documented, there is an enormous gap between attitudes and behavior, between what people say they will do in certain situations and what they actually do when the situation arises.[7]

This study is, however, an attempt to illustrate larger trends through the medium of a single case. The theory it builds is descriptive rather than explanatory. No serious attempt at prediction is made, beyond occasional speculation, because it is a single case. The explanations offered do not derive from this study only, but from the author's familiarity with a large body of behavioral research that has been conducted in this country since the end of World War II, in the areas of voting behavior, political participation and recruitment, attitudes and ideologies, and some of the many by-products of political sociology and psychology. It illustrates how certain political decisions—and blunders—may be made in the course of a campaign, and what calculations—rational, emotional, and political—may go into the making of those decisions. This study shows how some people behave in power situations, and how the context of American politics gives meaning to such behavior.

It is also an attempt at contemporary history. The citations in the body of the book are drawn mainly from the witnesses to these events and from the writings of those who had the opportunity to record them. The documentation in Appendix 1, however, was completed by the author according to the methodology of political research current at that time, and from the resources then available. Any shortcomings that may exist in either of these will, of course, be demonstrated eventually—but at this time little else can be ventured.

Nor does this case present a thesis that is then validated in the conclusion. Three issues were uppermost in the unfolding events: (1) a factional primary battle in which a reform element depicted itself as fighting a corrupt machine, and the machine's reaction in terms of possible retaliation in the general election; (2) a bigotry charge that aroused the politically active segment of a traditionally inactive minority group to threaten similar retaliation; and (3) a latent issue of the sex of one of the candidates. The election results referred to in Appendix 1 do not validate the effect of any of these factors as having been responsible for the final results. The facts presented attest *only* to the reactions of the individuals involved in the campaign—the protagonists, the party workers, the group leaders, the reporters, and others concerned.

Invariably such individuals, being professional opinion makers, believe that their opinions have an impact on those they attempt to lead—that since they are eminently rational human beings, their reasons, their perceptions, their values, being undeniably right, must be the ones that will carry the day. This is the essence of politics, and of conflict. To expect otherwise is to misunderstand the fundamentals of human behavior. Whether one emphasizes the cognitive-evaluative-developmental-psychological aspect

of that behavior, or the "sociology of knowledge" approach—
the cultural-ideological-collective links—what people perceive
influences what they believe. If they singly or collectively perceive
an injustice, they believe their attitudes and actions regarding it
are justified. Uncertainty is not something a person readily
admits to—not if one is a politician, and then certainly not in
public.

In this case there is much evidence of the publicly stated perceptions, attitudes, and actions of several particular political
elites; there is no (or very little) evidence that the public at large
saw things the same way and then acted upon those beliefs. This
latter link—between the attitude and the action—is extremely
difficult to establish even under well-controlled laboratory conditions; in fact, the opposite conclusion seems to have almost as
much validity (as Stanley Milgram's experiments on authority
have shown).[8]

Therefore, one cannot present the thesis that the three major
factors that the elites perceived as the controlling ones in the
primary and election campaign for the United States Senate in
Pennsylvania in 1964 clearly influenced the election's outcome.
Other factors may have been equally responsible. Lacking extensive in-depth evidence that just was not available then, or
today, one is forced to stay with the elite data. It may be unsatis-
factory, but it does show how individuals and elites did react
under certain circumstances. More than this it just is not possible
to do.

To state, for example, that under similar circumstances other
people would react in the same way would be going too far.
Before one could do so, one would have to conduct experiments
(simulations, perhaps) that would demonstrate that the reactions
of the individuals portrayed here were "normative" in the statistical sense rather than unique. At this point the question of
personality would inevitably arise, for how could one possibly
duplicate this situation in an experiment *without* programing in
the personal and perhaps unique reactions at certain strategic
points that both Senator Clark and Justice Musmanno exhibited?

Nevertheless, a study such as this still adds to our store of
knowledge of politics and human interactions in a substantial
and significant way. For even the unique has its message—as the

George and George study of Woodrow Wilson demonstrated some years ago.[9] Maybe some scholar of the future will, in reading this, be inspired to attempt a psychobiographical study of one of the protagonists — Justice Musmanno, perhaps. If the documentation were available (letters, diaries, notebooks) it might make a very worthy piece.

TWO SCENARIOS

In American political history 1964 was a most unusual year. After two decades of presidential politics dominated by New Deal liberalism, a revivified and reformulated conservatism made its first bid for the presidency in the person of Barry Goldwater. The new conservative movement did not affect the northeastern part of the country as much as it did the south and southwest, however, and in the Pennsylvania senatorial election — second in importance only to the presidential race that year — the clash was actually between a moderate-liberal Republican, Hugh Scott, and a "Stevensonian" Democrat, Genevieve Blatt.

Hugh Scott, of course, was the incumbent. The path by which Miss Blatt became his opponent in that race was a circuitous one involving one of the most bitter Democratic primaries in the state's history. It was a primary that at first simply juxtaposed a reform Democrat against the machine — a scenario so familiar to American politics that it might even have been considered a cliche. But the third major persona of this drama, party choice Justice Michael Angelo Musmanno, Miss Blatt's opponent, refused to play the traditional role of villain or pawn of the machine, and instead focused the election on a totally different and indeed far more contemporary scenario: that of the beleaguered and "oppressed" ethnic American fighting valiantly against the "evil and bigoted" establishment.

This second scenario was introduced too late to completely replace the first in the primary, but it did come in large part to dominate the general election. In the opinion of the majority of the political observers involved, it was one of the major causes of the defeat of the Democratic candidate, Genevieve Blatt, during the landslide Johnson victory of that year.[10]

The following narrative is not an attempt to measure definitively the effect of this new scenario in terms of actual votes (although something of this sort is attempted in Appendix 1). Pinning down the quantitative effect of any campaign strategy or technique is not as easy as it seems—even when one has a polling establishment to fall back on for validation: witness the difficulty of determining the effects of the television debates between Kennedy and Nixon in 1960.[11] Rather this is a case history of one particular battle for political power between a spokesman for an emerging vocal urban minority—in this instance the Italian-American—and the forces it believed to be the chief obstacle to that power and social acceptance, the liberal establishment. The fact that this split between two large segments of the New Deal coalition in the Pennsylvania Democratic party foreshadowed by four years a similar threat to the national party—the hardhats versus the liberals—is also significant. At that time the ideological and social alignments of the entire nation were in flux and in the process of being redefined. The final outcome of this process is not yet known, but in 1970 the Republicans thought they might be able to piece together a new majority coalition by applying a "southern strategy" and by appealing to "middle" (and "silent") "America."[12] The congressional elections of that year appear to have demolished that hope, but some sort of realignment may yet occur.

In this particular primary, however, one important factor that emerged was the failure of either side—liberal or ethnic group—to view the other in any saving light. Both sides saw themselves as right or good and depicted their opponents as wrong or evil, in the typical manicheist-adversary-paranoid style of American politics, but with one difference. Whereas prior to the mid-sixties, in most political battles in this country, bitterness of feeling may have run deep, it seldom went beyond the bounds of civility, where the opponents could no longer see each other as reasonable people and "kiss and make up" after the dust had settled. This had been (and still is basically) the prevailing tradition of politics in this country since 1800—except during the Civil War. It is, in fact, one of the few factors that makes politics in any democracy possible at all.[13] For so long as interests do not become too conflicting or the resulting enmities too blinding, compromise and peace are still possible and democratic government can still operate. But in the 1960s ideological, moral, social, economic, regional, and ethnic forces began to split this country along many different dimensions and the strident voices of unreason, dogma, and even anarchism seemed about to become dominant.

This case study records one such ugly confrontation. It came early in the 1960s so that no blood was shed and no barricades were built. But two long-established political careers were eventually destroyed and the barriers thrown up within the Pennsylvania Democratic party by this conflict continued to affect the politics of the state throughout the rest of the decade.

There were two major reasons for this effect: first, the party organization in Pennsylvania was so drastically divided by its defeat in the 1964 primary that it was unable ever again to win a major political battle against its own dissidents;[14] second, the scenario introduced by Justice Musmanno in this original confrontation was carried over into succeeding elections involving the other primary participants. That is, the "victim of intolerance and discrimination" (Justice Musmanno) won out in the end by relentlessly pursuing his "persecutors" with the "truth" of their evil. Thus, not only did Senator Scott defeat Miss Blatt in 1964 with the help of this issue, but these accusations of bigotry were reintroduced into her unsuccessful campaign for reelection as Secretary of Internal Affairs in 1966. And Senator Clark, her main source of support in that primary and indeed the major protagonist of the drama, met similar opposition in his unsuccessful bid to be reelected to the Senate in 1968.

It is no exaggeration to say that Justice Musmanno exulted in his role as the nemesis and punisher of the evil-doers, or that a considerable number of his most vocal supporters in the ethnic and public news media encouraged him in this role and did everything in their power to help him succeed. The justice, however, did not live to see his final victory over Senator Clark. He died three weeks before the 1968 election, on Columbus Day (ironically), the fourth anniversary of the end of the bitter primary of 1964.

Thus two major strands of political influence that historically tended to be mutually supporting and intertwined, big city machines and ethnic groups, had their solidarity tested. It was perhaps inevitable that the reformers should, in opposing the machine, also find themselves opposing those whom, ideologically, they had traditionally supported. In defeating the machine, therefore, they ran the risk of alienating a major portion of their own political base. To have expected the ethnic groups to react to the issue of reform in the same way that liberal suburbanites did was unrealistic to say the least.

The following case study illustrates the kinds of fissures that can occur in a party or any organization which, for one reason or another, is composed of two elements which refuse to admit any legitimacy to the other's complaints. The situation is a common one; only the details are different.

Italian-Americans, the particular minority that served as the focal point of this clash, were, relatively speaking, politically quiescent as far as major statewide elections were concerned in the early 1960s. They were just beginning to feel their strength in important local elections. For the most part, they had long been content to fill minor positions in county and municipal elections and to be appointed to whatever other offices their numbers seemed to entitle them to. The exceptions, of course, existed in those regions of the state where they were in sufficient strength to acquire considerable political power and where their absence from the upper echelons of political office would have been intolerable.

The Italian-Americans' impact upon state politics was still virtually nil, however, and this lag between numerical weight and political representation was one source of discontent for them. Although census figures indicated that they composed the largest white ethnic minority in the state, no Italian-American had ever been elected to any important statewide office, and until Governor William W. Scranton selected Walter Allesandroni, a Philadelphia lawyer, for the office of attorney general, only one other Italian, former Attorney General Charles J. Margiotti, had ever served in a high executive position in the state of Pennsylvania. Justice Michael Angelo Musmanno was the first person of Italian descent to be elected associate justice of the state's Supreme Court.

It was the Democratic Policy Committee's "last minute" choice of Justice Musmanno to run in the spring primary that led to the controversy forming the nucleus of this study. But first a brief review of the history and demographic composition of Pennsylvania state politics is essential if the events on which this study is based are to be properly understood.

NOTES

1. Elmer E. Cornwell, Jr., "Bosses, Machines, and Ethnic Groups," *The Annals* 353 (May 1964), 24ff.

2. See the introduction to the 1970 edition of *Beyond the Melting Pot* by Nathan Glazer and Daniel P. Moynihan (Cambridge: The Massachusetts Institute of Technology Press, 1970). See also Everett Ladd, Jr., "The New Lines Are Drawn: Class and Ideology in America," *Public Opinion* 1 (July/August 1978), 48-53.

3. For an excellent account of the recent history of ethnic politics in America and the importance of some of the factors outlined above, see Mark R. Levy and Michael S. Kramer, *The Ethnic Factor: How America's Minorities Decide Elections* (New York: Simon and Schuster, 1973).

4. Adam Clymer, " 'Conservatives' Share 'Liberal' View," *The New York Times,* January 22, 1978, p. 1, continued on p. 30.

5. See Arthur H. Miller, Warren E. Miller, Alden S. Raine, and Thad A. Brown, "A Majority Party in Disarray; Policy Polarization in the 1972 Election," *American Political Science Review (APSR)* 60 (September 1976), 753-778; David E. RePass, "Comment: Political Methodologies in Disarray: Some Alternative Interpretations of the 1972 Election," *APSR,* 814-831; and Arthur H. Miller and Warren E. Miller, "Ideology in the 1972 Election: Myth or Reality—A Rejoinder," *APSR,* 832-899.

6. An especially good source on this topic is Jane S. Jaquette, ed., *Women in Politics* (New York: John Wiley & Sons, 1974).

7. Irwin Deutscher, *What We Say/What We Do: Sentiments and Acts* (Glenview, Ill.: Scott, Foresman & Co., 1973).

8. Stanley Milgram, *Obedience to Authority* (New York: Harper and Row, 1974).

9. Alexander L. George and Juliette L. George, *Woodrow Wilson and Colonel House: A Personality Study* (New York: Dover, 1956).

10. See below p. 134ff, p. 161ff.

11. Sidney Kraus, ed., *The Great Debates* (Bloomington: Indiana University Press, 1962).

12. Kevin Phillips, *The Emerging Republican Majority* (New York: Doubleday, 1969).

13. Herbert McCloskey, "Consensus and Ideology in American Politics," *APSR* 58 (June 1964), 361-379.

14. Milton Shapp confronted and defeated the party's choice for the gubernatorial nomination in 1966 and in 1970; Arlen Specter switched his allegiance to the Republican party and fought the Philadelphia machine to become district attorney in 1965; Mayor Tate replaced the Philadelphia party chairman as the chief power in the city organization after his election in 1967; and in Pittsburgh itself, that bastion of organizational strength and rectitude, a young reformer, Peter Flaherty, dealt the death blow to the Lawrence-Barr organization by defeating it decisively in the mayoralty election of 1969.

2

Scenario I:
The Reformers
versus
The Machine

BACKGROUND

PRIOR TO 1947, Pennsylvania, with the sole important exception of the city of Pittsburgh, was a predominantly Republican state—in other than presidential contests. The New Deal had had very little impact upon state and local politics generally. Its major effects were felt only in Allegheny County, which embraces Pittsburgh, and the scattered coal- and steel-producing counties of the southwest and northeast. Philadelphia, the most heavily populated city in the state and its chief business and educational center, was still "corrupt but content" as it had been since the Civil War; it had to await a major upheaval among the civic and business leaders of the city before a shift to "reform" and Democratic politics was possible.

With the capture of the Philadelphia row office elections in 1949 by "reform-team" Richardson Dilworth and Joseph S. Clark,[1] a gradual shift began in the state balance of power toward the Democrats. The trend culminated in 1954 with the election of York County farmer George Leader, the first Democratic governor in twenty years, and only the second since the turn of the century. Another Democrat, Mayor David L. Lawrence of Pittsburgh, both a reformer and a party regular, successfully followed him four years later. Republican Congressman William W. Scranton recaptured the Governor's Mansion in 1962 by projecting a similar "good government" image.

By 1964 the state's political complexion resembled that of her sister states in the middle Atlantic region. Pennsylvania was

Democratic and liberal in the cities, Republican and conservative in the rural areas, with the suburbs predominantly Republican and moderate. In statewide campaigns the population of the cities so far outweighed that of the rural areas that a Democrat could now conceivably win an election by carrying as few as sixteen counties out of a total of sixty-seven; no Republican, in recent times, had won with fewer than forty-five counties. The suburbs, on the other hand, were somewhat unpredictable. In state and local elections (with a few exceptions) they were usually rock-ribbed Republican; in presidential elections they showed a tendency to become more and more Democratic.

Pennsylvania, as a whole, had been known to split its allegiance between the two major parties in certain types of elections. In the off-year election of 1958, Republican Congressman Hugh Scott defeated former Governor Leader for the United States Senate, while Lawrence was winning the governorship for the Democrats. In 1962, another non-presidential year, Democrat Clark was reelected to the United States Senate while Scranton defeated Dilworth for the governorship. Clark here repeated his even more impressive feat of six years earlier when he had bucked a presidential landslide (Eisenhower's in 1956) to win his senate seat the first time around.

Thus, since 1954 Pennsylvania could not be safely logged in either party's column. It had become a swing state of great importance to both national political parties and well worth the effort either party might expend to woo and win it. In fact, of all the observations one might make about politics in Pennsylvania, the tendency toward split ticket voting, certainly at the top of the ticket, might be the most valid. Row office votes might go one way or the other in a solid phalanx, but, given an opportunity to learn something about the candidates, the people of Pennsylvania seemed almost eager to demonstrate their independence by splitting their tickets.

The steady drift of the state toward the Democratic camp and the threat of a heavy Democratic sweep of all offices in the November election, resulting from the outcome of the Republican National Convention in July of 1964, are what caused Governor Scranton and Republican Senator Hugh Scott to engage in almost

heroic efforts to save at least one important office for the Republican party in the summer and fall of that year.

Pennsylvania's ethnic composition in 1964 had a great variety
of minority groups within, or about to enter, the state political
arena. According to the 1960 census, 7.5 percent of the population was Negro while 22.1 percent was of foreign stock (compared
with a national figure of 19 percent). "Foreign stock," according
to the Census Bureau, refers to both foreign-born and native-
born Americans of foreign or of mixed parentage. Of this latter
group, by far the largest number was of Italian extraction: 509,314,
as compared with 300,112 from Poland, 278,414 from the United
Kingdom, 260,358 from Germany, and 202,255 from the USSR.[2]
These figures do not include all those of the third and fourth
generation who might still have identified with those of "foreign
stock," nor do they indicate which of any generation or national
background might classify themselves as Jews. Thus the full
extent of ethnic voting cannot be measured exactly. However,
these figures do indicate the large proportion of Italian-Americans
in Pennsylvania and thus the importance they attached to their
role in the state. The figures also help explain their resentment at
their significant underrepresentation in statewide political offices.
Italian-Americans were rapidly gaining political experience in
local areas, and it would not be long before they would demand
power on the state level as well.

The steel regions of the southwest, the coal mines of the northeast, and the variegated business complex of the Greater Philadelphia region were the chief areas where the immigrants from
southern and eastern Europe had settled. The south-central and
northern tiers of counties were predominantly rural and German
in flavor—especially those farm areas inhabited by the "Pennsylvania Dutch." Politically the leadership of the urban regions of
the state revealed a pattern that remarkably reflected the length
of time particular ethnic groups had been settled in each area,
and the degree of social and political acceptance they had at-
tained. Thus, at the top of the political hierarchy in most of the
cities and urban counties in Pennsylvania the Irish or "Anglo-
Saxons" (in the eyes of the later immigrants the two were frequently identical) were in control. Lower-echelon positions were

generally filled by what one city official in the southwest referred to as "the Hunkies and the Dagos"—the Slavs and the Italians. In fact, in some counties, certain important patronage-laden positions were held traditionally by specific minority groups. In a typical county dominated by one major city,[3] for example, the mayor was expected to be Irish, the city tax collector German, the county prothonotary Italian, and the recorder of deeds Polish. Similarly, in a steel town of southwestern Pennsylvania, where the population was almost exclusively Italian (35 percent) and Slavic (45 percent), with blacks, Jews, and Greeks composing a very small minority, the Italian mayor was able to stay in power with the help of a coalition of Slavic leaders; he admitted that this was possible only because he had "given them representation" (by the use of patronage) in his administration.

It was this kind of politics that dominated the Democratic urban areas of the state and that any politician aspiring to statewide office in 1964 had to take into account throughout his campaign. Although the Democats and Republicans might be fairly evenly matched across the state as far as registration was concerned,[4] in a primary it was usually the much better organized city machines that produced a higher percentage of the vote on election day. Any Republican running for statewide office in a general election would have to have a great number of ticket-splitting Democratic votes[5]—including ethnic bloc votes—to win.

This fact became even more painfully obvious as the Democratic registration figures began to swell during the summer of 1964, reflecting the unprecedented unpopularity of the Republican presidential choice throughout Pennsylvania. By September, new Democratic voters were outnumbering new Republicans by two to one,[6] and Democratic State Chairman Otis Morse expected to go into the November election with an overall lead of 140,000 registrants.[7]

However, other than the overwhelmingly negative response of blacks to Barry Goldwater, no ethnic political questions would have arisen in Pennsylvania but for the peculiar situation that developed in the April Democratic primary.

Since 1954 Philadelphia has been able to produce a sufficiently large Democratic margin to carry the state into the Democratic

column with increasing regularity. For the Republicans to overcome Philadelphia's 100,000 to 400,000[8] Democratic vote plurality,
most of the other urban Democratic counties in the state would
either have to go Republican or turn in extremely low Democratic pluralities. In the three major elections during the eight
years prior to 1964, Philadelphia had never failed to give the
Democratic party at least a 100,000 vote plurality. The only other
area in the state that could approximate this record of fidelity to
the Democrats was the southwest, comprising Pittsburgh in
Allegheny County and its neighboring Democratic-controlled
steel-producing counties—Washington, Greene, Fayette, and
Westmoreland. But altogether these counties had barely turned
out a 150,000 vote plurality in the bonanza presidential election
year of 1960. The region's best effort could produce little more
than could the least effort expended by the Democratic organization in Philadelphia. This fact dominated the events that led to
the choosing of a Democratic candidate for the senatorial election
of 1964.

One other factor also influenced the decision-making process
within the party that spring: the need for the new leader of the
Philadelphia Democratic political organization to assert his
ascendancy over the state party.

Prior to 1947, Pennsylvania's Democratic party had always
looked to Pittsburgh for leadership and direction. It was there
that the first step in capturing the state from the Republicans had
been taken during the New Deal days. The Democrats did not
establish firm control of Philadelphia until the early 1950s, and
only gradually did Philadelphia attempt to wield statewide political
power. It was only a matter of time, therefore, before rivalry
between Philadelphia and Pittsburgh over the control of state
politics and patronage would erupt.

The Pennsylvania Democratic State Committee reflected the
weakness and diffusion of political control which existed because
of the party's failure to capture the Governor's Mansion for any
extended period. In fact, the party could hardly have been called
an organization at all. At most it was a mimeographing and mail-
ing outlet for the various statewide candidates during election
years. Understaffed and underfinanced, its chairman was seldom
more than a part-time figurehead. Actual administration of the

headquarters, oddly enough, came to be exercised by the secretary of the party, Miss Genevieve Blatt,[9] who, after 1954, also served as Secretary of Internal Affairs—the most important elective office in the Commonwealth after the governor. Pennsylvania's Democratic party was in fact little more than a collection of scattered feudal baronies loosely joined together by a common nomenclature and a dimly perceived allegiance to a shadow hierarchy of leaders. Without a Democratic governor in office to distribute the bounty of patronage and thus hold the vassals together, there was no state Democratic party.

Although the Democratic takeover in Philadelphia had at last enabled the state to go Democratic, the leaders of the state party (organized under the two Democratic administrations of 1954 to 1962) somehow continued to be related to the Pittsburgh or Lawrence-Barr[10] faction of the party. In 1961, however, the effect of the tremendous 300,000 vote plurality given to John F. Kennedy by the Philadelphia organization the previous year did begin to make itself felt. Former Governor Leader, who had been employed by the Philadelphia Democratic financier Albert M. Greenfield since 1958, managed to have his friend Otis Morse elected state chairman at the party organization meeting that June. Morse's main task was to revitalize and completely revamp the operation and coordination of the state party and headquarters in Harrisburg. A necessary result was the weakening of the control Miss Blatt—another Lawrence protégé—had previously held over party administration.

Morse was from neither Pittsburgh nor Philadelphia but from York County in south-central Pennsylvania. It was expected that he would try to steer a middle course between the two giants, but, as yet, he had little of the political experience required for such a delicate task. His greatest weakness was that he had no actual political base of his own from which to operate. A former radio announcer, he had held no elective position prior to his appointment, and was in fact little more than an administrator. Although he was the first chairman to act as a full-time, nonoffice-holding executive, his effectiveness as a coordinator and actual party leader could be seriously questioned when the party was no longer in control of the governorship and state patronage.

The following year was to see this situation come into being: the stage was then set for the battle for control of the state organization by the new Philadelphia leadership.

In 1962, Philadelphia once again attempted to put its favorite son, Richardson Dilworth, into the governorship. The first time Dilworth had run was in 1950, fresh from his 1949 victory over the Republican city machine. But his decision to run in 1950 may have been premature, since he lost. An effort had been made to balance the ticket between the southeast and the southwest with the choice of Pittsburgh Judge Michael Angelo Musmanno as the candidate for lieutenant-governor. Musmanno ran considerably behind the Philadelphian and, therefore, was considered to have been a "drag" on the ticket—but both Democrats were swamped by the Republicans that year. The same thing happened in 1962 when Dilworth ran with another westerner, Steven McCann from Greene County. In this instance, however, some felt it was Dilworth, not the Democratic party, who failed to attract the votes. Whereas his first loss had been by only 86,000 votes, his second saw him overwhelmed by 486,000 votes.

The 1962 election was particularly interesting, since the Philadelphia Democratic City Chairman, William Green, had tried to discourage Dilworth from running. Green had predicted that Dilworth would lose, primarily because, he said, Dilworth's rambunctious and unrestrained personality had been overexposed in the press and television during the intervening twelve years. Other political observers agreed that Dilworth would lose, but for an entirely different reason: since succeeding Clark in 1956 as mayor of Philadelphia, Dilworth had "toned down" the reform aspects of the new Democratic administration and had become closely connected with the Green organization. Under Green's leadership the Democratic party had begun to acquire a reputation for ward politics similar to that of the former Republican powers in City Hall. Thus two possible and seemingly contradictory explanations could be put forth for Dilworth's second loss of the governorship—personal and political—and both were invoked by persons of different persuasions.

When the election took place on November 8, 1962, Philadelphia turned out a 106,000 vote plurality for Dilworth, but Green's prediction came true and William Scranton was elected. After the election, Green's Philadelphia organization remained convinced that, despite some adverse publicity concerning its political activities, its own power had not been curtailed by the results of the election. Rather, the Philadelphia regulars seemed to think, the personal failure of one individual, Dilworth, was to be blamed for the loss. Philadelphia might yet attain control of the state's patronage the next time around. In the meantime, there was the state legislature and the United States Congress to concentrate on.

The most important statewide political office in the Commonwealth of Pennsylvania is the governorship. Rarely, if ever, does the position of United States Senator hold the same fascination for the political leaders of the state. The reason is obvious — a senator's patronage can by no means compare with the size of the payroll available to the party that controls the Governor's Mansion. Nor can it compare with the rewards that accrue to the local organization that retains control of its own municipal or county government.

A senate seat is not coveted with as much fervor nor is the effort that goes into the campaign as sustained and determined as the drive for a state or local office. But a contest to decide the candidate for the United States Senate can serve as a test of strength for a party's factions and leaders; it can act as a weathervane to tell which way the wind is blowing within a party preparing for a critical gubernatorial contest two years away. Such, it seems, was the original meaning of the senatorial election of 1964.

But, the question arises, why did such a test need to be undertaken at all? Wasn't the momentum that had been built up over the years sufficient to see the Philadelphia machine to its ultimate victory without a preliminary dress rehearsal in 1964? Why did the Philadelphia faction feel it had to test its influence in a senatorial primary in the spring of a presidential year?

The answer is that the Philadelphia faction of the Democratic party was itself anything but a monolith to begin with. In fact, in the spring of 1964, two and perhaps three distinct subgroups could very readily be distinguished within its ranks: one reform group popular among the "good Government" element that had wrested control from the Republicans in the first place; one "regular" group in control of the ward and precinct organizations throughout the city; and one "rump" group clustered around the new mayor[11] who was anxiously trying to walk the tightrope between the other two groups. A mayor without his own political base could not begin to operate effectively without the respectability of the reformers and the hard work of the precinct committeemen. But the primary cause of the split between the organization and the reformers was simply a congenital inability on the part of some reformers to come to grips with the ugly realities of political machine building.

Unlike David Lawrence in Pittsburgh, Clark, and later his partner Richardson Dilworth as well, failed to concentrate their efforts on constructing a strong ward and precinct organization throughout the city. They left this job to an independent city chairman[12] instead of undertaking it themselves. At first this expediency had worked quite well, since the man they had chosen—James A. Finnegan—was as much a reformer as an "old pol." But he soon lost control to a far more adept politician, Congressman William Green. In 1954 Finnegan was "promoted" to the position of secretary of the commonwealth in Harrisburg, and Green was formally installed as the new city chairman.

As long as Joe Clark had been mayor of Philadelphia (1952-1956), relations between the party regulars and the reformers, of whom he had become the chief guiding spirit, had gone from bad to worse. Clark had made no effort to mollify the organization or to try to work out some kind of compromise arrangement on patronage. Instead, he seemed to glory in his ability to antagonize the ward and precinct leaders of the city, and to treat their political requests with scorn. Clark's behavior, in fact, soon earned him the reputation among party workers of being a snob.

An old-line aristocrat, Clark had a finely developed social conscience and an ingrained sense of noblesse oblige. He seemed, therefore, the very ideal of the liberal patrician. But unlike others of this type who had entered politics, Clark could rarely bring himself to engage in the blintz-eating, baby-kissing practices of the typical American politician. He apparently viewed his role as that of the gentleman squire who assumes the distasteful burden of office out of a sense of public duty, but keeps his distance from the ward heelers and other unpleasant types one finds in politics. His unbending attitude toward the hard realities of backroom politics was not one to endear him to the ward leaders and committeemen in the city of Philadelphia—especially when he refused to undo the work of patronage reform, as requested by Bill Green, which had been incorporated into the new City Charter, and which had been the principal vehicle for the ouster of the Republicans from City Hall.[13] Therefore the political regulars were only too happy to "kick Clark upstairs" to the United States Senate in 1956.

When Dilworth then became mayor, he did arrange the patronage compromises with the organization, despite his equally aristocratic background. These compromises, however, ultimately helped Green gain greater and greater control over the political life of the city, and were in large part responsible for the demise of reform politics in Philadelphia. After Dilworth resigned to run for the governorship in 1962, Senator Clark felt himself free to become more and more critical of the "machinations" of the Democratic City Committee. The notorious "Green Grab" of 1962—a reapportionment plan in which Chairman Green had attempted to incorporate various sections of suburban Delaware and Montgomery counties into Philadelphia congressional districts—had raised an uproar throughout these heavily populated Republican areas, and had contributed substantially, some think, to Dilworth's defeat in 1962. Clark began to make his alienation from the city organization more and more pronounced. In the senatorial primary of 1964 the final break between the reform group and the city organization was effected—but the events which led to that break took place in the last few weeks of 1963.

THE CANDIDATES

On November 22, 1963, President John F. Kennedy was assassinated, and on the following December 21 William Green died at Graduate Hospital in Philadelphia. These two events had a tremendous impact upon the inner workings of the Democratic party of Pennsylvania: the first because it boosted the importance of the senatorial election as the instrument the party might have to rely on in order to carry the state for President Johnson; the second because it signaled the start of a battle for power within the city of Philadelphia which was to make the senatorial primary its chief battleground.

In December 1963 the Republican candidate for the presidency was still unknown. The chief contenders for the nomination were primarily northern liberals—Rockefeller, Lodge, Romney, and perhaps Scranton as well. All of these gentlemen were of the political persuasion most acceptable to Pennsylvania voters: liberal without being "socialistic," Republican without being immobile.

Johnson had done remarkably well stepping into Kennedy's job, but at the moment he was still an unknown quantity— undeniably southern and suspiciously resembling his conservative confreres. Therefore, in order to preserve some state patronage and to assure a healthy representation in the state legislature and in the Congress, the Pennsylvania Democratic party was going to have to choose a senatorial candidate who was both well-known and capable of boosting the statewide ticket—including the little-publicized fiscal and judicial offices—to victory independent of the presidential coattails. In fact, it was actually believed that a strong Democratic candidate would be needed if Johnson was to carry the state. Any possibility of a Goldwater candidacy was thought to have been effectively destroyed by the death of President Kennedy. The impact which Goldwater's success in the Republican National Convention six months later was eventually to have on Pennsylvania's statewide elections was completely unforeseen in December of 1963. Thus the senatorial election, and its necessary antecedent, the primary, came to be considered far more important to the Democrats than was usual.

On the other hand, Green's death had left a vacuum, at this most critical moment, in the very powerful Philadelphia Democratic city chairmanship. Without Green's strong leadership, which many believed had made possible that overwhelming margin of vote for Kennedy in 1960, the city could very well drift into indifference toward the Johnson-headed Democratic slate in November. The vacancy presented the two opposing factions with a sudden chance to improve their power positions. The reform group correctly sized it up as their one last hope to undo the damage done the party during the previous years by the scandals attributed to the Democratic city organization—scandals that Dilworth had been impelled at one point to characterize as "penny-ante stuff," a remark that had haunted him in the gubernatorial election of 1962.

To accomplish a cleanup the reformers were willing to ally themselves tentatively with the newly elected mayor, James H. J. Tate. Tate had by no means always been so independent as his 1963 election publicity had depicted him; he had come up through the ranks of the organization as a ward leader and member of city council. But without an independent power base he had had to project a far more acceptable image than that of a ward leader in order to achieve election to the mayor's office on his own, and in this he had been partially successful.

Some of the reformers now thought[14] that a coalition with Mayor Tate might prove to be just what was needed to change the direction of the leadership of the city committee, and perhaps even to achieve the same harmonious relationship between the mayor and the party that had been in effect for decades in Pittsburgh. The main difference in the power structures of the two cities had been that, whereas the mayor controlled the Democratic organization in Pittsburgh, the Democratic organization had increasingly controlled the mayor's office in Philadelphia. With Philadelphia's mayor aligned with the reform group, as was ostensibly the case in Pittsburgh, perhaps Philadelphia too could eventually achieve a high reputation for good government.

The organization, on the other hand, saw Green's death as a major threat to the continued existence of all that Green and others had struggled so hard to obtain: control of city patronage and the perquisites that went with it. Their bitter memories of Clark's city administration left them only too anxious to prevent any possible return to reform rule. The ward leaders and precinct committeemen were determined, therefore, not to give the opposition time to solidify its plans, consolidate its backing, or take over the city. Within six days of Chairman Green's death— a record by any calculation—they managed to dispense with all formalities and convened to elect one of their own members chairman of the city organization. With very few persons absent, fifty-seven of the sixty wards of the city voted for the party Finance Chairman, Francis R. Smith, to succeed Congressman Green. Thus Senator Clark, the reform element, and Mayor Tate were confronted with a fait accompli long before any but the most preliminary discussions could be conducted between them.

After partially recovering from the organization's blitz, the reformers began to assess the damage done to their position and to plan their next move. Both sides needed an issue or a contest of some sort to test the other's strength. The senatorial primary was just the instrument. But the reformers did not grasp the situation at once.

The next move was once again taken by Frank Smith, early in January, before the dust had quite settled over his recent coup. On January 14, at a dinner in Washington, D.C., honoring President Antonio Segni of Italy, City Council President Paul D'Ortona, a stalwart of the Democratic organization, asked Justice Musmanno, then serving on the Pennsylvania Supreme Court, what he thought of the idea of his becoming the Democratic senatorial candidate that year. "How would you like to be the Daniel Webster of the United States Senate?" is the way he expressed it at the time.[15] Musmanno responded in the affirmative, and it appears that the necessary exchanges of conversations and assurances between Frank Smith and Justice Musmanno took place shortly afterward.

A few days before the D'Ortona-Musmanno conversation, Mayor Barr of Pittsburgh and Mayor Tate of Philadelphia had both been in Washington testifying before a congressional committee on a matter of interest to urban officials. They decided to have lunch with Senator Clark and former Governor Lawrence, who was then in Washington as chairman of the President's Commission on Equal Opportunity in Housing. As Mayor Tate walked out of the lunchroom, a newspaper reporter asked him who would be the party's nominee for the United States Senate, and he replied that he thought it might be Genevieve Blatt. According to some sources,[16] Frank Smith saw this as an undisguised attempt by Senator Clark to join forces with Mayor Tate and the Pittsburgh branch of the party to choose the senatorial candidate without consulting him, and thus to "deal him out" of the most important decision to be made on the state level that year. Therefore, when Paul D'Ortona reported a few days later that Justice Musmanno was amenable to the suggestion that he run for the office, Frank Smith decided to make his move.

How was it that two citizens of Pittsburgh, Genevieve Blatt and Michael A. Musmanno, came to be the chief protagonists in what was primarily a battle for control of the Philadelphia Democratic organization?

For many years Miss Genevieve Blatt had been a loyal member of the Democratic party of Pennsylvania. A gracious and inherently courteous woman of fifty, Miss Blatt generally projected a public image of warmth and concern for even the smallest matters. She was not the kind of person, however, with whom one was likely to develop a sense of intimacy, or who took very many people into her confidence. To those about her, she frequently gave the impression of aloofness and distance; her manner was usually shy and dispassionate. For a politician she was frequently so "unflappable" that she often appeared to be bland.

As a young woman in college and in law school, she had helped establish the Intercollegiate Conference on Government, a statewide organization to interest students in the inner workings of state and national politics. By 1964 the organization had grown, over two and a half decades, to include some 500 students annually in over forty colleges and universities throughout the state. In the meantime, Miss Blatt continued to act as its executive director while advancing in various political offices. Therefore, she was well known to the academic community and to the many politically alert graduates of that community throughout the state.

Miss Blatt candidly attributed the start of her political career to Pittsburgh's former Mayor David L. Lawrence. After graduating from the University of Pittsburgh with highest honors at the age of nineteen, Miss Blatt went on for her Master's degree in political science and then switched to law. Her first political office came in 1938 when the then mayor of Pittsburgh, Cornelius D. Scully, asked her to serve as the secretary of the city's civil service commission. During the war years Miss Blatt took a position as an assistant city solicitor and was elected president of the Young Democrats of Pennsylvania. In 1944, David Lawrence, then chairman of the Democratic State Committee, reportedly insisted that she take the job of deputy treasurer of the commonwealth after she declined it several times. And when the Democrats lost the office of treasurer in 1948, Lawrence once again intervened, asking her to remain in Harrisburg as the secretary of the Democratic State Committee.

In 1954 Miss Blatt was elected Secretary of Internal Affairs along with Governor Leader in the first Democratic sweep in twenty years. In doing so she became the first woman ever to win a statewide office. When she ran for reelection four years later, she led the ticket in the number of Democratic votes received, at the same time that David Lawrence was being elected governor of Pennsylvania and Hugh Scott was defeating George Leader for the United States Senate. In 1962 she, along with Senator Clark, was able to buck the Scranton landslide and squeaked to victory by a 1,300 vote plurality.

Thus, not only had she served efficiently as party secretary for fifteen years, practically running the headquarters before the appointment of Otis Morse, but she also had had an opportunity to compile a fairly impressive political record as Secretary of Internal Affairs. Since this office had mainly to do with municipal and township affairs, statistics and geological reports of various sorts, she had gotten to know just about every village and township in the state, their economic and political problems, and many of their mayors, burgesses, commissioners, and supervisors by name. There were very few local and rural politicians of either party, and very few areas of the state, with which she was not personally acquainted. Thus she had acquired a considerable independent following as well as great power within the party and was considered in some quarters to be at the top of the list of all the persons likely to be asked to run for the Senate in 1964.[17] John Calpin, political columnist for the *Philadelphia Evening Bulletin*, had suggested on January 23, ". . . they should be drafting her, over her personal reluctance to push herself forward."

There was one other aspect of her personal life which may

also have been a factor propelling her to the fore. In a state such as Pennsylvania with an unusually high concentration of ethnic groups, Miss Blatt had a very appropriate name. As one of her staff expressed it later, "The Jews think she's Jewish, the Pennsylvania Dutch think she's one of theirs, and the Catholics know she's a daily Communicant—how can she go wrong?"

To this one might also have added that without being too liberal or too outwardly a feminist, Miss Blatt had also served as one of the founding members of the Americans for Democratic Action (a strong element in the Philadelphia reform faction) and was an untiring participant in women's organizations and activities. Her background as a well-known, loyal, but reform-minded Democratic politician seemed impeccable.

But whereas Miss Blatt's manner and approach to politics might almost be considered olympian, by contrast Justice Musmanno's was more like that of a firecracker—explosive and very much personally involved. Two more clashing personalities could not have been found to run against each other.

Justice Musmanno, a small, thin man of sixty-six, with a high-pitched voice, frequently intense mannerisms, and longer than average silvery white hair, had been on the political scene much longer than Genevieve Blatt, but not as a party worker making his way up gradually through the ranks. As a young man he had obtained several law degrees from American and European universities and had served six months shortly before and after the end of World War I in an army training camp in Virginia. In 1927, after trying unsuccessfully to win election to the state legislature, Musmanno went to Massachusetts and offered his services to the chief defense counsel in the by then notorious Sacco-Vanzetti case. He was appointed assistant counselor, worked furiously in their behalf, but to no avail.[18] They were electrocuted in August of that year. His efforts had made him a little better known, however, and the following year he ran once again for a seat in the Pennsylvania legislature as a Republican. He served one-and-a-half terms in the legislature and gained the gratitude of the unions by working to abolish the notorious Coal and Iron Police.[19] In 1931 he tried for a judgeship on the Allegheny County Court, received an overwhelming plurality, and a year later, decided to run for the Court of Common Pleas on both the Republican and Democratic tickets — a practice frequently used by judicial candidates in Pennsylvania. Once again his vote margin was enormous (320,000 out of 350,000 cast).[20]

It was at this point that his dramatic temperament began to be evident, especially in his handling of minor criminal cases. Once, while preparing to preside over the criminal court, he had had himself interned for three days in Western Penitentiary to see how the prisoners lived and behaved. While on the criminal court he conducted such an intensive crusade against drunken drivers that he occasionally tested the drivers himself in the absence of a doctor. He sometimes offered thirty days instead of forty-five to defendants who pleaded guilty, and he frequently made defendants go to the morgue to look at the bodies of traffic victims. In 1937, as a result of this, at that time, unusual judicial behavior, his fellow judges voted to discharge him from the criminal court and return him to more routine duties.[21] In the interim, he ran for and lost a seat on the state supreme court in 1935, and also lost two races for the superior court in 1941 and 1942 — each time as a Democrat, and once against the wishes of the state Democratic organization.

During World War II he was commissioned a lieutenant-commander in the navy and served as military governor of the Sorrentine Peninsula just south of Naples in Italy. It was while he was in this latter position that further controversy developed around the personality of Justice Musmanno. Frank Matthews of the *Pittsburgh Post-Gazette* later reported that at that time, "the United States Army in the field . . . had worked for a substantial portion of eight months to have Musmanno relieved of duty."[22] This was because, Gaeton Fonzi elaborated in *Greater Philadelphia Magazine,* "[they] complained that he had 'gone native' and was being oversolicitous to these Italian peasants."[23] Nevertheless, Musmanno was awarded the Legion of Merit, the Bronze Star, and the Purple Heart with a cluster for his military service in World War II, and was retired with the rank of rear admiral. He was also awarded the Silver Medal for Valor and the Cavalier's Cross of the Military Order of Italy by the Italian government. Later he was appointed a judge at the war crimes trials which followed the International Military Tribunal at Nuremberg, and won worldwide as well as statewide recognition for his work there.

In 1950 Musmanno announced he would be available as the Democratic candidate for governor, but since Dilworth had already been chosen by the party organization for that position, the judge was offered the lieutenant-governor's slot, over Dilworth's strenuous objections. A year after their defeat, Musmanno announced his candidacy for the Pennsylvania Supreme Court. This time, although the party backed the incumbent, Musmanno beat him by 88,000 votes in the primary. Because this election was one in which a justice from each party was to be elected, Musmanno faced no opposition on the ballot in November, and he was sworn in the following January.

Later that year, 1952, he continued his political activities by campaigning on behalf of Adlai Stevenson. At this point the Allegheny County Bar Association moved to censure the justice for engaging in political activities while serving on the bench.

In 1950, the Philadelphia Bar Association had filed a complaint with the American Bar Association accusing Musmanno of violating its Canons of Judicial Ethics for not resigning from the bench while campaigning for political office.[24] The ABA responded by suspending him from membership in its organization for one year, but Musmanno did not seek readmittance until 1963. In 1952, the Allegheny County Bar passed a resolution censuring him for his political activities as "tending to cause litigants and the public to lose confidence in and respect for the courts and the administration of justice in this Commonwealth. . . ."[25] Justice Musmanno replied that he considered the resolution ". . . barren of ethical responsibility and . . . so deep in the stream of prejudice and hate that reason flounders. . . ."[26] Thereupon he resigned from the County Bar Association as well.[27] All of this was to be used against him during the 1964 primary campaign.

The justice's record on the bench, similarly, was not always as wrinkle-free and noncontroversial as a candidate might wish. While still on the court of common pleas in 1950, he had been reprimanded by the state supreme court for barring a woman from serving on the grand jury because, while questioning her privately in his chambers, he had "determined" that she was a member of the Communist party. Her constitutional rights, the court held, had been abridged.[28] He was taken to task by the supreme court again the following year for holding an attorney in contempt of court and denying him the right to practice law before his court because he had refused to answer questions concerning his alleged membership in the Communist party.[29] On that occasion the court argued, "What the Judge has done, in his zeal against Communism, is to adopt the detestable method employed by Communists themselves in arbitrary and judicial proceedings contrary to all our cherished traditions of law and legal procedure."[30]

In line with his anticommunist courtroom efforts, Justice Musmanno once wrote to the manager of the Cincinnati Reds asking him to change the name of the ball club because of the communist implication. ". . . A headline like 'Reds Murder Yanks' might cause some 'terrible scares' in America,"[31] he was quoted as having said.

Thus, in addition to being a favorite of the liberals for his record on the Sacco-Vanzetti case, the Coal and Iron Police, and the Nuremberg Trials, Musmanno now appeared to be appealing for conservative favor with his stance on communism. Two other actions of his were to add to this semblance of a desire for equilibrium: his testimony before the Eichmann Tribunal in Israel[32] and his personal efforts to implant the American flag atop a post office in Fairless Hills, Pennsylvania, a modern community that had banned television antennas and flagpoles for aesthetic reasons.

The justice did indeed have a flair for the dramatic, and almost every act served to widen his reputation both in Pennsylvania and throughout the country. In 1964, at the age of sixty-six, soon to be sixty-seven, and with all the prospects of eventually becoming chief justice of the Pennsylvania Supreme Court when the current chief's term expired, Justice Musmanno was being asked to engage in an entirely new political drama—the race for the United States Senate.

What would cause the Philadelphia Democratic organization to choose him, above all others, as their candidate for the senatorial office? Frank Smith and other members of this group insist that it was solely his long and distinguished public record—his academic degrees, his antifascist and anticommunist reputation, and his frequent, if not always successful, political campaigns. Others, however, suggested another reason: the increasing dissatisfaction of the Italian-American community in south Philadelphia with the Democratic party, stemming from the time of Mayor Dilworth.[33]

Dilworth had at one time proposed an experiment in south Philadelphia whereby each car owner would be charged forty dollars for permission to park his car on the street outside his home. A mob scene complete with broken windows and shouted epithets resulted when Dilworth tried to explain his plan before a meeting of some of the residents of the area; the whole idea had to be dropped. Other disaffections developed over various other proposals Dilworth put forward regarding urban renewal: blacks were beginning to encroach deeply into Italian territory in south Philadelphia and the rapport between the races was not good. An ugly backlash situation was in the making in this important Democratic stronghold. Musmanno's candidacy, it was hoped, might well serve to keep the Philadelphia Italian community within the fold and to strengthen the party's defenses on its home ground.

In this way the desire of one political faction to increase its power throughout the state combined with the upward thrust of an emerging powerful ethnic group to produce the dramatic events of the spring primary.

DECISIONS

The Democratic party of Pennsylvania had long suffered under the handicap of being unable to devise a solution to the problem of choosing its statewide candidates. Some states use the convention method—a broadly representative, semidemocratic system in which the "bosses" in many instances substantially control the nominating procedure. In the period following the Progressive Era in American politics, Pennsylvania had succumbed to the "Wisconsin idea" and had established the closed party primary. The people of Pennsylvania soon discovered, however, that the genuinely democratic primary is a very elusive political instrument, and basically tends to weaken party control over the nominating procedure.

As in most other states throughout the nation, Pennsylvania Democrats eventually resorted to the extralegal device of a pre-primary meeting of the party leaders to settle the question of party endorsement, leaving all non-endorsed candidates with the stigma of being "mavericks" or antiparty independents.[34] In this way the very purpose of the primary—the assurance that the right to designate those persons who would bear the party label in the general election would belong to the rank-and-file and not to the party leaders—could be effectively circumvented. But the party, already heavily burdened by a lack of cohesiveness resulting from its chronic failure to establish a viable statewide organization, had, in the 1930s, hit upon this expedient as the only way to retain control over the nominating procedure for important state offices.

Originally, an ad hoc meeting of the state committee ten days before the date of filing for the primary was the device used to designate the party's candidates. Eventually, however, the rather small state committee proved too easy for one faction—the one with the most lucrative patronage—to control, and a broader, more representative body came into being. The policy committee, as it was called, was composed not only of thirty-two members of the executive committee but also of fifteen appointees of the state chairman (big contributors, former governors, and other important figures), plus the chairmen of all the counties that went Democratic in the preceding gubernatorial or presidential election, plus the chairmen of all Republican counties in which over 40,000 Democratic votes had been cast.[35] In 1964 the number reached sixty-four—not as large as a statewide convention of party regulars or as unmanageable as an undirected primary— but certainly preferable to a small handful of political yesmen. Its purpose was still to restore effective party control over the choice of the party's statewide candidates—primary or no. It was largely successful, however, until the spring of 1964 when it suffered a marked defeat.

The Segni dinner in Washington, where Philadelphia's City Council President Paul D'Ortona put the question of candidacy to Justice Musmanno, took place on January 14. The meeting of the policy committee to choose the party's candidate was scheduled to take place in Harrisburg on January 31. In the days intervening many telephone calls and consultations took place between Frank Smith, Albert M. Greenfield (a Philadelphia financier with a great deal of influence over the city's Democratic politics), and the justice—and between the justice and his Pittsburgh acquaintances—Governor Lawrence, Mayor Barr, and others. There is no evidence that, at that point, either Philadelphia's Mayor Tate or Senator Clark, despite their party eminence, were informed of this new development. In fact both Governor Lawrence and Mayor Barr attest to the lateness of the hour in which they themselves were brought into the conversation. Neither Miss Blatt nor Michael Byrne, Senator Clark's executive assistant, admit to any knowledge of the possibility that Musmanno might be a candidate until "forty-eight to seventy-two hours" before the policy committee meeting.[36]

On the other hand, what people were likely to have been considered for the nomination without Frank Smith's intervention? Very few were actively campaigning for it. The two most active were industrialist Milton Shapp, president of the Jerrold Corporation and prominent in Montgomery County politics, and State Senator Robert Casey, a young man from Lackawanna County considered by some party regulars to have exceptional political potential because of his youth and "Kennedy image."[37] Other names that had come up were Congressman John Dent from Westmoreland County, Judge Clinton Budd Palmer from Northampton County, and Prothonotary David Roberts, the latter not well known outside of Allegheny County. Some spoke of drafting Governor Lawrence or Congressman Thomas Morgan of Washington County for the job, but neither would allow his name to be considered.[38]

However, in the background but not pressing her candidacy was Genevieve Blatt. Many lower-echelon party regulars thought she was the only likely candidate and, therefore, did not see anything strange in her silence. The political correspondent for the

Pittsburgh Press acknowledged her to be the "front-runner."[39] As Miss Blatt was to explain later, "I was not really interested in the nomination. . . . I debated whether I would say yes or no should I be asked, but I certainly wouldn't go after it."[40]

From all indications only one person, before January 14, had given much consideration to the possibility that Musmanno might be the candidate. That was Milton Shapp who had thrown Musmanno's name along with a half-dozen others into a poll sampling taken by Joseph Napolitan in mid-December to determine who would be the strongest candidate to run against the incumbent Hugh Scott. Newspaper columnist John Calpin[41] mentioned Musmanno's name on January 23, but more as a part of a listing of all possibilities, and not as a person likely to take the lead.

Just before the endorsement meeting a curbside poll of the field might have shown: Democratic organization people outside of Philadelphia were attracted to Senator Casey; reformers, as Calpin's article indicated,[42] were drawn to Genevieve Blatt; labor and black groups might have been happiest with Shapp;[43] and Musmanno was the favorite of the Philadelphia regulars.

On the night before the policy committee met in Harrisburg, a dinner was held at the Bellevue-Stratford Hotel in Philadelphia in honor of City Councilwoman Mary Varallo. Most of the leaders of the state Democratic party were present—Governor Lawrence, Mayor Barr, Genevieve Blatt, Otis Morse, former Governor Leader, Michael Byrne, Senator Clark, Frank Smith, and others. Afterward, they convened in a hotel room and proceeded to discuss the next day's business.[44] By this time everyone knew that Frank Smith was backing Musmanno and that a great deal of pressure was being exerted on his behalf. Several of those present bitterly expressed their opposition to the justice's candidacy, and the meeting broke up at 12:30 A.M. with very little actually having been settled.

After the meeting several of those who were left, including Governor Lawrence[45] (Miss Blatt's mentor) and Mayor Barr (a good friend), stayed behind to "count the votes" and decide upon their course of action for the following day.

Party regulars in Pennsylvania traditionally have a special abhorrence for anything that might cause a primary split. They search about for any possibility that disputes can be satisfactorily settled "for the good of the party." Party harmony is usually too important a principle to be sacrificed to personal likes or dislikes— even when the question of the suitability of a particular individual for the office might be raised. "Musmanno was the man we could all agree on," Lawrence said later,[46] referring particularly to Pittsburgh and Philadelphia. An earlier primary split in 1938 had left the party crippled for years, and Lawrence did not wish to see the slaughter repeated. A primary fight at this time was, for some people at least, "unthinkable."

But Miss Blatt found that she just could not support Musmanno's candidacy. In her view he had fought the party on several previous occasions, he was already well into his sixties, he had a reputation for impulsiveness and controversial judicial behavior—in short, he could hardly be considered the ideal choice for the job of United States senator or an asset to the presidential ticket. She, therefore, concluded that Justice Musmanno, for all these reasons and because of his previous record of judicial censures, would have little chance against Senator Scott, a well-known, popular, and tough political infighter by anyone's standards. She was not inclined to sit by and watch silently while Frank Smith attempted to "steamroll" the policy committee into accepting what she considered to be an inferior candidate. She resolved to make a fight of it.

On the next day a political volcano erupted in the meeting room at the Penn Harris Hotel in Harisburg, and the fallout from the previous evening's consultations became evident. On the first ballot Justice Musmanno received twenty-two votes, Miss Blatt sixteen, Milton Shapp six, Senator Casey four, Congressman Dent four, Judge Palmer two, David Roberts one, with two abstentions. Miss Blatt had deferred her vote until the second ballot. Senator Clark, Governor Lawrence, Mayor Barr, Mayor Tate, and James Knox (chairman of the Allegheny County Democratic Committee) all voted for Genevieve Blatt; Frank Smith, Otis Morse, George Leader, and Richardson Dilworth cast their votes for Justice Musmanno. With seven members of the policy committee absent, twenty-nine votes were needed to endorse.

On the second ballot Miss Blatt voted for herself, but Lawrence and Barr, in a maneuver decided upon the night before,[47] switched to Musmanno; Mayor Tate and Chairman Knox held for Miss Blatt, as did some others. The final vote, however, read: Musmanno thirty-seven, Blatt sixteen, Shapp three, and one abstention.[48]

Ordinarily, that would have ended the matter. But several people present were very upset with the tactics of the Philadelphia delegation, claiming the entire process reeked of the "smoke-filled room."[49] Genevieve Blatt immediately made known her intention to give serious consideration to the possibility of filing for the primary—and she applied for the necessary petitions later that same day. As she was on her way out of the meeting room, however, Governor Lawrence was quoted as having said to her, "If you had only let us know earlier that you wanted to be the candidate, things might have been different."[50] The truth was that Miss Blatt did not know, until the Musmanno candidacy was all but sewn up, that she would want to run—and then it was primarily because the person to be selected was Musmanno.

At no time did any but her most ardent supporters seriously believe Miss Blatt had a chance of winning the primary against the combined forces of the Democratic organization throughout the state.[51] She might be popular in the rural areas, most of them thought, but Democratic votes are concentrated in the cities. How could she even think of going through with it? As she expressed her resolve in the hours immediately following the policy committee meeting: "I am going to determine how much support I have at the grass roots, and if I feel I have enough, I will run in the primary and I will win."[52]

Miss Blatt immediately circulated her petitions and sounded out her numerous party and independent contacts throughout the state to discover the extent of her support. On February 18, the final day on which nominating petitions could be filed, Miss Blatt showed up at a news conference with two prepared statements, one indicating she would not file, the other that she would. She chose to read the latter, and in doing so took many people—especially those who had long known her as a staunch party loyalist—by surprise. "The real target is victory in November for

President Johnson and for all the other Democratic candidates,"
she said. "I am afraid their [the policy committee's] candidate
will not enhance the possibility of a November victory."[53]

On February 21 Senator Clark announced his support for the
Blatt candidacy. His reason for doing so was quite frankly expressed: "To prevent the new boss of Philadelphia from taking
over the Democratic Party in Pennsylvania."[54] Thus the battle
was joined and Scenario I appeared to be unfolding in an orderly
manner, scene by scene.

The *Philadelphia Inquirer* (a conservative Republican newspaper
then owned by Walter Annenberg, Nixon's appointee to the Court
of St. James in 1969) strongly supported Musmanno in the primary
and later Scott in the general election. It attempted to turn the
tables on Senator Clark by asking, "Who Is Acting Like a Boss?"[55]
In this editorial Clark was characterized as a "boss" for intervening to overthrow the "majority decision" of the policy committee
to back Musmanno. Frank Smith also responded to Senator Clark
by issuing a statement purportedly signed by four of Philadelphia's
incumbent congressmen accusing Clark of backing Blatt only
because he actually wanted Hugh Scott to win in November.[56]
To this Clark countered that it was really Frank Smith who wanted
Scott to win and who had for this reason chosen so weak a candidate as Musmanno.[57] It is doubtful that either side really believed
the entire truth of what they were saying, but it momentarily
made interesting headlines in the newspapers.

In the meantime, Musmanno, who earlier had said he would
not become engaged in "any primary controversy,"[58] refused to
answer questions as to whether or not he would resign from the
bench now that a primary battle was shaping up.[59] After consulting with various colleagues, the justice issued a statement to
the effect that since he would officially become a candidate
only after his nomination, he would not resign until after the
primary and "on completion of judicial duties."[60] Later that
same month a group known as the "Reform Democrats of Philadelphia" pointedly raised the issue of Canon 30 of the American
Bar Association's Canons of Judicial Ethics, and publicly demanded that Musmanno resign as Justice of the Supreme Court
before the April 28 primary. The Canon in question reads:

While holding a judicial position a Judge should not become an active candidate either at a party primary or at a general election for any office other than a judicial one. If a Judge should decide to become a candidate for any office not judicial, he should resign in order that it cannot be said that he is using the power or prestige of his judicial position to promote his own candidacy or the success of his party.[61]

Chief Justice John C. Bell, Jr., of the Pennsylvania Supreme Court—one of the colleagues Musmanno had previously consulted—commented that the court had never adopted the American Bar Association's canons, but "if I were a candidate I would resign."[62] Thus the justice was once again ensnarled in an issue that had caused him considerable difficulty on previous occasions.

On February 25 it was reported that sixty-two of the sixty-seven county chairmen throughout the state were publicly backing Justice Musmanno for the United States Senate.[63] However, many of them unofficially informed Miss Blatt at the same time that they would not interfere with or hinder her campaign in any way.[64] Later, only Clarion County, where Miss Blatt was born, and Bucks County—a maverick area in many ways—refused to support the cause of party unity. Thus, it became obvious that the party was not united on this issue. Many telegrams and letters came from party workers all over the state asking Miss Blatt to withdraw from the race. But many others wrote expressing their support of her candidacy and many political amateurs as well urged her to "stick it out."

Miss Blatt's opposition to Musmanno, therefore, seemed to be pulling the party apart all over the state. Philadelphia suburban communities especially were showing signs of deep reluctance to go along with their county leaders in supporting the organization's choice. Too many of them recalled with bitterness the 1962 "Green Grab"[65] and the resounding defeat they had suffered at the polls because of it. They no longer wanted to be accused of "knuckling under" to the Philadelphia "machine," and accordingly, many township and even ward-level organizations served notice on their county leaders that they were going to support Miss Blatt. Later, when the June reorganization meetings were held in these counties following the primary, the momentum of this revolt carried some of them so far as to unseat a number of their county chairmen and to replace them with more independent spirits.[66]

The effect of Miss Blatt's candidacy was not so uniformly disruptive everywhere, but it did cause a disturbance within the party's ranks the likes of which it had seldom experienced. As one party staffer expressed it, "Gen Blatt has always been so much a part of the organization that many sleepy county chairmen must have thought that *she* was the organization candidate and Musmanno the upstart."[67] Despite Frank Smith's support for Musmanno, Genevieve Blatt was considered a far more loyal and hard-working party member than he, and resentment of the leadership's treatment of her went deep.

Miss Blatt was also to get quite a few volunteers and independents (lawyers, women's groups, professional people of various sorts) to support her and work hard for her throughout the state. This was especially true of the academic community which had come to know and respect her over the years through her work with the Intercollegiate Conference on Government.[68] Professors and college students, therefore, were speedily organized to work on her behalf, distribute literature, ring doorbells, and later to help conduct the investigations so vital to her court battles to secure the nomination.

In the meantime, Senator Clark was organizing his own forces to raise money and supply the kind of professional help Miss Blatt needed to conduct her campaign. That "grand old lady" of the Pennsylvania Democratic party, National Committeewoman Mrs. Emma Guffey Miller (who turned ninety during the campaign), also came forth to give her support to Genevieve Blatt, criticizing the way the state leaders had disregarded the wishes of women's groups in choosing Musmanno, and her moral suasion, if little else, was one more obstacle put in the way of the Philadelphia organization that spring.

Except for the *Philadelphia Inquirer*, the major newspapers throughout the state also approved Miss Blatt's decision to run, and in many instances criticized the party for having neglected her.[69] In some eyes Miss Blatt had become the "Joan of Arc"[70] of Pennsylvania reformers in her efforts to fight the big city machines.

When the last day to withdraw from the race had come, Miss Blatt's name was still on the primary list. All the pressures that had been brought to bear were not sufficient to cause her to withdraw — not even a threat to have her evicted from her long-held position as secretary of the state party organization.[71] She had counted her supporters and decided that they were adequate. Industrialist Milton Shapp, who had also filed but did not find his support as wide, had withdrawn in favor of Musmanno.[72] One other candidate, David Roberts, prothonotary of Allegheny County, did not withdraw, and many saw in his action an attempt to weaken Musmanno in southwestern Pennsylvania. Roberts, an extremely popular figure in that end of the state, had frequently joined with fellow-maverick William McClelland[73] to form the anti-Lawrence faction of the party regulars there. Roberts' staying in the fight, therefore, could very easily siphon off votes from the organization in that crucial section of the state.

Meanwhile, interest was high to see which way Philadelphia's Mayor Tate would go in this battle waging on his own doorstep. Would he continue his rapprochement with Clark and the reformers as his vote had indicated, or would he back the seemingly unbeatable Smith organization and thus risk his own political career? Tate managed to display considerable political skill in handling the matter. With but one gesture he placed himself in the position of being able to back Musmanno without antagonizing Clark, while at the same time appearing to be acting in the interests of good government: He asked each candidate to state his or her position on fifteen issues vital to the city of Philadelphia. After reviewing the answers of each contestant to this "test," he then announced which of them had given the "best" answers in his view, and thus, in a purely disinterested fashion, cast his support to the winner. Since rumors had been circulated for weeks[74] that he was thinking of supporting Musmanno, his ultimate decision to do so came as no real surprise.[75] But his method of extricating himself from a rather difficult situation was a clear indication of the skill he had developed during his years as a ward leader.

THE CAMPAIGN

The campaign, however, got off to a slow and somewhat listless start. What, for Justice Musmanno, was not to have been a campaign at all soon found itself a three-way (or two-and-a-half-way) battle. At first Musmanno was fearful of making any speeches whatever because of Canon 30; David Roberts did not go far beyond his home county in trying to win votes; and Miss Blatt was too busy opening a headquarters and recruiting volunteers to make very many speeches.

On February 27, the three candidates met in the Secretary of the Commonwealth's office to draw their positions on the ballot. Miss Blatt drew the first spot—usually considered to be worth at least 10 percent of the vote to the person drawing it—while Roberts placed second and Musmanno third.[76] This was a minor setback to the Musmanno effort, but apparently not enough to worry his organization.

Finally, on March 1, Justice Musmanno, Miss Blatt, and Senator Hugh Scott (who was facing only nominal opposition on the Republican ballot) each addressed a civil rights rally given by the Philadelphia branch of the NAACP. All expressed the appropriate sentiments, but Musmanno's presence gave Senator Clark the opportunity to criticize him a few days later for engaging in politics while still on the bench. To this Musmanno replied that he had not given a political speech at all,[77] but the newspapers had treated it as such, nevertheless.[78]

Clark was not going to let the justice off so easily, however. Later in the month the senator attacked Musmanno's age as being a serious handicap to one who would have to fight his way through the seniority system of the United States Senate if he was to be of any benefit to the state of Pennsylvania. The justice thereupon gave an impassioned defense of his "osseous joints" and enumerated a list of senators and statesmen who were well beyond the age of sixty—including Senator Clark.[79] Some political writers also thought an interesting way to compare the two candidates was to count their academic degrees, pitting Musmanno's seven against Miss Blatt's three;[80] other writers doubted if very many voters were impressed with such statistics.[81] And thus, the whole campaign appeared to be resolving itself into a compost of inconsequentialities.

But not for long. The real turning point in the campaign, the issue that may have won the primary for Miss Blatt in April and lost the election for her in November, was just around the corner. The stage was being set for Scenario II to be introduced.

Justice Musmanno's sharp sensitivity to any deprecation of religion, nationality, or race, actual or simply perceived, soon became a major factor in the April primary. In fact, the justice was sometimes apt to see slurs where none existed at all. A typical story frequently told of his hypersensitivity was repeated by Frank Matthews in an article in the *Pittsburgh Post-Gazette* on April 15, 1964:

> One outspoken critic [of Musmanno] . . . was acid-tongued Hiram G. Andrews, at Johnstown, long-time Democratic leader in the House of Representatives. He described Musmanno as a "heel!" Musmanno responded that Andrews "hates me because I am a Catholic." Reporters learned that Andrews, too is a Catholic, and Musmanno adopted a new reason for Andrews' alleged hate: "Andrews hates me because my ancestors were born in Italy," Musmanno declared.

Perhaps not every Italian-American would have reacted the way he did to Representative Andrews' statement. But the justice does not appear to have been the only one involved in this campaign who was aware of the kind of sensitivities which might be aroused when the issue of nationality is invoked. On February 28, Frank Smith urged his committeemen to play upon such sensitivities of the Italian-Americans within their districts in a letter which began:

> The forthcoming Primary and Special Elections on Tuesday, April 28, will be the *FIRST* major Party test for Philadelphia's Democratic Organization since we sustained the doubly tragic loss of President John F. Kennedy and City Chairman William J. Green, Sr. . . . In the *last week* of Voter Registration, we should make every effort to enroll *Republican and non-partisan voters, as well as others in the Democratic Column* so that they may have an opportunity of supporting Judge Musmanno's candidacy. This can be done in the following ways: . . . 2. *Urge all Republican Italo-Americans* [sic] *to register Democrat so they can Support Musmanno in the Primary. Remind them that Pennsylvania has never had an Italo-American in the U.S. Senate.* . . .[82]

On March 12, one Italian-language newspaper published in Philadelphia, *Il Popolo Italiano,* carried the headline clear across its front page: "2.4 MILLION ITALO-AMERICANS IN PENNSYL-VANIA COULD SPELL LANDSLIDE FOR JUDGE MUSMANNO." The article which followed claimed to be based upon material taken from the United States Census, but one would be hard put to track down the actual source of the figures it cites[83] — for example, "the official total population for the State of Pennsylvania in 1960 was 11,319,336 and of this total there were 2,419,240 or 21.3 per cent Italo-Americans. Thus Pennsylvania has more Italo-Americans than any other one nationality or race."

A follow-up article in a later edition of the same paper repeated these claims but with a ward by ward breakdown of the city of Philadelphia showing figures purporting to represent the percentage of Italian-Americans in each. The implication of the importance of these figures was the same as in the previous article.

On March 27, a Pittsburgh Italian newspaper, *Unione,* published an editorial entitled: "WHY IS SENATOR CLARK OPPOS-ING JUSTICE MUSMANNO'S CANDIDACY AS DEMOCRATIC PARTY NOMINEE?" Complaining bitterly of Clark's attacks on the justice, the article wonderingly asked "Why?" and then proceeded to give its own answer:

> It is difficult to explain Senator Clark's attitude *except perhaps on the basis of intolerance.* No one knows better than he of Justice Musmanno's superb qualifications. . . . Frenziedly seeking some issue upon which to base his criticism, Clark has said that Justice Musmanno was selected by "bosses." A more ridiculous assertion it would be difficult to find. . . . This newspaper appeals to Americans of Italian lineage to show their resentment of Senator Clark's unprincipled attack. By defeating Senator Clark's candidate, Senator Clark will be taught a lesson he apparently needs to learn, namely, that *snobbery and intolerance can no longer be a part of the American scene,* as we carry on the traditions of this great and glorious country as the land of the free and the home of the brave.[84]

An article in the New York newspaper *Il Progresso,* which carries an insert page for Philadelphia news, quoted Charles G. Notari, president of the Federation of the Sons of Columbus in

Pittsburgh, as saying, "All Americans of Italian descent have a *duty* to vote for Musmanno in the Democratic primaries on April 28 because, in a manner of speaking, their own prestige is at stake."[85]

It is necessary to quote at length from each of these sources[86] to show that the stage had long been set for an ethnically motivated reaction to anything the senator or anyone else might say directly or indirectly to criticize Musmanno. So sensitive, indeed, were some spokesmen for the Italian-American community in certain sections of Pennsylvania that virtually any criticism of Justice Musmanno was going to be construed by them as a personal affront and a symptom of bigotry.

At any rate, such appeared to be the substance of the warning sounded by the Italian-American press in this its first opportunity to rally behind a statewide candidate of Italian lineage. It was not surprising, therefore, that when actually confronted with what appeared to be a genuine slight to Musmanno's nationality, they should pounce upon it at once as a vindication of their worst suspicions.

THE BLUNDER

On April 6 these spokesmen for the Italian-American community were given their opportunity. On that day, Senator Clark, fulfilling his promise to campaign widely for Genevieve Blatt, gave a speech before a luncheon meeting of the Pittsburgh branch of the newly organized "Voters for Genevieve Blatt." A few remarks had been hurriedly jotted down by the senator while on the plane from Washington, and he had not refined his talk or given much thought to the way in which it would be expressed. Nor, for that matter, had there been time for his staff to compose a release for the press. One reporter was later to comment, "The almost casual remarks dropped by Clark at Monday's luncheon have been blown up by the contending Blatt-Musmanno factions into the largest pre-election furor of the campaign. . . ."[87] The senator, however, repeated these controversial remarks on a television program that same night, and it is from that taped broadcast that the following transcription[88] has been taken. This is the substance of what the senator said:

QUESTIONS FOR JUSTICE MUSMANNO

1.   What makes you think you were "drafted" for the nomination? On the first ballot a majority of the Policy Committee was against you.

There was no draft in the smoke-filled room in the Bellevue Stratford Hotel where Frank Smith the big boss of Philadelphia dictated your selection to reluctant Western Pennsylvania leaders who feared a primary fight.

There was only the spread of cancer for the Democratic Party in that smoke-filled room. The cancer of big city bossism which thinks of politics as a road to personal power, not a means to the end of decent government.

2.   Why do you refuse to obey Canon 30 of the American Bar Association Code of Judicial Ethics which reads: ... [Here Senator Clark read the text of the canon, which was reproduced previously].

3.   Did you not become an active candidate for the United States Senate when you signed and permitted to be filed your nominating papers in Harrisburg on February 20 on knowing that two other candidates had also filed?

4.   Are you not the only Democrat in the history of our party who has violated this Canon of Judicial Ethics? Remember John Morgan Davis was not opposed for Lieutenant Governor in 1958.

5.   Why have you not told the voters whose support you seek:

   (a) When and where you were born?

   (b) Where and at what age and under what name and for how long and in what rank you served in the Armed Forces in World War I?

   (c) Where, when and under what name you were admitted to the Pennsylvania Bar?

   (d) The only non-judicial office you have ever held was as a Republican in the legislature.

   (e) Whether you have ever been censured for your public behavior by either your superiors in the Armed Services, by the Board of Judges of the Court of Common Pleas of Allegheny County or by the Supreme Court of Pennsylvania.

The Democratic voters of Pennsylvania are entitled to your answers to these questions before they go to the polls on April 28.

It is interesting to note just how the Pittsburgh newspapers reported Clark's speech to the people on the following day. James Helbert of the *Pittsburgh Press*[89] headlined an off-the-cuff remark made by Clark, "LBJ TO STAY NEUTRAL IN STATE SENATE FIGHT," and devoted most of his column to this and to Clark's criticism of Musmanno's violation of Canon 30. Bossism and Smith's pressuring of Lawrence and Barr were the only other major points reported.

Pat O'Neill of the *Pittsburgh Post-Gazette* emphasized Clark's reference to "The Last Hurrah" as characterizing Pennsylvania politics, once again stressing the "bossism" issue. The major portion of his column reported Miss Blatt's speech on Musmanno's "latest" political activities while still on the bench in detail.[90] Only the Associated Press picked up the potentially ethnic implications in the questions Clark had asked, and in one small paragraph reported: "He called Musmanno to answer a number of questions, among them 'when and where he was born and at what age and under what name he served in the armed forces in World War I.' "[91] The rest of the column had to do with "bossism" and Miss Blatt's speech.

Thus, without a press release in hand, very few reporters and presumably fewer spectators knew exactly what it was that Clark had said. The evening television program probably had greater impact than the newspaper stories, but the effect there is not so easily measured.

However, on Sunday, April 10, the Italian paper *Unione,* the official organ of the Order of Italian Sons and Daughters of America, which bills itself as the "Oldest Italian-Language Newspaper Published in the United States," printed this headline clear across its front page: "IF YOU . . . YOUR PARENTS . . . YOUR GRANDPARENTS . . . OR GREAT GRANDPARENTS WERE BORN IN ITALY, SENATOR JOSEPH S. CLARK, D. PA., INSULTED YOU! WHAT ARE YOU GOING TO DO ABOUT IT?" The editorial which immediately followed was entitled "WHAT'S IN A NAME?" Next to the editorial was an article reporting that "800 OFFICERS OF ISDA WESTERN PA. LODGE APPROVE STRONG PROTEST." And on the following day leaders of eleven ethnic group organizations in Pittsburgh joined in adopting a resolution condemning Senator Clark for his "bigoted and intolerant attacks on Justice Musmanno."[92] What had happened in the four days that intervened?

On the night following Senator Clark's speech, Justice Musmanno had gone on television to deliver his rebuttal. "Senator Clark's implications about my name and birth place constitute an insult to every person whose parents or grandparents came from Europe to America, the land of equality and opportunity. . . ."[93] On another broadcast he continued: "The inevitable implication was that I was born in some far away forbidding place like Patagonia, or the North Pole. . . . It so happens, however, that I was born in Stowe Township, only five miles away from where Senator Clark was indulging in his McCarthyism."[94] On April 8, Mayor Barr had joined in the fray charging Clark with " 'McCarthyism,' . . . in his use of innuendo rather than facts."[95] No attempt was made at this time to reply directly to Clark's "implied allegations."

What factors actually caused Senator Clark to make his "notorious" statements on April 6, and why did he express them in such an inflammatory fashion? This, as far as the public's level of consciousness was concerned, remained the unprobed mystery of the campaign. Of course Senator Clark later tried several times to clear up the matter, and it is very doubtful that he ever realized just how inflammatory such statements could be. But no amount of ex post facto explanation was able to clear up the fog and confusion once the initial charges and counter charges had been made. Senator Clark had blundered into the major faux pas of the campaign, and Genevieve Blatt was later to pay the consequences. But the reasons behind Clark's attack did have some substance.

During the opening days of the campaign several pieces of literature had been put out by the Philadelphia Democratic County Executive Committee and the statewide Pennsylvania Democratic Victory Committee—both working for the candidacy of Justice Musmanno. In one, a biographical outline distributed by Frank Smith to all his committeemen, Musmanno's military service was referred to in these terms: " 'Mike' Musmanno served as a combat infantryman in World War I." In another, a brochure distributed throughout the state, the reference was in these terms: "He served in World War I as an infantryman, enlisting as a private and achieving a captain's rank." In both instances there was a slight ambiguity in phrasing which might give the reader a false impression. First, it was later revealed, Justice Musmanno had never left the United States during World War I and, therefore, could not properly be considered a "combat" infantryman in the usual sense of the term. Second, he had been discharged from the army while still a private but had joined the Army Reserves as a first lieutenant in 1925, and in 1930 had achieved the rank of captain. This is the answer to Senator Clark's question 5(b).

Question 5(a) "When and where were you born?" was asked, according to Clark's aides, only to point up the fact that nowhere, in any of the justice's biographical materials, was any reference made as to the date of his birth. The question "where," they said, was actually superfluous, not necessary to accomplish the purpose of the inquiry, which was simply to elicit the justice's age.

Parts of 5(b) and 5(c) alluding to Musmanno's name resulted from a check of various documents, school, army, and bar records showing that the justice had at one time spelled his name "Musmann." In a nation of immigrants an error in spelling—deliberate or not—is hardly a matter for deep concern.[96] But whatever point the senator may have been attempting to make, these questions were not actually phrased in such a way as to reveal his belatedly explained intent. All sorts of implications could be, and in fact were, derived from them—most of which put the senator in a position of being everything from a "society snob" to a "bigot."[97]

Questions 5(d) and (e) referred to matters in the justice's past which have already been discussed—in particular his having been reprimanded on several occasions for his treatment of a juror in one instance and a lawyer in another for alleged membership in the Communist party, and for his method of conducting drunk-driving cases. What specifically was intended by the reference to the supposed censure by his "superiors in the Armed Services" is anyone's guess. Both Frank Matthews and Gaeton Fonzi, in articles previously cited, had referred to some disaffection which developed between Musmanno and the army while he was military governor of the Sorrentine Peninsula, but the question of whether or not he was actually censured was never satisfactorily clarified. However, over radio Station KDKA in Pittsburgh on April 8, Musmanno called the charge "a base canard and contemptible to the last degree"[98] and offered no further elaboration of the matter.

The four other "questions" which Senator Clark asked in the same speech require little or no explanation: they were merely ways of rephrasing in shortened form several of the points of controversy already touched upon in earlier speeches by both himself and Miss Blatt. They had, in fact, composed the major theme of the campaign until that moment. The next three weeks, however, were to see a radical change in approach by both factions.

MUSMANNO RETALIATES

Until this time, Justice Musmanno had been rather sparing with his speeches and press releases. At one point he had promised Mayor Tate that he would step up his political activity, and after Clark asked his "questions," he speedily did so.[99] Releases began issuing forth from his office at the rate of at least two a day. On Sunday, April 12, he became particularly loquacious and fired this battery of words at Senator Clark:

> He continues to fire at my ship below the water line, revealing every evidence of wanting to sink that ship. I will not let him do that, I will return shot for shot. And my projectiles will not be loaded with McCarthy falsehoods, distortions, misstatements and half-truths as his are. They will be filled with factual shrapnel which will cool away the vindictive, vituperative vapors rising from his pirate ship of vilification and personal slander.
> I wish to assure the people of Pennsylvania that very soon the standard of skull-and-crossbones flying from Senator Clark's pirate craft will be torn away, and they will see that his truth is one of erratic egotism, vicious vanity and snobbish self-assumed superiority. Ever since his childhood he has been sailing his slandering, sniping schooner through a sea of oil gushing from wells he never dug. Thus, from the golden depths of his swollen wealth and affluence he haughtily looks down upon me because from the age of 14 I have had to make my own way through sweat, toil and tears. . . .[100]

On April 13 the justice delivered a fourteen-page release at a news conference held at the Bellevue Stratford Hotel in Philadelphia. It was the longest of the entire campaign. In it he did raise the question about his service as military governor in Italy but only to counter the charge with a list of his commendations and medals. To the question of his ever having been censured by the Supreme Court of Pennsylvania, he replied with an emphatic negative—although this and other like censures had long been a matter of public record.[101] On the question of running for office while holding a judicial post, Musmanno stated that Judge John Morgan Davis had had two opportunities to step down in the 1958 primary and still had not done so. He called this citation by Senator Clark "a deliberate falsehood" and "a brazen attempt to deceive the people." He also labeled "a monumental lie" Clark's statement that he had "changed his name," explaining that his name had always been Musmanno but that he had had to ask the Philadelphia Court of Common Pleas to "correct the misspelling" of his name because of an error on his father's employment record made by a railroad foreman. The correction was not formalized until 1924, however, by which time he had completed the greater part of his formal education and his World War I military service, and had been admitted to the Bar.

Referring to an intermediate attempt by Clark to clarify this question, Musmanno proclaimed:

> For him now to say that if I object to this particular question about my name, he will withdraw it, represents appalling hypocrisy. After sinking his axe into the trunk of the truth, he now wants to say that he really didn't intend to damage the tree. . . . Senator Clark is giving evidence every day of being less and less a Democrat but I never thought that he would take a leaf from the notebook of the Communists. . . . There could have been no purpose in Senator Clark's making an issue of my name except to stir up the forces of intolerance and bigotry.

On the question of the place of his birth, Justice Musmanno referred Senator Clark to the *Pennsylvania Manual* and *Who's Who*. As to his age, he replied:

> Senator Clark's derogatory remarks about age are an insult to over 40 per cent of his Senatorial colleagues, who, like myself are in their sixties. The age between 60 and 70 represents the golden age of life because it is then that man reaches the highest peak of his mental powers. It is then that he is best ballasted by experience, which is man's best teacher.

And so on, similarly, for six more pages, replying with ridicule to even the most rhetorical of the senator's questions. The final jibe began with the assertion that "there is just no limit to Clark's mendacity. . . ."[102]

Clark, in the meantime, was trying desperately to recover lost ground. The matter had really gone far beyond anything he was reported to have anticipated. His statements, too, were long and detailed, but they could not begin to match the justice's for volume.

On April 12 the senator stated the basic reason that he had endeavored to ask those five questions to begin with:

> The questions which I put to Justice Musmanno which he does not answer, were for the sole purpose of getting at the basic facts about the Justice's qualifications for the office he seeks. They were an honest effort to elicit from the candidate himself answers to questions which are not available to the public because— unlike most candidates—he has been unwilling to make them available. The point is not how old the Justice is, or where he was born, or when he was in the Army—I don't care about these specific data. What I care about, and what I think Democratic voters have a right to care about is why those facts have never been available to the public. It is the Justice's candor and veracity that are the issue, not his name.

It was to this statement that Musmanno had issued his fourteen-page reply. On April 16 the senator responded with his own eight-page rebuttal. He opened with an analysis of Miss Blatt's qualifications for the position of United States senator, remarking that she was ". . . of unimpeachable integrity, unquestioned veracity and emotional stability. . . . In her public career she has always told the truth, the whole truth, and nothing but the truth." In referring to the questions he had asked in Pittsburgh, he asserted that they had been "misinterpreted" and "their purpose distorted by Justice Musmanno." He continued:

> I spoke not one single word in Pittsburgh about ethnic minority groups, about national origin, about race or creed or color or religion. I only asked questions . . . which the Justice has either not answered at all, not answered fully, or not answered accurately. He accuses me of deliberate falsehoods. . . . I do not intend to answer him by defending myself. . . . I am content to leave the

judgment of my character and integrity to the people who have twice elected me to the high office he now seeks. . . . The Justice in his press conference in Philadelphia on Tuesday added the question of his emotional stability to the other issues of the campaign. His statements were close to hysterical. They were also lacking in candor. I must accordingly set the record straight.

On the question of Musmanno's having been drafted for the campaign, Senator Clark once more emphasized the "smoke-filled room" aspect of his selection, stating:

Thirteen out of the twenty-two votes for the Justice on the first ballot in the Democratic Policy Committee were controlled by Boss Smith. On the second ballot, Frank Smith's threat to tear the party apart if he did not have his way worked with some friends of mine in Pittsburgh who cast their vote for Secretary Blatt on the first ballot. . . . The fact is that what was supposed to look like a draft did not work out as such. The plan to prevent a primary contest has failed.[103]

On the matter of the justice's qualifications, the senator once again raised the issue of Canon 30, quoting it at length and pointing out that ". . . the argument that others were similarly obtuse in their ethical standards in the past is no answer to the demand that he resign from the bench or get out of the race." As for Judge John Morgan Davis in 1958, "Judge Davis did not campaign until he resigned from the bench in late August. . . ." The senator then cited the several times the justice had been suspended for politicking by the different bar associations, and quoted various newspapers criticizing him: "This is the public record. One can imagine what use his Republican opponent would make of it in the general election."

Once again Senator Clark cited the justice's "record for candor," especially with regard to his age. "If elected to the Senate, he will be 73 by the end of his first term when he would be beginning to acquire some of that seniority so important for success. Incidentally, Miss Blatt is 50. If a lady will tell her age, without being asked why won't the Justice?" Clark then commented on the inaccuracies found in Musmanno's literature, and the question of the correct spelling of his name, commenting, "I do not care what his name was. The issue is his truthfulness and candor. Why has he been so ashamed all these years to be open and frank about matters of which he has no cause to be ashamed?"

Pointing out that Justice Musmanno had also not mentioned the fact that his terms in the state legislature were served as a Republican, Clark went on:

> The Democratic voters have a right to know that, while the bosses backing the Justice are reviling Miss Blatt . . . for fighting in the primary against the organization-endorsed candidate, their own candidate spent a lifetime running either as a Republican or in primaries against candidates endorsed by the Democratic Organization. If the charge of disloyalty to the organization is an issue then Justice Musmanno must live with it because he has made a career out of it.

Senator Clark then proceeded to discuss the times the justice had been reprimanded or "censured" by his fellow justices on the Pennsylvania Supreme Court. On the matter of his army career the senator made this comment:

> Just as his passionate crusade against drunken drivers led the Justice beyond the bounds of judicial conduct in Pittsburgh, so did his humanitarian concern for hungry civilians under his charge in Italy after World War II *lead him into violation of the military law sufficiently serious to raise the question of his fitness for further service overseas.* Fortunately, his superiors finally recognized his humanitarian motives and he was only transferred to other duty where he rendered valuable service as a Judge at the Nuremburg Trials.[104]

One gets the impression after comparing this version with those of Fonzi and Matthews that perhaps more was being hidden than revealed by these three accounts. However, the only comment reported to have been made by the justice on this delicate matter was included at the very end of a report on one of his news conferences in the *Pittsburgh Post-Gazette:* "Musmanno also belittled his troubles with the Army, when he was accused of repeatedly flouting orders while military governor of the Sorrentine Peninsula during World War II. *He blamed it all upon a vindictive British officer.*"[105] At any rate, the senator then ended his statement with a resume of his previous charges against the candidacy of Justice Musmanno and urged the voters to support Miss Blatt on election day.[106]

Later, in assessing the effects of this exchange between Musmanno and Clark, one of the senator's aides concluded that it had had at least one "beneficial" effect from their point of view: it had forced the justice to come out of his corner and fight. It had revealed his fiery temperament, his low boiling point, and his penchant for florid prose. And by some reports,[107] many who saw him on television for the first time were indeed deterred from voting for him, not only because of these characteristics, but also because of his aged appearance, his high piercing voice, and his intense mannerisms. And the election was only two weeks away.

BLATT RESPONDS

In the meantime, Miss Blatt had gotten lost in the publicity shuffle. There is evidence that she did find herself somewhat embarrassed by the controversy between the justice and the senator, but that she did not think she could readily denounce the one staunch supporter she had in the primary campaign. On April 17 the Associated Press quoted her as having downgraded the entire issue by characterizing both the questions and the answers as "irrelevant . . . casual and parenthetical"[108] but further than this she was not inclined to go. When asked by the *Unione* to "disassociate" herself from Clark's "inferences and innuendoes," she complied with the statement that, although her own grandparents had come from four different countries and they were proud of their homelands, they were prouder still to be Americans, and that she believed that everyone voting for candidates of either party would vote as Americans. ". . . And while I do dis-associate [sic] myself with any inference or innuendo which would reflect upon any citizen's country of origin I must in all fairness say that I believe Senator Clark's questions reflected only upon my opponent's candor, and not upon any national or ethnic group." She ended with the assertion that ". . . I deplore bigotry and bias in any form whatsoever. . . . I am grateful to you for giving me the opportunity to tell you so."[109]

This letter, however, was never published in the *Unione,* and later, during the fall campaign, several of the same people to whom she addressed it were to inquire in injured tones, "Why didn't she ever deny it? Why did she sit by while Clark made his accusations?" And: "Who could have turned her down if she had said 'Please don't judge me by what Senator Clark said?'"[110] Obviously, Miss Blatt did not feel she could condemn Senator Clark for unethical behavior when she did not believe him guilty of it. But whatever she did say, and the extent to which she did go in trying to soothe injured feelings, were not sufficient. Genevieve Blatt's "silence" was to be the key to the fall campaign.

Throughout the final two weeks before the primary, Senator Clark and Miss Blatt generally let Musmanno's charges go unanswered. Each day new headlines appeared in the papers with the epithets "MUDPILE CLARK,"[111] "HYPOCRITE AND SCANDAL-MONGER,"[112] "MONTEBANK,"[113] "VILIFIER,"[114] "CONSPIRACY"[115]—and at one point, "MUSMANNO OFFERS POLKA TO DEFEND AGE: CHALLENGES CLARK TO MARATHON DANCE TO PROVE FITNESS."[116] But Clark's reputation and record as a liberal both in the Senate and as a reform mayor of Philadelphia acted as a buffer for himself and Miss Blatt at this point. It was not until weeks and months later that the charges were felt to have a cumulative effect.

Miss Blatt proceeded to issue position papers on various questions—unemployment compensation, mass-transit aid, urban renewal, consumer protection, and the like—but did not attempt to engage in countering the justice salvo for salvo. At one point she did challenge him to a debate, but Musmanno rebuffed her for her effort with the accusation that she was displaying "high school immaturity and puerility."[117] And so the matter was dropped.

Finally, on the Friday before primary day Justice Musmanno released a story to the newspapers which was to cause a minor earthquake in the offices of Senator Clark and Miss Blatt. As the Associated Press related it:

> Supreme Court Justice Michael A. Musmanno yesterday received the "blessing" of Prime Minister David Ben-Gurion of Israel in his bid for the U.S. Senate. "From the bottom of my heart I send you my Jewish blessing for your success. . . . I am sure you will bring to the Senate an ardent passion for peace, justice and welfare for all."[118]

Members of Clark's staff in Washington immediately telephoned the Israeli Embassy to protest the release of what, they strongly objected, was a private communication. On Saturday morning, April 25, 1964, the *Philadelphia Inquirer* carried a story headlined, "BEN-GURION BID TO MUSMANNO STIRS TEMPEST," in which it was related that: "The Israel [sic] Embassy was embarrassed. Musmanno's political opponents, notably Senator Joseph S. Clark (D. Pa.) were furious. And the general public, presumably from the large number of inquiries made, was curious and wondered whether the note existed at all." On reading this Justice Musmanno

> . . . went to the Inquirer's offices and asked that they reproduce David Ben-Gurion's letter so that the public would know that it did exist. Otherwise there might be engendered the idea that the letter was a mere invention. The City Desk agreed. A photographer was assigned to take many pictures of the letter. Later, however, when the picture did not appear in the first edition I called the Inquirer's offices, and I was informed that they would not publish the letter or make any further reference to it.[119]

A source "close to the embassy" had commented that "The control by a government over a former Prime Minister, especially one who is at an advanced age, is not very great."[120] It would appear that someone had had better success with the *Philadelphia Inquirer*.

By the time the primary day rolled around several of the state's major newspapers had declared for Genevieve Blatt. Only the *Philadelphia Inquirer* and the *Scranton Times* had come out squarely for Justice Musmanno. Most papers contented themselves with cheering the lady on for giving the people a real choice in the primary but declined to take sides. Few newspapers or politicians declared publicly that they thought she would be able to do little more than throw a good scare into the organization.

62   "BIGOTRY!"

As the *Philadelphia Inquirer* put it on April 26, "Most observers figure Musmanno to win the State by a 100,000 to 125,000 edge." Such optimism for Musmanno's chances might have been discounted as preelection wishful thinking, but the professional polls had come up with mixed results. In January a poll taken by Joseph Napolitan for Milton Shapp found that Musmanno would make a better candidate against Hugh Scott than Miss Blatt by 1 percent.[121] In March a poll by E. John Bucci for the Republican party showed Miss Blatt to be the better candidate by 3 percent.[122] Even so, except for one brief comment from Senator Scott,[123] these polls were neither widely disseminated nor generally made available to the public. Had they been so, a truer picture of the probable outcome of this primary might have been obtained by greater numbers of the informed citizenry, and especially by the Philadelphia Democratic organization.

Imagine everyone's surprise on electon night, when the broadcast tabulations seesawed back and forth, giving now Musmanno and now Miss Blatt a lead of 200 or 500 or 2,000 votes. By the following morning it still was not clear who would finally win, but Miss Blatt had taken the lead, according to most press reports, by about 3,500 votes.[124]

Most people were stunned—and incredulous. The Philadelphia margin for Justice Musmanno, which many had believed would be overwhelming, had turned out to be a bitter disappointment to the organization.[125] Smith had predicted a 100,000 vote plurality, but Musmanno actually received just slightly more than 60,000, according to the unofficial returns.[126] In the Philadelphia suburbs Miss Blatt "swamped" the justice by better than two to one.[127] When votes in all sixty-seven counties had been reported, Miss Blatt was ahead in a total of fifty-seven, while the justice led in only ten. Except for Greene County, these ten were the most heavily organized Democratic counties of the southeast, southwest, and northeast. But obviously, not even in these sections of the state had they been able to turn in a vote sufficiently heavy to outweigh the anti-organization sentiment of the suburbs and rural areas.

After the bulk of the figures were in, political commentators began to discuss what John Calpin had called the "Black Eye"[128]

Miss Blatt had dealt the party leaders. Clark's next move, his power so demonstrably enlarged, became a matter of increasing speculation. The condition of the Democratic party of Pennsylvania was in a state of flux.

None of the newspapers, however, editorially or in any other way, attributed Miss Blatt's apparent success to bigotry. To disaffection with the organization—yes. To displeasure over a jurist's not relinquishing his seat on the bench—yes. But to intolerance? For the Italian-American press (and Justice Musmanno himself) this was true, but no other paper thought Miss Blatt's success was due to Clark's arousing the prejudices of the suburban and rural electorate. Only in the midst of the general election campaign, when Senator Hugh Scott made it the chief weapon in his political armory, was this to be projected into the public consciousness as a major factor in Justice Musmanno's defeat. And only in this way did the bigotry issue become the focal point of the Pennsylvania senatorial election in the fall of 1964.

NOTES

1. Dilworth was elected city treasurer and Clark city controller.

2. U.S. Bureau of the Census, *Congressional District Data Book (Districts of the 88th Congress)—A Statistical Abstract Supplement* (Washington, D.C.: U.S. Government Printing Office, 1963), p. 427.

3. Lackawanna County whose county seat is the city of Scranton.

4. Registration returns from the state's sixty-seven counties gave the Democrats a slim majority of 12,981, compared with 83,013 the previous fall and 195,935 in the fall of 1962. *Philadelphia Evening Bulletin,* April 19, 1964.

5. Interview with Robert L. Kunzig, administrative assistant to Senator Hugh Scott, March 25, 1965.

6. *Philadelphia Evening Bulletin,* September 27, 1964.

7. *Harrisburg Patriot,* September 28, 1964.

8. The new record set by President Johnson in 1964; the previous record was 300,000 for John F. Kennedy in 1960.

9. In 1964 Miss Blatt was to become the eventual winner of the disputed senatorial primary recounted in this study.

10. Joseph A. Barr, who succeeded Governor Lawrence as mayor of Pittsburgh in 1958.

11. James H. J. Tate, former president of city council, succeeded Dilworth in 1962 and ran for election on his own merits in 1963.

12. The terminology here may be confusing. Because Philadelphia is both a city and a county the county chairman is more commonly referred to as the city chairman.

13. See James Reichley's account of this controversy in *The Art of Government* (New York: The Fund for the Republic, 1959), pp. 16-17.

14. Senator Clark wrote a memo to his staff after the primary on this very point. Joseph P. Browne, *Pittsburgh Post-Gazette,* June 19, 1964. Much to the chagrin of the reformers, however, Mayor Tate did eventually establish mayoral control over the city organization—but with the cooperation of the ward leaders as it finally turned out.

15. Interview with Paul D'Ortona, City Council President, March 24, 1965.

16. Frank Smith denied the truth of this report in an interview, April 21, 1965. There were many variations put forth by those interviewed about this event. The one presented above is necessarily that which appears to be the most plausible in view of later developments.

17. L. R. Lindgrenn, *Pittsburgh Press,* January 26, 1964.

18. Gaeton Fonzi, "Musmanno Rides Again," *Greater Philadelphia* 55 (April 1964), 62.

19. A book he wrote about his battle against these company strike-breakers was made into a movie, "Black Fury," and starred Paul Muni.

20. Fonzi, "Musmanno Rides Again," p. 62.

21. *Pittsburgh Post-Gazette,* February 4, 1937.

22. Frank Matthews, *Pittsburgh Post-Gazette,* April 15, 1964.

23. Fonzi, "Musmanno Rides Again," p. 64. Said Fonzi: "The care and feeding of the people was the important thing. He went to all lengths to get them food and supplies, even if it wasn't strictly by the book."

24. The resolution passed at the quarterly meeting of the Philadelphia Bar Association reads as follows: "Whereas Canon 28 of the American Bar Association Canons of Judicial Ethics, as adopted by the Pennsylvania Bar Association, provides in part that a judge 'should avoid making political speeches, making (except for his own campaign) or soliciting payment of assessments or contributions to party funds, the public endorsement of candidates for political office. . . '; and

"Whereas Canon 30 of the American Bar Association Canons of Judicial Ethics, as adopted by the Pennsylvania Bar Association, provides in part: 'While holding a judicial position he [a judgd] should not become an active candidate either at a party primary or at a general election for any office other than a judicial office. If a judge should decide to become a candidate for any office not judicial, he whould resign. . . '; and

"Whereas Judge Michael A. Musmanno of the Common Pleas Court of Allegheny County was a candidate in the spring primary election of 1950 for nomination as the Democratic Party choice for Lieutenant Governor of Pennsylvania and, having been nominated thereat, is now the Democratic Party candidate for that position in the fall general election of 1950 without having to this date resigned his judicial position;

"Be it resolved that the Philadelphia Bar Association condemns the action of Judge Musmanno in becoming a candidate for nonjudicial office while retaining his judicial position as a flagrant violation of the established ethics of the legal profession and hereby calls upon him to resign his judicial position forthwith; and

"Resolved, further, that copies of this resolution be forwarded to the appropriate authorities of the American and Pennsylvania Bar Associations for such action as they may see fit." *The Legal Intelligencer* 123 (October 4, 1950), 5 and 335.

25. *Pittsburgh Post-Gazette,* December 12, 1952.

26. Frank Matthews, *Pittsburgh Post-Gazette,* April 15, 1964.

27. The justice's own account of these incidents follows: "In 1950, when I contemplated being a candidate for lieutenant governor, I called on the Chief Justice of the Supreme Court of Pennsylvania and the President of the Pennsylvania Bar Association, and received assurance that I could stand for election to that office without censure. On October 3, 1950, a handful of Republican lawyers (81!) in Philadelphia met and passed a resolution censuring me for being a candidate. I was not notified there would be such a meeting. I do not live in Philadelphia. I was hundreds of miles away. I was not notified of the meeting but these 81 partisan Republican lawyers passed their resolution in violation of every principle of law and ethics, to say nothing of precedent and fairness. Up until then there had been countless cases of judges who ran for governor, mayor, and other political offices throughout the State but there was no censure. . . . But these individuals were not a Musmanno, they were not of 'foreign extraction,' they were not Roman Catholics, they were not men of modest economic origin. And so these 81 lawyers, out of the vast Philadelphia bar [the auditor's report for that year indicated a total membership of 2,243], passed their partisan, prejudiced resolution and it went to the American Bar Association which approved it. I appealed the decision and asked for a hearing on my appeal, which was denied. I was then suspended for one year from the American Bar Association. I was restored to membership on July 1, 1952. And on September 27, 1952, I resigned voluntarily from the American Bar Association . . . [About the censure by the Allegheny County Bar Association in 1952] it wasn't the County Bar. The Allegheny Bar consisted in 1952 of more than 2,000 members. On

December 10, 1952, the Allegheny County Bar Association had a meeting attended by 217 lawyers. These 217 passed their resolution. I was not notified to be present to defend myself, nor was any of the other four judges [involved]. The action of that handful of lawyers was shameful, violating every rule of fair play." Letter to the author from Justice Michael A. Musmanno, March 7, 1965.

28. 364 Pa. 359 (1950); *New York Times,* March 31, 1950.

29. 367 Pa. 476 (1951).

30. *Ibid.,* p. 483.

31. *New York Times,* October 4, 1961.

32. According to Homer Bigart of the *New York Times,* May 16, 1961, Justice Musmanno testified that many Nazi leaders, whom he had interviewed in connection with the writing of a book on his Nuremberg experiences, had spoken to him of Eichmann's role in the extermination of the Jews and of his influence on Hitler in that regard. However, when asked by the presiding judge of the Eichmann tribunal whether he had mentioned Eichmann in his book *Ten Days to Die* (since revised and retitled, *The Eichmann Kommandoes*) the justice suffered his "most embarrassing moment. . . ."

"Justice Musmanno conceded that the book contained no reference to Eichmann because he had not considered Eichmann important when he wrote it." When the defense attorney objected to his testimony as hearsay, Musmanno insisted "often with vehemence that . . . it must be true because so many jailed Nazis had told him of Eichmann's power."

33. Pat O'Neill, *Pittsburgh Post-Gazette,* February 4, 1964. Miss Blatt also thought this was the overriding consideration in their choice. Interview, December 17, 1964. So, also, did many political and newspaper commentators throughout the state. The suggestion was adamantly denied by Frank Smith in an interview, April 21, 1965.

34. "In Pennsylvania . . . the party organizations completely dominate the primary elections in their parties. The real choice of public officers is made by the party organizations and whoever controls them," was James Reichley's assessment of the situation in *The Art of Government* (New York: The Fund for the Republic, 1959), p. 36.

35. I am indebted to former Governor Lawrence for the history of the development of the Policy Committee of the Democratic Party of Pennsylvania; the information was received in an interview on March 6, 1965.

36. Governor Lawrence, Mayor Barr, Miss Blatt, and Mr. Byrne were all quite clear about this in their interviews. Robert Taylor in the *Pittsburgh Press,* February 2, 1964, upholds this point of view, claiming that it was not until the day before the January 31 meeting of the policy com-

mittee that the report of Smith's agreement with Musmanno was released, but Joseph Miller of the *Philadelphia Inquirer* had already had the entire story of Smith's "big push" for Musmanno published in the January 26 edition of his paper.

37. These two personalities later clashed in the 1966 primary for the gubernatorial nomination, and again in 1970 for the same office. In both cases Milton Shapp won.

38. Chaiman of the House Foreign Affairs Committee in 1964.

39. H.L. Lindgren, *Pittsburgh Press,* February 1, 1964.

40. Interview with Miss Genevieve Blatt, Secretary of Internal Affairs of the Commonwealth of Pennsylvania, December 17, 1964.

41. *Philadelphia Evening Bulletin,* January 23, 1964.

42. See passage quoted above, p. 31.

43. Interview with Michael Johnson, Executive Vice-President, Pennsylvania AFL-CIO, December 12, 1964.

44. The account which follows was derived from various interviews, confidential and otherwise, with those actually present. Where contradictions in their accounts have occurred, I have noted them in the notes.

45. Lawrence denied the following ever took place. Interview, March 6, 1965.

46. *Ibid.*

47. As Mayor Barr put it later, "We wanted to save Gen Blatt's feelings on the first ballot." Interview with Joseph A. Barr, Mayor of Pittsburgh, April 5, 1965.

48. Dr. William McClelland of Allegheny County refused to vote after David Roberts' name was withdrawn from the field because he had received only one vote on the first ballot.

49. National Committeewoman Emma Guffey Miller was the first to refer to it as such.

50. Frank Matthews, *Pittsburgh Post-Gazette,* February 1, 1964.

51. Sources from all over the state strongly indicated that this had been their judgment of the situation. Opinions given in personal interviews with the author after the election.

52. Frank Matthews, *Pittsburgh Post-Gazette,* February 1, 1964.

53. Frank Matthews, *Pittsburgh Post-Gazette,* February 19, 1964.

54. Milton Jacques, *Harrisburg Patriot,* February 22, 1964.

55. *Philadelphia Inquirer,* February 22, 1964.

56. John G. McCullough, *Philadelphia Evening Bulletin,* March 10, 1964.

57. John Calpin, *Philadelphia Evening Bulletin,* March 12, 1964.

58. Joseph H. Miller, *Philadelphia Inquirer,* January 31, 1964.

59. L.R. Lindgren, *Pittsburgh Press,* February 1, 1964.

60. *Philadelphia Inquirer,* February 4, 1964. A later article indicated that Justice Musmanno would resign before August 2. Joseph H. Miller, *Philadelphia Inquirer,* April 7, 1964.

61. Harmon Y. Gordon, *Philadelphia Evening Bulletin,* February 28, 1964.

62. Harmon Y. Gordon, *Philadelphia Evening Bulletin,* February 28, 1964. Although endorsed by the Pennsylvania, Philadelphia, and Allegheny County Bar Associations, this canon was not officially adopted by the Pennsylvania Supreme Court until after the election of November 1964.

63. Joseph H. Miller, *Philadelphia Inquirer,* February 25, 1964.

64. John C. Calpin, *Philadelphia Evening Bulletin,* February 27, 1964.

65. See above, p. 26.

66. Montgomery County had been "split wide open" (*Philadelphia Evening Bulletin,* April 24, 1964) by the primary as had Chester and Delaware counties. In June two of these counties changed chairmen and one one nearly did so. In the case of Delaware County the main reason for replacing him, as reported to me by several of my acquaintances among the ward leaders and committeemen, was the beating the organization had taken in the primary.

67. Interview with Robert Sabbato, Publicity Director, Democratic State Committee, November 18, 1964.

68. The author had been a faculty moderator of one chapter of the Intercollegiate Conference on Government for several years while teaching at Immaculata College and believes this to be a fair summation of their general attitude at that time.

69. As Gaeton Fonzi stated in "Musmanno Rides Again," "He [Musmanno] and that newspaper have always been very close." p. 70.

70. A label given her by Senator Clark during the primary.

71. Joseph H. Miller, *Philadelphia Inquirer,* February 23, 1964.

72. Two years later he was to take on the machine himself in the primary and run on the slogan "The Man Against the Machine."

73. Who alone had voted for him in the Policy Committee.

74. Joseph H. Miller, *Philadelphia Inquirer,* February 22, 1964.

75. Joseph H. Miller, *Philadelphia Inquirer,* April 2, 1964.

76. Joseph H. Miller, *Philadelphia Inquirer,* February 28, 1964.

77. *Philadelphia Evening Bulletin,* March 5, 1964—a position which the justice later took in a written reply to several questions put to him by me in March of 1965.

78. The *Philadelphia Evening Bulletin* headlined Paul F. Levy's story of the rally, "Rivals in Race for Senate Ask Negro Support," March 2, 1964, and the *Philadelphia Inquirer* reported that "The political speeches were the first of the primary campaign," March 2, 1964.

79. Rudy Cernkovic, *Pittsburgh Press,* March 19, 1964.

80. *Harrisburg Patriot,* March 23, 1964.

81. Editorial, "A Matter of Degrees," *Valley Daily News* (Tarentum, Pa.), April 7, 1964.

82. Emphasis in the original.

83. The U.S. Census Bureau does not cite all Italian-Americans but only those who are of "foreign stock" — that is, foreign born or having one or both parents born abroad. Nowhere does the Census Bureau list that figure as being higher than 509,000, or give more than 22.1 percent for the *total* of all those persons enumerated as being of "foreign stock," Germans, Poles, and so forth; to state, therefore, that there were 2.4 million Italian-Americans in Pennsylvania, one would have to present some kind of statistical evidence of there being almost four additional Italian-Americans in the state for every first- *and* second-generation Italian enumerated by the Census Bureau.

84. Emphasis added.

85. Undated release provided by Justice Musmanno; emphasis added.

86. The only Italian newspaper for which the *N.W. Ayer and Son's Directory* listed a circulation figure in its 1965 edition was the *Unione:* 15,047 (William F. McAllister, ed., Philadelphia: N.W. Ayer and Son, Inc., 1965). This paper is the official organ of the fraternal organization known as the Order of Italian Sons and Daughters of America, which because of its many lodges in western Pennsylvania is generally conceded to have considerably more political influence than this figure suggests.

87. Pat O'Neill, *Pittsburgh Post-Gazette,* April 8, 1964.

88. Tape provided by Senator Joseph S. Clark.

89. April 7, 1964.

90. April 7, 1964.

91. "Miss Blatt Called Foe of Bossism," *Harrisburg Patriot,* April 7, 1964.

92. *The Philadelphia Inquirer,* April 12, 1964.

93. Associated Press , *Harrisburg Patriot,* April 8, 1964.

94. United Press International, *Williamsport Sun-Gazette,* April 8, 1964.

95. Pat O'Neill, *Pittsburgh Post-Gazette,* April 8, 1964.

96. One of Senator Clark's aides expressed the opinion shortly after the election that "Musmanno tried to pass himself off as Jewish in Philadelphia when he was looking for a job." The justice indignantly denounced this as false. As false as it may be, it nevertheless provides a motive for Clark's accusation.

97. Three years later, another aide of Senator Clark commented on this matter: "He wanted to prove that the blurb put out on Musmanno by the party was filled with lies — that Musmanno was not a hero of World

War I, that he had, in fact, once changed his name to 'Musman,' that he was not a *paisan* but was American-born." Greg Walter, "It is Necessary for a Politician not to get so far Ahead of His Troops that He Gets Shot in the Ass," *Philadelphia Magazine* (June 1967), p. 61.

98. Release provided by Justice Musmanno.

99. John G. MuCullough, *Philadelphia Evening Bulletin,* April 6, 1964.

100. Release provided by Justice Musmanno. A major portion of this statement was quoted by the *New Yorker* magazine under the heading, "Metaphors We Hated to Come to the End Of." May 23, 1964, p. 136.

101. Technically speaking he had been reprimanded by the court in two of its decisions; no *vote* of censure had ever been taken in these cases. Formal censure votes *had* been taken, however, in the Allegheny Bar Association and other bar actions cited above.

102. Release provided by Justice Musmanno.

103. Release provided by Senator Clark.

104. Emphasis added.

105. April 21, 1964. Emphasis added.

106. Release provided by Senator Clark.

107. In particular, one ward leader in suburban Philadelphia was extremely distressed by the fact that in canvassing one precinct after another within her domain, and in going from home to home talking to those with whom she had worked for years in her own neighborhood, she found she was unable to get anyone to vote for the justice who had seen him on television. At least, such was her account to this author of her failure to carry her ward for the organization in the primary.

108. *Harrisburg Patriot,* April 17, 1964.

109. Letter dated April 22, 1964, provided by Miss Blatt.

110. In fact the gentleman who solicited the letter from her stated later that he had never received it. If he had, he said, it would not have satisfied him, but he would have taken it into consideration in his later remarks. Had she disassociated herself completely from Senator Clark as he had asked her to do, he would have had no reason to write about her the way he did in later editions of the newspaper. "Our battle then would have been only with Clark," he said. Interview with John B. Di Giorno, National Secretary of the Order of Italian Sons and Daughters of America, July 7, 1967.

111. *Philadelphia Evening Bulletin,* April 17, 1964.

112. *Philadelphia Inquirer,* April 18, 1964.

113. *Harrisburg Patriot,* April 18, 1964.

114. *Philadelphia Evening Bulletin,* April 13, 1964.

115. *Philadelphia Inquirer,* April 21, 1964.

116. *Pittsburgh Press,* April 23, 1964.
117. John G. McCullough, *Philadelphia Evening Bulletin,* April 21, 1964.
118. *Harrisburg Patriot,* April 24, 1964.
119. Letter to the author, March 7, 1966.
120. *Philadelphia Inquirer,* April 25, 1964.
121. Richard A. Doran, interview, November 25, 1964.
122. E. John Bucci, "Political Outlook in Pennsylvania," unpublished, March 1964. Swarthmore, Pa.
123. *Philadelphia Inquirer,* April 28, 1964.
124. For instance, *Philadelphia Evening Bulletin,* April 29, 1964.
125. Saul Kohler, *Philadelphia Inquirer,* April 29, 1964.
126. John G. McCullough, *Philadelphia Evening Bulletin,* April 29, 1964.
127. *Philadelphia Inquirer,* April 30, 1964.
128. John C. Calpin, *Philadelphia Evening Bulletin,* April 30, 1964.

The Tragicomic
Interlude

On APRIL 29 Miss Blatt, Senator Clark, and their campaign team rejoiced, but with a sense of disbelief. The primary was over and they had won!

Or had they? It wasn't long before their exuberance died and a feeling of depression set in; the following months were to become among the most tedious and exasperating of their entire lives. Indeed the primary was *not* over, nor would it be officially at an end until twenty-two weeks later on October 12. The seemingly unending days of legal maneuvering and vote recount that followed appeared calculated, like the Chinese water torture or guerrilla warfare, to tire out the victim until he would give up of his own accord.

All planning by Miss Blatt's aides for the election campaign ahead—all fund-raising, all recruiting of volunteers, all scheduling of appearances, and all the tiny details that are usually taken care of during the period following a primary—was slowed down to a snail's pace. The participants appeared to be dream-walking through their assignments, partially paralyzed by the legal spectacle unfolding before their eyes in all its Kafkaesque absurdity, confusion and irony.

The senatorial election took place only three weeks after the final court ruling ending the primary, and while few people expect any political campaign to be a model of organization and dispatch, Miss Blatt's turned out to be a model of disaster. In this sense then, Justice Musmanno did ultimately obtain his victory—not by winning the battle himself—but by making it possible for another to deliver the death blow. In the years that followed the election the justice continued to dog the footsteps of his opponents, entering from the sidelines every campaign they were involved in, reminding his Italian "constituents" of the "evil of their ways," until they were both defeated.

Thus the justice came close to fulfilling his dream of rewriting the final chapter of his autobiography.[1] Instead of its ending with his primary defeat, it could now depict the true moral of his life — that good will always conquer evil — as demonstrated by the ignominious destruction of his enemies.

Such was the scenario that was to be enacted in the months ahead. How it came into being, and how it developed into the elaborate drama just discussed is the topic of this chapter. The steps were tiny, the details involved and interwoven with confusing legalisms, but the end result was nevertheless forthcoming. With Senator Scott's help during the election the strategy gradually took hold, and Justice Musmanno was, in his own mind, and in the minds of many others, vindicated.

Prolonged election disputes, when the identity of the victor is unknown for months while the recount goes on and on, occur every now and then in American politics,[2] but there has seldom been a long primary recount. The Blatt-Musmanno litigation over the outcome of this primary became so involved and confused that at one point the State Board of Elections wondered if it might not be necessary to postpone the senatorial election indefinitely until the courts were able to determine who had won the primary.[3]

The first indication that the race might require a "recount" came from the justice on the day after the election. Miss Blatt was considered to be some 3,000 votes ahead of her opponent, but there were an estimated 10,000 absentee ballots yet to be counted, and about twenty-five precincts unreported. The justice's "tearful"[4] indecision of the night before had given way to a determination not to concede until the final votes were in. After berating Clark once again for his campaign of "vilification" and "bigotry,"[5] the justice returned to his chambers and maintained a judicious silence.

Miss Blatt, in the meantime, refused to claim a victory until her margin should become larger, the mail vote recorded, or the justice conceded. Under Pennsylvania law, the official vote count in all electoral divisions does not take place until the Friday after the election (May 1 in this instance), while the absentee ballots are not counted until the following Friday (May 8).

Under a new law, effective for the first time in 1964, absentee voters could mail in their ballots anytime after the day of the election—provided they marked their ballots no later than election day, and provided also that the county election board received their ballots on or before the day they were to be counted.[6] It was entirely possible, therefore, for a person to wait until the unofficial election returns were in, on April 29 or 30, to then mark his ballot saying that he had done so on the proper day, and mail it in at anytime sufficient for it to get to its destination by May 8. For this reason Michael J. Byrne, Senator Clark's executive assistant and Miss Blatt's chief campaign counsellor, had earlier decided to check the party registration of all those who applied for such ballots and the numbers of ballots sent to each election division within the city of Philadelphia. Later, he and his assistants actually compared the signatures of each applicant with his voter registration record to determine the possible number of "forged" ballots which might have been sent in.[7]

Newspaper reports, however, soon revealed other sources of difficulty for Miss Blatt. As the official tally was being conducted statewide, her margin of victory gradually began melting away. First she lost 257 votes in Lackawanna County,[8] then 680 in Philadelphia, and then 623 in Allegheny County.[9] By May Miss Blatt was ahead by only 1,587 votes.[10] Then, on May 9, Venango County discovered a 1,048 vote error in favor of Miss Blatt.[11] With so much variation between what was originally reported and what the sealed returns were showing, the Blatt forces decided to look into the legality of the official count.

Long before the election had taken place, several of the Blatt workers in Philadelphia foresaw the possibility that some of the voting machines in heavily Democratic areas might not be "read right"[12] by the precinct election officials who usually owe their positions to the local organization committeemen. Similar occurrences in previous city-wide primaries had warned them that a close race could be stolen through "errors" in reading the results off the backs of the voting machines. The only way to check such errors, once the vote was in, was to pay fifty dollars and present three signatures on a petition to have each division's (or precinct's)[13] machines reopened and the vote count rechecked. With over 1,640 divisions in the city of Philadelphia alone, the sum required would be prohibitive.[14] The volunteers, therefore, had decided to put as many poll watchers as possible into every polling place and to send letters to various judges of election urging them to read the numbers correctly. After the election they thought it obvious that their precautions had not been sufficient, so they very carefully began to study the returns, division by division, to look for signs of tampering. The method used was simple but not obvious.

In Pennsylvania, candidates running for the supreme court may cross-file on the different parties' tickets. Campaign literature and individual party workers, in making their rounds, usually identify the allegiance of the candidates, urging certain ones on their own party faithful. But on the ballots the candidates may be listed in both parties' columns. Thus, if a particularly strong Democratic division lost more votes to the Republican candidates for the supreme court than to independent Democrat Genevieve Blatt, the Blatt volunteers were more likely to suspect those divisions of errors than others. In some instances, anonymous phone calls gave tips on where votes may have been stolen. So the stage was being set for a wide-spread investigation into possible vote frauds.

THE ABSENTEE BALLOTS

In the meantime, the count of absentee ballots began through-out the state. A spot check of the ballots in the city of Philadelphia had revealed some rather interesting data. Of the total number of civilian ballots throughout the city (1,243), an incredibly high number (302), almost one-fourth to be exact, had come from one single ward—the 42d. One member of Miss Blatt's legal team of five young lawyers[15] made a house-to-house check of a single division and found that of twenty-one persons interviewed, seventeen had illegally voted by absentee ballot.

Pennsylvania law is quite specific as to who may use the absentee ballot and who may not. Only military personnel, those unavoidably absent from their voting districts on election day because of "duties, occupation or business," or those who are ill and cannot go to the polls may apply for an absentee ballot. A voter who pleads illness must provide the signature of a witness who may be either the attending physician or a resident of the same ward of the city but unrelated to the voter. According to Miss Blatt's investigator, many people had been asked by their committeemen whether or not they intended to vote on primary day. If they replied "No," they were told, "Well, you can vote by mail this time, just sign here."[16] They were then given applications for absentee ballots that they signed, and when the ballots came in the mail they marked them and turned them over to the committeemen, whether they were entitled to them or not.[17]

As a result of this preliminary check, thirteen teams of volunteers—most of them college and law students—were organized and sent throughout the city to interview absentee voters in districts returning a heavy proportion of such ballots in comparison with previous years. Similar investigations were inaugurated by volunteers in other areas, particularly in Scranton.

On the fourth day of counting absentee ballots from Philadelphia, only the military ballots were completed, and these went surprisingly in favor of Allegheny County Prothonotary David B. Roberts. Roberts received 196 of the military votes, Musmanno 157, and Blatt 137.[18] This gave rise to speculation that it was Roberts' clearly Anglo-Saxon name and the fact that he was not a woman that caused him to receive a disproportionate number of military votes in Philadelphia where Musmanno was still 60,000 ahead. This speculation, in turn, reinforced Musmanno's conviction that the election had gone against him for purely ethnic reasons. (But Miss Blatt could similarly have complained that her rather slim share of this vote was due to her sex. Which of the two types of prejudice actually determined the outcome in November is another question.) Musmanno's chagrin over Roberts' candidacy had already been pointedly expressed on election night when, speaking about Roberts' 70,000 votes culled mainly in southwestern Pennsylvania, the justice had complained, "They were all my votes . . . votes that would normally have gone to the organization's candidate. Something should be done about Roberts in the party."[19] Musmanno's contention was substantially boosted by an unsigned article in the *Pittsburgh-Gazette* calling Roberts a "champion vote-wrecker, " an opinion with which former Governor David Lawrence substantially agreed.[20] At the moment, however, the civilian ballots, not the military ballots, were the center of contention.

On the following Monday, Michael Byrne and his team of young lawyers decided to challenge the legality of 550 absentee ballots before the Philadelphia County Board of Elections, or the City Commissioners as they were also called.[21] A dispute immediately arose over the procedure to be followed in challenging each ballot under the new law.

The Blatt forces held that a simple statement of the reason for the challenge, in general terms, plus the word "challenged" should be written on each ballot so designated. More specific evidence on the nature of the challenge would be given at a later hearing at which, according to the election code, the elector casting the ballot would have an opportunity to reply to the challenge before the elections board.

But Musmanno's lawyers, State Senator Benjamin Donolow and Abraham E. Freedman, argued that a simple statement in general terms was not sufficient to delay the count. If any ballot was to be set aside, they argued, the persons so challenging should first be required to establish a *prima facie* case as to its invalidity by means of a signed affidavit before the elector could be put to the inconvenience of coming to a hearing. Not to require some proof of invalidity first would be to encourage all sorts of "frivolous or captious" challenges having a purely dilatory effect, they said. Since the board of elections was supposed to certify results of the primary by May 18, the affidavits would eliminate all challenges not made in "good faith" and would thus speed up the process of counting the ballots.[22]

To this Miss Blatt's lawyers, headed by Ferdinand P. Schoettle and Gregory M. Harvey, argued that an affidavit was nowhere called for by Pennsylvania's election laws and that the procedure outlined in those laws did not specify that evidence was actually to be given until the individual hearing on each challenged ballot took place. As a physical matter it would have been impossible for the volunteers to put together 550 affidavits on the spur of the moment, but they could have been able to produce substantial evidence of their contentions by the time the challenged voters were to appear before the elections board.[23] The commissioners, however, ruled that the affidavits had to be presented ahead of time, so the Blatt team appealed to President Judge Vincent A. Carroll of the court of common pleas. The following day the judge handed down a rather ambiguous ruling to the effect that no affidavits per se would be required, but for the hearings beginning on the following day a "memorandum" would need to be presented for each challenged ballot indicating:

> Why this man is not a qualified absentee elector; that he was within the county where he is entitled to vote on the day of election; three, that he was able to appear personally at the polling place on the day of the primary election. . . . He [Harvey] will state in writing in each case why this vote is challenged . . . [and will] hand them to them [the elections board and Musmanno's lawyers] when they [the ballots] come up for a hearing.[24]

He also commented, "I think they [the Blatt lawyers] ought to give it a little in advance, but I won't insist upon that. . . . He will have to furnish them, *and* the hearings are being fixed for tomorrow morning at 11:00."[25] When asked by Harvey, "My understanding was that at the time each one came up I would then submit to the voter citing the reasons . . . ," the judge intervened, "Yes."[26]

This simple colloquy was to give rise to contradictory interpretations by both sides. The Blatt team understood the judge to mean that a simple statement ("memorandum") of the reasons for each challenge would be presented the following morning as the voters came forward for the individual hearing on each ballot. They would try to have as many challenges as possible ready for presentation to the elections board and Musmanno's lawyers by 11 A.M., but it would not be necessary to have all of them completed at that time. The judge had agreed, they felt, that a statement would not have to be ready until the individual ballot was presented at the hearing.[27]

The lawyers for Justice Musmanno, on the other hand, believed that Judge Carroll had required that a detailed statement of evidence be presented on each of the 550 challenges at 11 A.M. the following morning—before the hearing had begun—so that they would have information on which to act before each case was presented. When the transcript of the previous day's court proceeding was read, it was revealed that Judge Carroll had agreed to allow the challenges to be delayed until each case was presented. The commissioners proceeded to examine the individual "memoranda" submitted by the Blatt attorneys. Instead of a detailed statement of evidence, each memorandum consisted simply of a single mimeographed sheet with checks beside one or more of seven possible reasons for invalidating each ballot. Each sheet gave the name, ward, and division of the elector, and provided little more information for the challenge than the Blatt attorneys had originally intended to give on the opening day of the proceedings. The bulk of the evidence was to be revealed later in the form of oral testimony from their door-to-door investigators as each case was presented. The memoranda were only "indications," not "evidence," of the points to be proven.

When Musmanno's lawyers objected that this was not what Judge Carroll had intended, the board of elections sustained them and ordered all challenges to be dismissed and the vote count to proceed.[28] Miss Blatt's attorneys immediately filed an appeal to the court of common pleas.

On the following day, May 14, at 4:00 P.M., Judge Charles A. Waters handed down a decision upholding the ruling of the board of elections to dismiss the challenges as a "sound one."[29] The commissioners immediately proceeded to open the challenged ballots, and a general free-for-all ensued.

In an effort to stop the separation of the ballots from their identifying envelopes while an appeal of Judge Waters' decision was being filed before the Pennsylvania Supreme Court, the Blatt team insistently read to the commissioners that part of the election law that prohibited any count from being conducted pending all appeals before the courts and demanded that all action cease.

Musmanno's lawyers countered that before the board could order the slitting of envelopes to be stopped a writ of supersedeas would have to be obtained from Chief Justice Bell to halt the action. After one hour of frantically searching for the justice, a writ was formally obtained by telephone, and the separation of the ballots from the envelopes was ended—but only after almost the entire mass of ballots had been opened.

In the process, the following exchange complete with pushes, shouts, and punches had taken place, and the next morning's newspapers had a field day:

> Schoettle (Attorney for Miss Blatt) : . . . we have evidence, and I plan to read some of it now, that many of these absentee ballots were obtained unlawfully.
>
> Wolov: We will not have you reading that.
>
> Kalodner (Attorney for Miss Blatt) : Continue to read it despite the decision of the Deputy City Solicitor.
>
> Wolov: In that case, remove the stenographer.
>
> Schoettle: I have a right to present—
>
> Commissioner Osser (interposing): Let me stop this right here and now.
>
> Donolow (Attorney for Musmanno): I am not going to let him talk when the count is going on. We are going to make—
>
> Osser (interposing): I am going to clear the room in a minute. He has no right to read it.
>
> McGlinchey (Democratic leader of the 42d Ward): This Commission is running this count. I have not seen anything like this in twenty years.
>
> Donolow: I agree with you it is disgraceful. . . . Don't push me (to Kalodner), don't you go pushing me. I have as much right to this Bar as you do. You have no right to push me. With your father on the High Court you think I am scum, I'm not scum. I'm at this Bar and I am standing here to speak, you are not going to push me.
>
> Osser: All right, let's clear this courtroom. Only employees and watchers are to stay in here, everybody out. . . .
>
> Kalodner: I have no intention of removing myself, unless I am removed.
>
> Schoettle: I would like to point out that as I started reading our evidence, that except for the fact that Mr. Donolow started pushing—
>
> Donolow (interposing): That is absolutely a lie. . . .
>
> Kalodner: On the record, we have no intention of removing ourselves from here while the count is going on. That constitutes a

violation of the United States Constitution, this is an open proceeding and the public is permitted to attend . . . .
Donolow: When you were in the District Attorney's office, you
framed everybody and wired everybody up. You wired everybody
up and now you are coming here pushing me around.
Kalodner: Put that down as that was said by the Senator, put that
down. . . . I suggest you file a formal complaint, Mr. Donolow, as
a member of the Bar you know how to do it. The Committee of
Censors will be interested in this.
Donolow: You can go to the Committee of Censors, and there's one
more thing. I'm going to take you outside. I'm only a little guy,
but you are a big guy, you and I are going outside, you are a
yellow-belly, and I want to take you outside. . . .
Commissioner McHenry: The only thing I am waiting for is the
policeman so I can order you out, that is it. I am not going to
have a prize-fight in front of this Court. . . .[30]

The next morning the newspapers cheerfully announced that
Donolow had punched Kalodner several times and that three car-
loads of police had been required to establish order.[31] However,
the vote count had been stopped despite the fact that most of
the ballots had been separated from their identifying envelopes;
the two teams now retired to prepare their briefs on the absentee
ballot question to be argued before the Pennsylvania Supreme
Court on May 25.

THE MACHINE COUNT

In the meantime, the other counties throughout the state were
continuing with their count of official machine returns and un-
challenged absentee ballots. On May 16 Justice Musmanno
pulled ahead of Miss Blatt by 179 votes,[32] and on the basis of the
discrepancies noted earlier between the official and unofficial
returns Ferdinand Schoettle succeeded in having Judge Carroll
order a reopening of the voting machines in twenty divisions of
Philadelphia's 42d ward. This was the same request which the
County Board of Elections had turned down a few days earlier,
despite the fact that the law requires the board to do so on its
own motion (without charging appellants the fifty dollar bond
per division) wherever such discrepancies exit. Schoettle had

chosen the 42d ward in particular because of an anonymous tip,[33] but decided to concentrate on those divisions within the ward whose committeemen were jobholders—just on a "hunch."

As it turned out, in five of those divisions the machines showed totals entirely different from those *officially* reported. Miss Blatt was found to have been denied seventy-two votes that had been credited to Justice Musmanno, thus giving her a net gain of 144 votes. On the basis of these "errors," Commissioner Osser ordered all the machines in the 42d ward reopened and another ninety-seven votes were found to have been similarly miscounted or "misplaced"[34]—a net gain of 241 votes for Miss Blatt from that ward alone. An observer, James Duffy from the United States Senate Subcommittee on Privileges and Elections (called in by a petition from the Blatt team and authorized by the Senate to report whatever irregularities might have arisen in the possible election of a future member of the Senate), commented that this particular recanvass showed a "definite pattern in the 42d ward to record votes for Justice Musmanno which rightfully belonged to Miss Blatt."[35] This matter was later to be the subject of a federal grand jury investigation into possible vote fraud.[36]

On the following day the County Board of Elections, on its own volition, ordered the reopening of every voting machine in the city—a total of 3,300.[37] In the process, sufficient "errors" were discovered to cause Miss Blatt to overcome Musmanno's lead. A total of 995 votes were recovered for Miss Blatt from the machine recount alone,[38] 196 of them from a single division of the 52d ward.[39] During the process of counting the votes in the reopened machines, several other discrepancies were discovered; for example, in some divisions more Democratic votes were cast in this primary than there were registered Democrats.[40] But the difference between the 996 votes recovered for Miss Blatt and her final margin of 491 votes resulted from the continuing count of absentee ballots throughout the state.

Before the Pennsylvania Supreme Court heard the two sides argue the correct procedure for counting the challenged absentee ballots in Philadelphia, however, the Musmanno team thought up another method of obtaining votes for their client—that of tallying the votes cast in "blank spaces" on the Jamestown machines used in certain wards of the city of Philadelphia.

Approximately half the polling places of the city were equipped with the Jamestown voting machines that list the candidates for each office horizontally on a single line with each party having its own row of listings. Persons voting on these machines are supposed to pull the small levers directly *above* the names of the candidates. The other half of the city used Shoup machines that list the candidates vertically; in the controversy that developed, the Shoup machines were involved in only two wards. Most of the arguments and explanations used in the following litigation were based upon the Jamestown machines.

Since Pennsylvania law requires that primaries be open only to registered members of the parties, it is the custom of the election officers at each poll to prepare the machines before the elector casts his vote so that he cannot vote in the primary of the other party. Thus a voter who is a registered Democrat will not be able to vote for a candidate in the Republican primary, and vice versa. However, in April of 1964 one congressional and one state senatorial district in Philadelphia, thirteen wards in all, were holding special elections to fill vacancies that had occurred since the previous general election. The voters in those districts had to be given access to both parties' levers in order to vote properly in the special elections.

To reduce the confusion, in those districts where the Jamestown machines were used, the congressional and state senatorial elections were printed on separate rows beneath the regular primary listings, with the names of the candidates placed to the far right and beyond the columns used for the primary. The result was that two whole rows immediately below the names of the primary candidates, blank except for the special elections being conducted at the very end of each row, were completely accessible to anyone who, mistakenly or otherwise, cared to depress a lever. It was revealed later that the machines could very easily have been fixed by the board of elections so that those blank spaces would have been blocked off and their levers locked in place, but the matter had not been taken care of because it would have cost $3,000—hardly a tremendous sum for a city of almost two million people.

The Musmanno legal maneuver, therefore, was to try to have all the votes cast in the blank spaces immediately below the names of the United States senatorial candidates (Row C)[41] counted as having been intended for them. The voters' honest confusion on entering the voting booth is what caused them to pull the levers below instead of above the names of the candidates, it was argued, in spite of the fact that the particular row referred to was labeled "Republican—Special Election." It was entirely possible, however, and in fact it was intended that Republicans as well as Democrats be able to depress the levers in the row immediately below the names of the Democratic primary candidates so that, as Miss Blatt's lawyers were later to argue, they, rather than Democrats, might be more inclined to make such errors.

The Democratic City Committee, which was sponsoring and was reliably reported to have paid the entire cost of the Musmanno litigation[42]—a questionable procedure during a primary—admitted later that they had gotten the idea for this latest move from their study of similar results in a previous primary. In 1963 a state senatorial candidate whose name happened to be listed directly under Mayor Tate's received what was considered a surprisingly high number of votes. The city organization concluded that many of these votes had been intended for Mayor Tate but because of the confusion of the voters, had mistakenly been logged in the row beneath.[43] On this basis they decided to make a court test of the present situation, claiming that where the intention of the voter can be demonstrated he should not be disfranchised because of a mere technicality—that of having cast his vote in a blank space. To this, one of Miss Blatt's attorneys replied, "You cannot . . . attempt to 'guess' what a voter had on his mind when his vote ended up in a blank space."[44]

The City Board of Elections completely refused Donolow's proposal to count the Row C votes. Musmanno's attorneys, therefore, commenced a series of appeals that carried the issue all the way to the Supreme Court of the United States, and served to delay the final determination of the Democratic candidate for the United States Senate until October 12. In the meantime several other developments rapidly moved to their conclusion.

APPEALS

As a result of all the investigations into voting irregularities conducted by the Blatt volunteers throughout the state, Miss

Blatt's legal army was able to put together a catchall contingency petition to be acted upon in the event that Musmanno should be certified the winner of the primary by the State Elections Bureau. Submitted to the Dauphin County Court in Harrisburg on the last day for filing protests stemming from the primary,[45] the petition concentrated on specific voting irregularities discovered in Lackawanna, Fayette, and Philadelphia counties. It alleged fraud and forgery in certain instances and urged the court to declare Musmanno's election illegal. Sixteen pages were required to outline the specific vote frauds and irregularities alleged to have been perpetrated in those counties, and an additional twenty-nine pages were consumed in detailing the nature of the specific challenges to the absentee ballots in Philadelphia still pending before the Pennsylvania Supreme Court.[46] Since Musmanno was never certified by the State Elections Bureau this petition was never acted upon. But had it been, it is a certainty that this appeal, combined with Musmanno's blank space appeal, would have consumed sufficient time before the courts of Pennsylvania and the United States to have prevented any election for the United States Senate from taking place in Pennsylvania in November.

By this time, some of the party's statewide leaders had become so frantic over the maze of intermingled court appeals confronting them that several were reported to have called for both candidates to step down and allow the party leaders to choose a compromise candidate to run against Hugh Scott. Needless to say, neither candidate reacted very favorably to such reports, and Chairman Otis Morse had later to admit that this proposal, coming after the rank-and-file Democrats had already made their wishes known at the polls, "might be a serious handicap . . . and would give Hugh Scott a ready-made campaign issue."[47] Such were the woes of the Democratic party of Pennsylvania in mid-May.

On May 25 the Pennsylvania Supreme Court, minus Justices Musmanno and Cohen,[48] heard arguments from all three participating sides (Blatt, Musmanno, and the Philadelphia County Board of Elections) on the challenged absentee ballots case that had been so abruptly interrupted by Chief Justice Bell's telephoned writ of supersedeas in May.[49]

Arguing on behalf of Miss Blatt, Philip Kalodner presented a brief[50] asserting that she and her lawyers had been denied the right, by the County Board of Elections, to present evidence at individual hearings concerning 550 challenged absentee ballots because of the board's misunderstanding of the Pennsylvania election code. Stating what they considered to be the proper interpretation of the law—that detailed evidence to back up each challenge was not required until the time of the actual hearing—they appealed to the court to overturn Judge Waters' decision and to permit the hearings to proceed.

Musmanno's lawyers (Abraham E. Freedman and Senator Benjamin Donolow), on the other hand, argued that for strictly technical reasons the appellants had no right to appeal the decision of the elections board citing authorities into evidence other than those referred to by the Blatt attorneys to support their case.[51] They argued further that there were no irregularities in the proceedings before the County Board of Elections, that the board had acted correctly, and that Judge Waters' decision should be upheld. With this position, Levy Anderson, first deputy solicitor for the city of Philadelphia and acting counsel for the board of elections, substantially agreed.

At one point in the two-hour debate, Chief Justice Bell rather plaintively commented about the opened ballots, "I don't see how we can do anything but allow them to be counted once they have been opened."[52] But he reserved judgment until the court had had a chance to study a plan put forth by the Blatt attorneys to circumvent this difficulty.[53]

The formula the Blatt people had worked out first called for the challenged ballots to be separated by ward and division. Then, if all absentee ballots of a particular division were found to be invalid, all would be cast out. If all votes counted from a particular division were for the same candidate, the board of elections would deduct the invalid votes from the total number of ballots within that division. Next, if a substantial number of absentee ballots from a particular division were found to be invalid, all of the absentee ballots in that division would be discarded. The number that might be considered substantial enough to invalidate a whole division's ballots was suggested to be anywhere from 25 to 50 percent. Finally, if a significant number were found to be invalid, but not enough to invalidate the entire division, the votes for each candidate would be reduced proportionately to the number given to each candidate by the whole division.[54]

This was the plan submitted by the Blatt attorneys to the supreme court, but until the board of elections had had an opportunity to study it most people thought the task an insoluble one. How could anyone be expected to subtract invalid ballots from valid ones when they were no longer identifiable except by ward and division? The challenges, after all, were to be based on specific complaints as to the legitimacy of the voter's application for the ballot, his using the absentee ballot correctly and in good faith, and so on. Indeed it was a hard nut to crack—so much so that in time the true practicality of the Blatt proposal came to be appreciated and was ultimately adopted.

In the meantime, the supreme court took two days to reach a decision. Agreeing substantially with the Blatt brief, but without mentioning her attorneys' proposals for counting the ballots, the court unanimously overturned Judge Waters' decision and ordered the board of elections to proceed with the hearings, commenting: "There is no requirement in the Election Code that a challenge to an absentee ballot be supported at the time of the challenge, or prior to hearings, by an affidavit *or memorandum.* . . ."[55]

On hearing of the court's decision, Commissioner Osser complained, "I just don't know any way of matching the votes with the envelopes." When asked if he would possibly resort to asking a voter how he voted in order to do so, he replied, "I have no right to ask him; I wouldn't ask him; and if I were foolish enough to ask him, I hope he'd tell me to go to hell."[56]

Two days later the board of elections met to hold the hearings ordered by the court. The instant the galvanized box in which the ballots had been stored for safekeeping was opened, however, the newspapers had another field day. On counting the ballots and the envelopes from which they had been separated it was discovered that there were 561 ballots but only 549 envelopes.[57] Michael J. Byrne, Miss Blatt's chief advisor, was quoted as having said, "We had expected this would happen." Earlier, watchers for Miss Blatt had spotted an envelope with four ballots and another with two. "This is definitely illegal," Byrne continued, "I guess there were more we didn't catch."

The explanation for such an occurrence was being independently uncovered by a Philadelphia newspaper pursuing its own house-to-house investigation of the absentee ballot controversy. For days the *Philadelphia Evening Bulletin* had been carrying unsigned stories, one of which was headlined "ABSENTEE BALLOTS FORCED BY DEMOCRATS, VOTERS SAY."[58] The series described how the ballots had been solicited by the committeemen, whether the voters needed them or not, who later picked them up to be mailed. The conclusion that the committeemen just might have thought it much more convenient to mail several ballots back in one envelope, rather than individually, seemed to gain currency as a result of these stories. Why they might have taken the risk in doing so was never adequately explained.

At any rate, Republican State Attorney General Walter Alessandroni immediately urged the city's Democratic district attorney, James C. Crumlish, to hold a grand jury investigation into all aspects of the alleged vote frauds. But Crumlish simply passed the ball back to the attorney general, saying that he would be happy to present any petition Alessandroni might prepare, on the basis of his own investigations, before the proper court.[59] The district attorney, in substance, had declined to conduct his own inquiry and had left the entire matter to the Republican. The attorney general responded by assigning his own investigator to observe the proceedings, "for the purpose of discovering all evidence of criminal violations of the Election Code." Before the issue was closed, even the FBI was called into the case.[60]

The County Elections Board was still having no luck deciding on a method to determine which absentee ballots should be counted. They went back to the supreme court to request some guidance in the matter, but Chief Justice Bell ignored the previously submitted Blatt plan and merely referred them to the election code.[61] Then, in order to waste no more time, the elections board and the Blatt and Musmanno teams of lawyers decided to put aside, for the time being, the question of counting ballots and concentrate instead upon the immediate problem of a compromise procedure for hearing the individual challenges on each ballot.

At first the Blatt attorneys proposed to subpoena all those who had used absentee ballots, but then relented and permitted simple "invitations" to go out.[62] At one point Miss Blatt's attorneys even wanted the elections board itself subpoenaed and required to produce the improperly filled out ballot applications that would help prove their contentions.

During the process one commissioner came down with a bad case of hypertension and another begged to be relieved of his duties because of a cardiac condition. Finally, the last of the three-man board of elections, Commissioner Osser, lamented, "It looks like I might be the third victim."[63]

In time, however, the proceedings moved ahead and the board conducted as many as forty or fifty hearings in a single day. Even so, it was August 12 before the last hearing was completed. Of the 550 absentee ballots originally challenged 429 were found to be defective and only 121 were declared valid. To count the valid ballots, attorneys Kalodner and Harvey once again submitted their vote-count formula, this time urging that all the ballots in a particular division be discarded if more than 30 percent were found to be invalid.[64]

This formula, finally, was substantially accepted—the only difference being that the proportionate vote condition was lowered to 25 percent—and the vote count proceeded. Of the total remaining valid votes, then, Justice Musmanno received seventy-two, Miss Blatt sixteen, and David Roberts three.[65] So ended the absentee ballot phase of the litigation in Philadelphia.

BLANK SPACES

The remaining major issue to be settled before a candidate could be certified for the November election—the Row C "blank spaces" controversy—was already well under way by mid-May. At the same time that the County Elections Board was ordering all the voting machines in the city to be opened,[66] Judge Vincent A. Carroll of the common pleas court was hearing an appeal from the Musmanno attorneys to have the Row C votes counted. Taking advantage of the opportunity, Judge Carroll ordered the elections board to tally the Row C votes on the machines in the thirteen wards involved, but not to include them in the overall totals for each candidate. Instead, they were to be turned over to him as the basis for further consideration when additional legal arguments could be heard.[67]

In the meantime, the Committee of Seventy—an influential nonpartisan (but bipartisan) self-proclaimed watchdog committee of private citizens interested in maintaining good government in the city of Philadelphia[68]—urged Judge Carroll not to include the "blank space" votes in the final tabulation. "Those who allege that these figures were put on the voting machines by persons who intended to vote for candidates in an adjacent row or column," they stated in a letter sent to the judge, "are merely asserting what they are attempting to prove."[69]

On June 4 the results of the Row C count were in and Judge Carroll heard further arguments from both sides on the issue. Since almost 6,000 votes were involved, which would have given Musmanno a plurality of better than 1,200 votes and thus the election, the Blatt lawyers were very anxious to have the entire batch discounted. They therefore presented most unusual testimony from two psychology professors from the University of Pennsylvania, Doctors Robert D. Luce and Julius Wishner, experts in mathematics and statistical analysis,[70] to discredit the arguments of the Musmanno team.

On being asked the hypothetical question as to whether the percentage of Row C votes cast for each senatorial candidate could lead to the conclusion—as the Musmanno team had asserted—that the voters had indeed intended to vote for the names appearing in Row B, the professors replied that it could not. Referring to a chart comparing Row C with Row B figures, they stated in their report that:

> This chart . . . shows that Roberts received nearly twice the percentage of Row C "votes" as were received by Blatt and Musmanno. Assuming that the hypothesis of a constant proportion of dropdown vote was correct, the chance of a discrepancy as large or larger than that shown on the table is *less than 1 in a billion chance* that all the Row C "votes" have resulted from a constant proportion of the voters mistakenly moving the Row C lever under the name of a Democratic Senatorial candidate in Row B.[71]

The Blatt attorneys then went on to argue that some of the "blank space" votes were the result of other factors, specifically "indiscriminate voting" by electors and registered Republicans voting for Democratic candidates.[72] The university experts also pointed out that there were a significant number of votes cast in blank spaces on Row D—two rows below the candidates' names—and that "there is no obvious interpretation of these votes ... " but they are clearly not "votes 'dropped down' ... from Row B."[73] Examination of the voting machines had also shown a considerable number of votes cast in blank spaces where no candidates were listed in the row above. Also, some sixty votes had been cast under the names of Democratic candidates on machines reserved (as was the custom in some divisions) for use by Republicans only. By projecting this number throughout the rest of the wards using the Jamestown machines, the Blatt attorneys were able to estimate that more than 1,300 of the 6,000 votes which the Musmanno team wanted counted had been illegally cast by Republicans.[74]

Finally, on June 8, Judge Carroll handed down his decision on the matter affirming the ruling of the County Board of Elections not to count the Row C votes: "[A] judicial pronouncement that a particular voter has not complied with the regulations does not disfranchise the voter, rather the voter by failing to observe the regulations has rendered his vote a nullity."[75] He relied not on the testimony of the professors, but on a precedent set in 1897 at a time when only paper ballots were in use throughout the state. In that case voters in a primary who marked their ballots in boxes adjacent to blank spaces instead of adjacent to the name of the candidate had their votes invalidated. The judge declared the principle to be the same in both cases ("We must presume the voter knew where and how to vote.").[76]

An editorial in the *Philadelphia Evening Bulletin* a few days later pinpointed the issue exactly when it pointed out:

> ... a vote is a vote and a mistake is not. ... In practical terms, a ruling the other way would have been a voyage into the tricky territory of interpreting intention. ... If there was wholesale error, the situation reveals a sorry gap in voter education which should be plugged before the next election.[77]

Nothing daunted, however, the Musmanno team, backed by the Philadelphia Democratic Committee with Frank Smith at its head, decided to appeal Judge Carroll's decision to the Pennsylvania Supreme Court. Asserting on behalf of Musmanno that "inherent justice" requires that the votes be counted, Abraham E. Freedman reiterated that "no voter should be disfranchised just because he made a mistake and voted on the wrong line." He continued: "There is no possible explanation for so numerous a number of voters on Row C except that the voters believed this was the row on which they were to pull the levers. . . . No other reasonable explanation exists."[78] As to the argument that Republicans were more likely than Democrats to flip the levers in a row labeled "Republican-Special Election," Freedman replied, "For a Republican to vote in a Democratic primary would be to violate the law, and in the absence of any proof of such a violation . . . it must be presumed that no Republican violated the law."[79]

On July 1 the Pennsylvania Supreme Court met to hear arguments on the case that, by this time, was clearly meant to determine the outcome of the April primary. Assuredly, the forthcoming decision by these five colleagues of Justice Musmanno would settle once and for all the matter of who would receive the majority of the votes cast. Miss Blatt's plurality at this point was less than 500; the justice's margin of 1,200 in the Row C votes would definitely throw the election to him.

The lawyers for Musmanno presented four major arguments—several of which had already been utilized in the proceedings before the court of common pleas: (1) that the intent of the voter is the controlling factor in determining the effect of the ballot ("The law requires every presumption to be applied in favor of the validity of the ballot and the voter may not be disfranchised for minor irregularities or technical violations.");[80] (2) that the voting machine is more complicated and more subject to human error than the paper ballot; (3) that where the board of elections fails to take all precautions to avoid human error such neglect may not operate to disfranchise the voter; and (4) that all Row C votes must be regarded as Democratic votes because, in the absence of evidence to the contrary, all voters must be presumed to have voted legally as Democrats, Republicans, or nonpartisans, and not to have violated the law by crossing party lines.[81]

The second argument obviously was designed to answer Judge Carroll's assertion that the voter must be presumed to know how to cast his vote, while the third argument was raised to point out the blame that should be shared by the County Board of Elections for not locking the Rows C and D levers in the first place.

To the rather novel fourth argument, the Blatt brief replied:

> Any argument that a Republican who moved a lever over a blank space in the row marked "Special Election - *Republican*" would thus "violate the law" is completely fallacious. Such an action by Republicans would violate the law only if Row C were reserved for Democratic electors. That conclusion is demonstrably false, because Row C, being a special election row, was not reserved for any particular party.[82]

The Blatt team also argued, of course, that it was impossible to determine the actual intent of the voters because of the erratic nature of the evidence. They urged the supreme court to follow Judge Carroll's line of reasoning since "under the Constitution of Pennsylvania the rule applied to paper ballots applies equally to voting machines."[83] Philip Kalodner was then reported to have said in summation, "We cannot let Republicans or Non-Partisans decide who the Democratic candidate for the United States Senate is going to be."[84]

Levy Anderson, representing the County Board of Elections once again, basically agreed with the Blatt attorneys on this occasion, saying, "It is pure speculation . . . as to who the votes were intended for."[85]

DELAYS

The court then retired to consider its decision. Surprisingly, one week passed, then two, and then three—and still no opinion was forthcoming. One source reported that Chief Justice Bell had gone fishing. Another said that the judges were having a very difficult time trying to reach a conclusion. Rumors abounded that the vote was going first one way and then another. In exasperation the *Philadelphia Evening Bulletin* berated the court for its "dawdling," saying, "the State Supreme Court has frequently been critical of the backlog and delays in the lower Courts. In this instance, it doesn't seem to be practicing what it preaches."[86] Finally, on July 27 the court handed down its decision, three to two, not to allow the Row C votes.

The court did not immediately reveal the reasons behind its split vote; its majority opinion was to be published later. But the newspapers immediately concluded that Genevieve Blatt had won the primary, and euphoria reigned once again in the Blatt headquarters. On the following day, however, Justice Musmanno labeled the decision "erroneous" and declared his intention to file a petition immediately, asking his colleagues on the court to hear a reconsideration and reargument of the matter. He based his request on the United States Constitution that requires the counting of all votes cast in an election to a federal office, and on his assertion that the voting machines, as set for the primary, were a "trap for unsuspecting voters."[87] In another interview, Abraham E. Freedman stated that a 1937 Pennsylvania law required only that the voting lever had to be "upon" or "adjacent" to the candidate's name and that therefore, ". . . these votes were cast in full accord with the Pennsylvania Statute"[88] — no matter how the machines themselves had been constructed. He thus was laying the foundation for an appeal to the United States Supreme Court on constitutional grounds.

Generally (outside of the Musmanno camp) the ruling of the court was well received. One newspaper called it "A Prudent Decision";[89] another said there was "no other reasonable decision."[90] A columnist in the Philadelphia Inquirer even characterized the ruling as upholding the contention that ". . . mind reading has no standing in the eyes of the law."[91]

But Freedman disagreed and proceeded to file his "Petition for Reconsideration and/or Re-argument"[92] and later amendments, and the Blatt attorneys countered with a "Motion to Quash." Levy Anderson, on behalf of the board of elections, stated in his reply to Musmanno's petition, "the appellant presents nothing new except a constitutional argument which it failed to present in the Court below or before your Honorable Court and which argument is without merit."[93]

On August 5 the Supreme Court released its opinions to the public: one for the majority by Chief Justice J. C. Bell, Jr., with a concurring opinion by Justice Samuel J. Roberts; and one dissenting view by Justice Benjamin R. Jones.

The majority opinion forcefully stated that in reaching his conclusion that the vote should be counted Justice Musmanno had misinterpreted or ignored:

> (1) the clearer (pertinent) election laws, and (2) the setup of election machines which are clear to everyone except to a careless or an absent-minded or a hurried or an unthinking voter, and (3) the marked sample ballots which contained (a) very brief, clearly worded instructions, instructing a voter *twice* in clear, simple, brief language which lever to pull *down* in order to vote for the Democrat or Republican candidate of his choice, as well as (b) a crystally clear illustration and (4) words at the left end of Row (C) which state in small capital letters *"Special Election"* and in very large capital letters *"Republican,"* and (5) the line through the middle of Row C, with an arrow at the right end where the name of the candidate . . . appears, and (6) many prior decisions of this Court which, we repeat, in principle directly rule in the instant case. Furthermore, appellant has not been deprived of any right ordained or guaranteed by the Constitution of the United States.[94]

Justice Roberts, in his concurring opinion, called the assumption that voters who pulled Row C levers intended to vote for candidates in Row B an "exercise of retroactive clairvoyance."[95] Only Justice Jones expressed the belief that justice was more likely to be done by counting the votes than by refusing to count them.[96] All three opinions concurred in condemning the failure of the elections board to block off the blank spaces, however.

Two days later the court refused to hold a rehearing on the Row C question. But they did give Justice Musmanno ten days in which to file an appeal to the United States Supreme Court, staying all further proceedings on the state level for the time being. This meant that Miss Blatt could not be certified as the official Democratic candidate for the next ten days. However, the stay would not work an immediate hardship since the absentee ballots had not been completely disposed of, and the proceeding in the Lackawanna County vote disputes had only just been settled.

Musmanno's lawyers tried two more times to get the Pennsylvania Supreme Court to grant a rehearing, but Chief Justice Bell sharply turned them down, warning at one point that further delays "will not be tolerated."[97]

While attorney Freedman prepared his petition for certiorari to be presented to the United States Supreme Court, all other disputes were rapidly coming to a close. Miss Blatt was declared the winner by the State Elections Bureau after the ten-day stay expired on August 19—115 days after the April primary. This declaration was not, however, an official certification of Miss Blatt's candidacy, but just a notification by the director of the State Elections Bureau of the vote count. The instant it was announced Musmanno filed a suit in the Philadelphia Court of Common Pleas to force the counting of the 550 challenged absentee ballots.[98] Since the Pennsylvania Supreme Court had already ruled on this issue[99] the tactic was interpreted as a device to further delay Miss Blatt's certification.

The next day Judge Carroll dismissed the appeal without an opinion, and Philadelphia, the last county in the state to do so, certified its results to the State Elections Bureau.[100] But to prevent the state from certifying Miss Blatt's election during the first week of September when the state bureau was to notify the counties of the names to be placed on the November ballot, attorney Freedman once again appealed to the Pennsylvania Supreme Court for a stay. He argued that the printing of the ballots with Miss Blatt's name as the official candidate would result in "great prejudice" to the candidacy of Justice Musmanno.[101]

One important effect of all these court actions was pointed out by Ingrid Jewell in the *Pittsburgh Post-Gazette* on August 28, while the National Democratic Nominating Convention was in progress in Atlantic City:

> Because he will not concede defeat . . . the Democratic National Committee does not officially recognize anyone as Senatorial candidate from Pennsylvania. So Miss Blatt has been denied the television exposure during the convention which would have been hers had she been officially certified. State officials have gone as far as they can go in this regard. But the Supreme Court appeal prevents an official closing of the case. . . . With the obvious approval of

President Johnson, this . . . convention has been used as a show case for Democratic candidates for Governor, for Senate, for the U.S. House of Representatives. Candidates in close races have been put on camera to introduce other speakers or to speak in their own right. . . . But all this passed Miss Blatt by because Justice Musmanno will not concede his defeat.[102]

Miss Jewell then reported that some party leaders had tried to get the justice to resign "gracefully." "But," she said, "the Judge won't budge."[103]

At any rate, on August 31 the Pennsylvania Supreme Court denied, once again, the justice's plea to stay certification of Miss Blatt's candidacy. But on the following day the justice reiterated his intention to continue in the race until the ultimate appeal had been concluded. By all indication this final appeal would not take place until the United States Supreme Court reconvened for its fall term in October. The justice had requested the Court to hold a special session to dispose of the case immediately, but since the Court rarely did so, short of a national emergency, the possibility of its acceding to his request was slim indeed. The first day, therefore, that the Court could possibly consider the petition was October 5, and under the Monday rule then in effect, the first day that a decision could be handed down on whether or not to grant certiorari was October 12. Should the petition on certiorari have been granted, it would have been anyone's guess as to when the case would ultimately have been settled and the senatorial election held. Fortunately, the suspense was not prolonged beyond Columbus Day.

On September 5, Justice William J. Brennan, speaking for the United States Supreme Court, rejected Musmanno's plea to have the federal Court stay Miss Blatt's certification pending its disposition of the petition on certiorari,[104] and on September 8 Miss Blatt was formally certified the senate nominee by the State Elections Bureau. Thus the penultimate major hurdle was surmounted. The last was still a month away.

The petition for certiorari that Abraham E. Freedman filed on behalf of Justice Musmanno had some very interesting hurdles of its own to surmount. First, there was the matter of federal jurisdiction: In 1948, when President Johnson made his first successful bid for the Democratic nomination for the Senate in Texas, he won by only eighty-seven votes; his opponent also appealed all the way to the United States Supreme Court, but in that case the Court ruled that all aspects of a primary election were not subject to federal jurisdiction since it was primarily a party function. A series of civil rights cases had brought party primaries under partial federal control, and one case, *United States* vs. *Classic*,[105] extended the constitutional protection over any outright fraudulent attempts to change primary results. But, lacking a civil rights issue or evidence of tampering with election returns by the Blatt team, it was questionable just whether or not the Court would take cognizance of the case.

Therefore, Freedman had to broaden the scope of his constitutional issue to overcome this jurisdictional handicap. To do so he based his argument strongly on the possible disfranchisement of the voters. "The Elections Board," he said, "failed to issue any instructions to the voters not to use Row 'C', and, arbitrarily refused to block off that row because of the cost of $3,000. Nor did it affix any instructions on the voting machine itself. . . . [The] Elections Board by its actions had thus set up a trap for the unsuspecting Democratic voters."[106] Quoting from Justice Jones' dissent in the Pennsylvania Supreme Court, Freedman asserted once again that the United States Constitution (Article I, sections 2 and 3, and Amendment 17) guarantees not only the right to vote but the right to have one's vote counted. Thus 5,624 voters had been denied their right as citizens of the United States to "participate in a federal election."[107]

On this point the Blatt attorneys replied:

> That assertion is not only unsupported by the record but is also contradicted by the statements made by the petitioner's counsel in his argument to the trial Court. Nothing in the record establishes the time at which any request was made of the Board by the petitioner that Row C be blocked by the use of specially-made devices manufactured for that purpose. No evidence was introduced to establish that such a request was made or that the Board refused such a request.[108]

At any rate, the justices of the Supreme Court held their own counsel as to what they thought of these and all the other arguments that both sides had put forth. On October 12 the Court issued a denial of certiorari, merely asserting that it would not take jurisdiction,[109] and thus the case was closed. The ultimate effects of this long drawn-out series of court clashes were not to be felt, however, until November 3.

NOTES

1. Interview with John B. DiGiorno, July 6, 1967. The justice did not get the opportunity to rewrite that chapter, however, since he died three weeks before Clark's defeat, on October 12, 1968.

2. For example, see: Ronald F. Stinnett and Charles H. Backstrom, *Recount* (Washington, D.C.: National Document Publishers, Inc., 1964), on Minnesota's gubernatorial election of 1962.

3. Richard L. Graves, *Harrisburg Patriot,* May 13, 1962.

4. Hugh E. Flaherty, *Philadelphia Evening Bulletin,* April 29, 1964.

5. Pat O'Neill, *Pittsburgh Post-Gazette,* May 1, 1964.

6. 379§1308a, 1963 Pa. Laws 743 (1963).

7. Interview with Gregory M. Harvey, Esq., Morgan, Lewis, and Bockius, Philadelphia, December 3, 1964.

8. *Philadelphia Evening Bulletin,* May 5, 1964.

9. *Philadelphia Evening Bulletin,* May 6, 1964.

10. Joseph H. Miller, *Philadelphia Inquirer,* May 7, 1964.

11. Joseph H. Miller, *Philadelphia Inquirer,* May 9, 1964.

12. Interview with Ferdinand P. Schoettle, Esq., one of Miss Blatt's lawyers during the summer-long litigation. December 3, 1964.

13. In Philadelphia each voting district is called a "division" while in the rest of the state it is known as a "precinct."

14. Miss Blatt had spent only $34,000 for her entire primary campaign; a vote check would have cost $82,000.

15. Robert Bray. The four other "kids," as their opponents came to call them, were Ferdinand P. Schoettle, Philip Kalodner, Stanhope Browne, and Gregory M. Harvey.

16. Schoettle interview, December 3, 1964.

17. See above, p. 88, on independent evidence of the same sort collected by reporters for the *Philadelphia Evening Bulletin.*

18. John G. McCullough, *Philadelphia Evening Bulletin,* May 8, 1964.

19. Hugh E. Flaherty, *Philadelphia Evening Bulletin,* April 29, 1964.

20. "Musmanno Can Blame Roberts—If," *Pittsburgh Post-Gazette,* May 11, 1964. Governor Lawrence confirmed his agreement on that score in our interview, March 6, 1965.

21. Philadelphia, being both a city and a county, has a rather awkward system of county government superimposed upon its city government—hence the confusion in the title. The County Commissioners also serve as the County Board of Elections, but are more commonly referred to as the City Commissioners.

22. "Proceedings before Judge Vincent A. Carroll, Common Pleas Court No. 2," unpublished, May 12, 1964, pp. 14-17. Provided by Gregory M. Harvey.

23. Interview with Gregory M. Harvey, Esq., December 3, 1964.

24. "Proceedings . . . ," May 12, 1964, pp. 31-33.

25. *Ibid.*, pp. 33-34. Emphasis added.

26. *Ibid.*, p. 34.

27. Summarized from "Petition to the Supreme Court of Pennsylvania, Eastern Division, No. 303." Provided by Gregory M. Harvey.

28. "Hearing before Board of Elections," unpublished, May 13, 1964, p. 11. Provided by Gregory M. Harvey.

29. "Opinion of Judge Waters, Common Pleas Court No. 3," filed May 20, 1964. Provided by Abraham E. Freedman.

30. "Proceedings before Board of Elections," unpublished, May 14, 1964. Provided by Gregory M. Harvey.

31. Donald A. McDonough and Leonard J. McAdams, *Philadelphia Inquirer,* May 15, 1964.

32. Associated Press, *Harrisburg Patriot,* May 16, 1964.

33. Schoettle interview, December 3, 1964.

34. Donald A. McDonough and Leonard J. McAdams, *Philadelphia Inquirer,* May 21, 1964.

35. *Ibid.*

36. The grand jury, however, was able to turn up nothing definite after several months of trying, and so was dismissed in July of the following year.

37. Associated Press, *Pittsburgh Post-Gazette,* May 22, 1964.

38. Schoettle interview, October 3, 1964.

39. Daniel J. McKenna, *Philadelphia Evening Bulletin,* May 26, 1964.

40. *Philadelphia Evening Bulletin,* June 7, 1964.

41. All Republican primary candidates were listed on Row A; Democratic primary candidates on Row B; the Republican Special Election candidates at the end of Row C; and the Democratic Special Election candidates at the end of Row D. Thus, while a voter might be restricted to voting on *either* Row A or Row B, nothing prevented him from depressing the levers on *both* Row C and Row D.

42. Justice Musmanno denied this last point in our interview by mail, March 31, 1965, but another source, also privy to the actual events

of the litigation but who does not wish to be identified with this quote, claims otherwise.

43. Interviews with Francis R. Smith, Chairman, Philadelphia County Democratic Committee and his Administrative Assistant Joseph Lockard, April 21, 1965.

44. John G. McCullough, *Philadelphia Evening Bulletin,* May 17, 1964.

45. May 18, 1964.

46. "Petition to Contest Election," provided by Miss Genevieve Blatt.

47. Associated Press, *Harrisburg Patriot,* May 20, 1964.

48. Who stepped down from the bench throughout the vote controversy for some undisclosed reason.

49. See above, pp. 49.

50. "Brief for Appellants," unpublished, May 25, 1964. Provided by Gregory M. Harvey.

51. "Answer to Petition Under Rule 68½ for Allowance of Appeal Nunc Pro Tunc," unpublished, May 25, 1964. Provided by Abraham E. Freedman.

52. Inquirer Harrisburg Bureau, *Philadelphia Inquirer,* May 26, 1964.

53. "Appellants' Memorandum Sur Further Proceedings Should the Supreme Court Reverse the Order of the Court Below," unpublished, May 25, 1964. Provided by Gregory M. Harvey.

54. Substance derived from "Appellants' Memorandum . . . ," pp. 2-6.

55. *Philadelphia Evening Bulletin,* May 27, 1964. Emphasis added.

56. *Ibid.*

57. Donald A. McDonough and Leonard J. McAdams, *Philadelphia Inquirer,* May 30, 1964.

58. May 25, 1964. The series ran from May 24 through mid-June.

59. Saul Kohler, *Philadelphia Inquirer,* May 29, 1964.

60. Paul Levy, *Philadelphia Evening Bulletin,* July 24, 1964.

61. *Philadelphia Evening Bulletin,* June 2, 1964.

62. Donald A. McDonough and Leonard J. McAdams, *Philadelphia Inquirer,* June 21, 1964.

63. *Ibid.*

64. *Philadelphia Evening Bulletin,* August 13, 1964.

65. Harmon Y. Gordon, *Philadelphia Evening Bulletin,* August 14, 1964.

66. See above, p. 82.

67. Donald A. McDonough and Leonard J. McAdams, *Philadelphia Inquirer,* May 22, 1964.

68. Some representative members (selectively chosen by a membership subcommitte) in 1964 were John B. Kelly, Jr. (the brother of Princess Grace), Hal L. Bemis, chairman of the Greater Philadelphia Chamber of Commerce, Brandon Barringer, retired treasurer of the Curtis Publishing

Company, Robert I. Ballinger, architect, Raymond S. Short of the Political Science Department of Temple University, W. W. Keen Butcher of the brokerage firm Butcher and Sherrerd—all prominent businessmen and civic leaders.

69. *Philadelphia Evening Bulletin,* June 2, 1964.

70. *Philadelphia Evening Bulletin,* June 4, 1964.

71. *Philadelphia Inquirer,* June 4, 1964. Emphasis added.

72. *Philadelphia Evening Bulletin,* June 4, 1964.

73. *Ibid.*

74. "Answer of Genevieve Blatt to Petition Under Rule 68½ for Allowance of Appeal," pp. 12-13, unpublished, June 4, 1964. Provided by Abraham E. Freedman.

75. "Opinion of Carroll, P. J., Commons Pleas Court No. 2," June 8, 1964, p. 3. Provided by Abraham E. Freedman.

76. *Ibid.,* p. 5.

77. "A Vote Is a Vote Is a Vote," *Philadelphia Evening Bulletin,* June 10, 1964.

78. Associated Press, *Harrisburg Patriot,* June 18, 1964.

79. *Ibid.*

80. "Appellant's Brief on Writ of Certiorari," unpublished, July 1, 1964, p. 8. Provided by Abraham E. Freedman.

81. *Ibid.,* summarization of "Appellants' Brief."

82. "Answer of Genevieve Blatt . . . ," unpublished, July 1, 1964, p. 14.

83. *Ibid.,* p. 24.

84. Associated Press, *Pittsburgh Post-Gazette,* July 2, 1964.

85. *Ibid.*

86. "The High Court Dawdles," *Philadelphia Evening Bulletin,* July 19, 1964.

87. Paul Levy, *Philadelphia Evening Bulletin,* July 28, 1964.

88. *Pittsburgh Post-Gazette,* July 29, 1964.

89. *Pittsburgh Post-Gazette,* July 28, 1964.

90. *Allentown Chronicle,* July 28, 1964.

91. John M. Cummings, "Mind-Reading and the Law," *Philadelphia Inquirer,* July 30, 1964.

92. Copy provided by Abraham E. Freedman.

93. Paul F. Levy, *Philadelphia Evening Bulletin,* July 31, 1964.

94. C. J. Bell, "Opinion of the Court," reprinted in "Petition for Writ of Certiorari," pp. 20a-21a, unpublished, October 5, 1964. Provided by Abraham E. Freedman. Emphasis in original.

95. J. Roberts, "Concurring Opinion," *ibid.,* p. 24a.

96. J. Jones, "Dissenting Opinion," *ibid.,* p. 51a.

97. Paul F. Levy, *Philadelphia Evening Bulletin,* August 8, 1964.

98. *Philadelphia Inquirer,* August 19, 1964.

99. See above, p. 89.

100. Leonard J. McAdams, *Philadelphia Inquirer,* August 21, 1964.

101. *Philadelphia Inquirer,* August 28, 1964.

102. *Pittsburgh Post-Gazette,* August 28, 1964. Before the end of the convention, however, Miss Blatt did get an opportunity to say a few words of introduction for Adlai Stevenson, and was interviewed briefly on a national TV hookup. The degree of her exposure, however, was not considered commensurate with the fact that she was a senatorial candidate from a major northeastern state.

103. *Ibid.* Mayor Barr personally acknowledged his own and Governor Lawrence's many efforts in this regard in a personal interview, April 5, 1965, but the justice denies that anyone ever approached him on the subject. Interview conducted by mail, March 31, 1965.

104. *Philadelphia Evening Bulletin,* September 5, 1964.

105. *United States* vs. *Classic,* 313 US 299 (1941).

106. "Petition for Writ of Certiorari, " p. 6. Provided by Abraham E. Freedman.

107. *Ibid.,* p. 12.

108. "Brief for Respondent Genevieve Blatt in Opposition," p. 11. Provided by Abraham E. Freedman. The author personally requested such evidence from Frank Smith and his administrative assistant, Joseph Lockard, during two interviews on April 21, 1965, since they were the only ones who could have demanded this action of the Elections Board prior to the election. This request arose only after they had first raised the issue and insisted that they had so urged the board. I was assured that they would send me a copy of their correspondence with the board on this matter within the next few days. However, no such material was ever received.

109. *Philadelphia Evening Bulletin,* October 12, 1964.

4

Scenario II: Down with Bigotry!

THE BIGOTRY ISSUE had of course been important to the senatorial campaign up to this point, but it had had only a peripheral effect in the primary. Its potential in the general election was not yet fully realized.

In retrospect, it seems clear that the bigotry issue alone could not have caused Senator Scott to defeat his opponent. But added to the senator's other assets, and to the fact that Miss Blatt is a woman, it probably carried sufficient weight to tip the balance in his favor against the seemingly overwhelming coattail power of Johnson's landslide victory.

The importance of the bigotry issue, while largely ignored by Senator Clark and Genevieve Blatt, was recognized by the Scott team from the very beginning,[1] and much of their strategy was planned around it. While not neglecting the more staple bread and butter appeals — labor, the Jewish vote, business, the black vote, the farm interests, etc. — they acted to forge a solid statewide Italian bloc vote, where before one had existed only in an amorphous and unstructured form. By emphasizing the "injustice" perpetrated upon one of their own, enough traditionally "straight-ticket" Italian-American voters might be persuaded to split in Scott's favor and thus enable him to survive what was to become an historic deluge.

It would not be entirely accurate, however, to depict the fall campaign as having had one issue only or as having played *solely* upon the sensitivities of one minority group. No campaign ever is that simple, nor can any candidate afford to place all his eggs in one such basket. This particular senatorial campaign had many issues—some irrelevant, some insignificant, some unconnected—but it also had several that were very important, interrelated, and effective. At the time it was not always possible to discern the difference, but, in retrospect, the events can be unscrambled and a design discovered and described with a fair degree of accuracy.

To begin with, Senator Hugh Scott—medium-sized, not quite rotund, and approaching sixty-four—was not by any means the kind of man to go into a campaign unprepared. Famous for his sharp tongue and witty rejoinders, he had often exchanged barbs with Senator Clark on their weekly television program, "Your Senators Report." Usually civil, he could nevertheless deliver a swift "blow to the gut" when suitably aroused, and was usually able to discover his opponent's weaknesses with ease.[2]

A native of Fredericksburg, Virginia, Scott graduated from Randolph-Macon College in 1919 and then went on for his law degree at the University of Virginia. Soon after passing his bar exams he went to Philadelphia and took a job as an assistant district attorney. In 1940 he ran for Congress against Frank Smith and won, but was defeated in 1944 by another Democratic party regular, Herb McGlinchey (leader of the 42d ward in 1964). After serving two years in the navy he emerged a lieutenant-commander and returned to reclaim his seat in Congress. In 1948 he was brought to the attention of Thomas E. Dewey by Pennsylvania Republican "boss" Joseph Grundy and was appointed chairman of the Republican National Committee; Scott was immediately blamed for the party's spectacular defeat that year, and shortly afterward he resigned.

In 1952 he was among those who strongly urged General Eisenhower to run for the presidency, and he became one of Eisenhower's floor managers, thus helping to erase the loser's stigma he had acquired in the previous election. Finally, when the Republican incumbent, Senator Edward Martin, decided to retire Scott put on a hard-hitting fight against the popular Democratic Governor George Leader, and by hammering away at Leader's "lenient" pardons board, managed to defeat him by 113,000 votes—at the time when Lawrence and Blatt were carrying the state for the Democrats.

Since then Hugh Scott has been strongly connected with the liberal wing of his party, setting up the now-defunct "Republican Alliance" in 1962 to oppose the tired and largely discredited GOP leadership in Philadelphia.

By working closely with Governor Scranton in July 1964 at the Republican National Convention, Scott fought hard first to stave off the Goldwater juggernaut, and failing this, to strengthen the party's platform on civil rights and labor, and to change its stand on extremism. When none of these moves succeeded and Scranton capitulated and openly pledged his support for Goldwater, Scott too withdrew his opposition and agreed to support the Republican ticket. However, his pledge turned out to be more of a formality than an actuality, as Genevieve Blatt soon discovered.

THE BLATT CAMPAIGN

The Blatt strategy, if one may call it that, was very simple— perhaps too simple—and in many ways far weaker than the "holy war" approach of the primary campaign. It had two prongs of attack and one line of defense, and all three suffered from some rather fatal defects. The attack plans were based on Scott's strengths rather than his weaknesses: his legislative record in Congress and his recent opposition to Goldwater. The idea behind the first prong was to reveal Scott's "Janus-like" voting record in Congress[3]—his propensity to vote for crippling amendments to major bills before voting for the bills themselves, thus presenting both a conservative and a liberal image to his diverse constituency. It was a tactic, however, that had won him much more admiration than criticism since it had marked him as a "true moderate." As if to show just how effective this type of maneuver could be, Scott resorted to it once again just prior to the opening of the campaign: on September 3 he voted against the medicare amendment to the social security bill; on September 4 he voted for the bill with the medicare amendment included. His own explanation of his action, when criticized by Miss Blatt, was quite simple:

... She has distorted my record on so-called Medicare without pointing out that I introduced what I believed to be a far better

health and medicare bill, offered it and it was voted down. Had my
amendment been accepted . . . you would have had a workable bill
without the limiting bonds and burden of social security payments.[4]

In this fashion the senator was placed in the position of basically
agreeing with the American Medical Association while at the
same time having the true interests of the aged at heart. Unfortunately for Miss Blatt, such criticism aroused little resentment
on the part of the Pennsylvania voter; instead it only served to
confirm Scott's middle-of-the-road image.

Another facet of this attack on the senator's record was an
attempt to belittle his work in Congress by alleging that the senator
had not been the author or chief sponsor of any piece of major
legislation throughout his twenty-two years as a representative
and a senator on Capitol Hill, and that he had only cosponsored
most of the legislation for which he claimed the principal credit.
The Blatt forces pointed out that cosponsorship in many instances
meant simply the act of adding one's name to a bill while it rested
on the desk of the secretary of the Senate. No major responsibility
for a bill was essential to the role of cosponsor, Miss Blatt asserted.

Senator Scott countered by merely producing pictures of himself
at different bill-signing ceremonies receiving pens from various
presidents in gratitude for his active assistance in the passage of
these bills. The senator also complained to the Fair Campaign
Practices Committee that Miss Blatt's use of his record was blatant-
ly unfair. The Philadelphia Inquirer, with its characteristic acerbity
toward any political figure whom its publisher, Walter Annenberg,
happened to dislike,[5] supported Scott with an editorial entitled
"MISS BLATT IS UNFAIR."[6] Finally, the entire tactic was given up.

The second prong of her attack on the senator had to do with
his battle against the Goldwater forces at the San Francisco
convention and then his "complete about-face" a few months
later when he announced—reportedly because of pressure from
Governor Scranton[7]—his support for the Goldwater-Miller ticket.[8]
His "about-face," however, was anything but complete. He excused
his endorsement of Goldwater as a requirement of the "rules" of
the Republican party "that officers . . . support all candidates on
the Republican ticket"[9] and pointedly refused several times
during the campaign to appear on the same platform with the

Republican presidential candidate. Not once did he include Goldwater's name in any of his literature. In fact, it required an ultimatum by the Philadelphia Republican city chairman to get him to add the words "Vote Republican" to his poster.[10]

Therefore, Miss Blatt's attempts to tie Scott to Goldwater, asking whether or not he now agreed with Goldwater's more conservative positions, had little effect. Miss Blatt could not boldly state that Scott was a Goldwaterite since this "would have raised a question of ethics; I don't think he is like Goldwater on all points."[11] But her repeated queries as to "where my opponent stands"—with Goldwater or with Johnson—only served to emphasize Scott's disaffection with the head of his ticket. As one of Miss Blatt's aides expressed it later:

> Scott got his independent image from Blatt. . . . She should have tied him in with Goldwater, without mentioning his ambiguity, just emphasizing those issues on which he agreed with Goldwater. . . . People ended up voting for Scott because Blatt convinced them he didn't support Barry Goldwater. Her continually questioning his position fits in with the two faces approach, but it's a bad point. . . . One would disassociate Scott from Goldwater only if Goldwater were going to win Pennsylvania, not if one expected him to lose. . . . The whole issue was misplayed.[12]

Miss Blatt's one positive approach, the presentation of her own independant legislative program should she be elected, also suffered from a serious flaw: It was too detailed and too academically expressed. Most of her releases were excessively long and complicated. Few newspapers could get brief but comprehensive headlines out of them, and as a result, they were either cut drastically or strung out over several columns under rather dull leads. This led to many complaints on the part of her leading supporters in the field. "We had no idea what Miss Blatt's campaign theme was," one said.[13] "I don't know what Gen Blatt was for," said another. "I know she's a good sound liberal thinker, one of the best state officials we've ever had—but she presented no outstanding issue or idea in this campaign."[14]

Miss Blatt later commented: "There was no campaign strategy. If there was any it was mistakenly based on Quayle."[15]

The "Quayle" referred to was the late-summer poll taken by the nationally known Oliver Quayle and Company and paid for by COPE, the political action arm of the Pennsylvania American Federation of Labor-Congress of Industrial Organizations. The poll indicated that Senator Scott was leading Miss Blatt in statewide popularity by fifty-four to forty-six, and that her greatest weakness was her sex. But it nevertheless asserted that Miss Blatt could overtake and defeat her opponent if she followed certain prescribed lines of attack. For one of these, the "key theme must always be, Scott the two-faced moderate who was one day fighting the good fight, and another in a posture of complete and total appeasement. . . . [He is definitely] vulnerable to charges he capitulated after San Francisco."[16]

The poll also urged Miss Blatt to concentrate her efforts on Philadelphia and the northeastern part of the state because the southwest was 64 percent for her and in no danger of falling to Scott.[17] On the day after election day, the exact opposite appeared to be true: The northeast and southeast produced close to their usual[18] Democratic majorities for Miss Blatt; it was the southwest that failed her drastically.

On one point, however, Miss Blatt would have been wise to have heeded Quayle's advice. "Senator Scott has a good job rating and is not vulnerable on his record," the poll stated.[19] But Miss Blatt followed other counsels. "Frank Smith, Dave Lawrence, and labor were always saying, 'Stress Scott's phony record,'" she recalled later. "They always contended that he was a good electioneer, but if he ever voted right it was because the votes were already there."[20] A late summer meeting of the Blatt team's key staff strategists had, therefore, decided to attack Scott's voting and legislative record. Without enough time to research thoroughly all aspects of the record—good and bad—to determine whether such an attack was feasible, a fiasco resulted.[21]

Needless to say, Miss Blatt's strategy suffered most from a lack of clearly thought out advance planning. Her speeches were largely written on the spur of the moment by one man, and he had difficulty communicating with the traveling candidate to get her thoughts and consent to each release. The long drawn out primary litigation had left her without the time, money, and staff needed to plan and schedule her campaign appearances throughout the state.[22]

She had no press relations aide and her scheduling was done chiefly on the basis of invitations received. There was no one on her staff (mainly composed of volunteers or persons borrowed from Senator Clark) who was familiar enough with the candidate's mind and method of operation to feel free to make emergency decisions, no matter how petty, whenever Miss Blatt was not available. Bottlenecks inevitably developed over the simplest matters.

In many instances her speech writer did not know until the last minute what kind of audience the candidate would be facing for a particular address. And if it were not for the efficiency of the Greyhound Bus Lines' parcel delivery service, many of her speeches would not have arrived on time. As the speech writer said later: "The campaign was very badly organized. The primary took its toll . . . the main factor which plagued the staff . . . and the candidate . . . was fatigue."[23]

There was one other very serious gap in the Blatt campaign: There was no overall campaign manager. No one person was solely responsible for determining and coordinating the policies and tactics for her campaign. Senator Clark's executive assistant, Michael J. Byrne, had been designated for the role, but because of the primary's alienation of Clark and Blatt from the Democratic State Committee, Byrne had also been chosen — in a meeting of the state committee that was supposed to "heal all wounds" — to replace the state chairman as campaign manager for the entire Democratic slate. Mike Byrne, therefore, had not only Miss Blatt's campaign to handle but those of two judicial candidates and two fiscal candidates[24] as well. Additionally, in the middle of the campaign the man most responsible for the finances of the Democratic party's entire statewide effort — fomer Ambassador Matthew H. McCloskey, the state finance chairman — was completely immobilized by the Bobby Baker scandals.[25] This development thrust the entire job of raising campaign funds upon Byrne's already overburdened shoulders. The result? "We had disorganization in buckets," said Miss Blatt.[26]

Under the circumstances, how her campaign got under way at all is something of a mystery. Without McCloskey, the usual sources of revenue for Pennsylvania's Democrats all but dried up. And the fact that Lyndon Johnson was expected to win handily over his opponent did not bring in the extra money from the small contributors that usually shows up only during a presidential campaign.

When the final accounts were rendered it appeared that Miss Blatt had been able to scrape up only $150,000 for her entire campaign; only $75,000 came from state committee sources.[27] The rest she raised herself through the "Voters for Genevieve Blatt" and the "Volunteers for Johnson-Humphrey-Blatt" organizations.[28] The crippling effect of such a basic lack of money on the conduct of a campaign is obvious. In her own words:

> Television got top priority. But you've got to pay for it ahead of time. We originally had a six or seven week program planned by the end of September. This had to be pared down to a four week program because we had no money. When the four weeks came around there still was no money. The result was that we had to further pare it down to a three week program. Finally we bought our time just prior to the beginning of the third week before election day. The quality of the time periods we were able to buy then was far worse than if we had been able to buy it earlier. The things we did on television were of far poorer quality than we wanted. We wanted a staff member exclusively for television; an agency cannot do the job adequately. But there was no use putting someone on the staff when there was no money for the time. By the time the money was raised, we had no staff.[29]

The resultant television spots were not only brief and awkward and at off moments of the day and night, they were also poorly done from a public relations standpoint. They were badly staged, poorly lighted, and the props and clothing were of a rather inferior selection. Miss Blatt was by no means a beautiful woman in the "Hollywood" tradition, but in several of these spots all traces of femininity seemed to disappear. Her usual self-assurance and everyday approach to the problems of her office were nowhere in evidence. Many observers thought the programs were, at best, a waste.

In just about every aspect—time, money, staff, and strategy—Miss Blatt's campaign was woefully inadequate. Her opponent's campaign, however, enjoyed just the opposite qualities. Senator Scott's planning, fund-raising, and staff-collecting activities all began in the summer of 1963[30]—thirteen months prior to his competitor's. The competent, professional results he achieved showed it.

THE SCOTT APPROACH

First of all, Senator Scott's chief aides were not borrowed from someone else or enlisted on the spur of the moment as were Miss Blatt's. They all were members of his own staff in Washington. Scott's campaign manager was the man best equipped for the job —his own administrative assistant. His press secretary conducted the campaign's press relations, and his executive secretary did all the scheduling. As Senator Scott's aide Robert Kunzig commented, "Our press relations were well handled—much better than Gen Blatt's, and we got four to one over the Blatt material in newspaper space."[31]

Senator Scott had enough money to equip a mobile trailer and a helicopter for the duration of the campaign ("We could cover fourteen counties in one day and could saturate whole areas with publicity," said Kunzig). But Miss Blatt had to hire whatever small planes were available, and once was barely spared a crash.[32] By the end of the campaign Scott had traveled over 40,000 miles and had visited all the state's counties except one. Miss Blatt had been able to log only 13,000 miles.[33]

Miss Blatt had to rely principally upon the somewhat hastily contrived and loosely organized "Volunteers for Johnson-Humphrey-Blatt" and a few stalwart coordinators left over from her primary campaign for whatever work might be done on her behalf in the field. Senator Scott had his "own people all over the state, parallel to and in addition to the state organization."[34]

Nevertheless, Senator Scott reportedly "had a money problem" too.[35] His statewide resources, including a Washington testimonial dinner held in the fall of 1963, were able to furnish him with a campaign fund of only $500,000,[36] despite the fact that the state

Republican organization had raised the "largest amount ever —over $4.5 million."[37] Still, he had several times the money that was available to Genevieve Blatt.[38]

The senator's television purchases were noticeably better placed and much more professionally constructed. One particularly effective spot considerately showed the voters how they could split their tickets by admonishing: "Ah, ah, ah! I mustn't touch that big [straight ticket] lever. I'll vote for Senator Scott first, and then for President—let's see. . . . " His campaign literature was equally lavish and plentiful. His major brochure was a twenty-two-page, two-color glossy magazine bearing pictures of Scott talking to Pope Pius XII, President Dwight D. Eisenhower, Chancellor Adenauer, President Johnson, Franklin D. Roosevelt, Jr., golfers Arnold Palmer and Jack Nicklaus, the late President John F. Kennedy, President Chung Hee Park of Korea, former Prime Minister David Ben Gurion of Israel, some coal miners, and a boy scout.[39]

As for strategy, the Scott team was able to call upon one of the most prominent and experienced pollsters in the state to lay the groundwork for their campaign: E. John Bucci. Not just one, but three separate and complete polls were conducted in March, August, and October of 1964. The senator was thus able to gauge fairly well the effectiveness of his own campaign efforts and the areas in which those efforts would be most efficiently deployed.

The pre-primary March poll showed that Genevieve Blatt "would make a stronger candidate against Senator Scott" than Justice Musmanno, but only by three percentage points. Scott was ahead by 58 percent to Blatt's 42 percent at that moment.[40] In August, Bucci agreed with Miss Blatt's Quayle poll on one very important point; that Scott's greatest weakness was Goldwater, for, said Bucci, "a majority of Republican voters are committed to Johnson. . . ."[41] This particular poll also advised the senator not to criticize the Democratic party as such, since 36 percent of its adherents were switching to him. He could, however, criticize Johnson as a "wheeler-dealer" because that would place him in the position of keeping an eye on the president and on such things as the Bobby Baker shenanigans.

On the whole, Bucci's comments proved far more accurate

than Quayle's and hence should have been far more valuable to his client. For example, in March Bucci commented, "Blatt is a woman—and that fact just about washes out any real chance she may have had. . . . Blatt's sex was not an important factor in previous races because she was not a major candidate. This year it will be."[42] And in October, when citing a list of reasons why voters favored Blatt and Scott respectively, he asserted that the data showed a "Pro-Women" sentiment expressed by 10 percent of those polled and an "Anti-Women" sentiment expressed by 17 percent. With all other factors combined, the over-all composite picture of the factors affecting the outcome, according to Bucci's calculations, showed the impact of the "Pro-Women" sentiment to be 5 percent and that of the "Anti-Women" sentiment to be 8 percent, or a pro-Scott differential, on this point alone, of 3 percent.[43] The Scott team did not, however, rely as heavily on the polls for strategy as for basic statistics. For where Bucci's October poll commented that "Scott can benefit indirectly from the bigotry and anti-Italian sentiment exhibited by opposition to Musmanno in 57 of the 67 counties,"[44] Senator Scott chose to take the opposite tack and stress his own "Italianness" wherever it might be profitable.[45]

Despite the polls few people believed Scott could defeat Genevieve Blatt if Johnson garnered more than a 600,000 vote plurality in Pennsylvania.[46] Had this been any other year it is doubtful that anyone could have defeated Senator Scott. He was too well-known and well-liked, and there were few Democrats in the state of equal stature. But 1964 was generally conceded to be another matter.

It was on strategy, therefore, that the Scott campaign truly depended. Money, staff, and preparations, of course, were very important to this aim. But more important was the senator's need to convince the voters of the state that they should take the time and the trouble to single him out, in what obviously was going to be an overwhelming Democratic victory, as the one exception worthy to be rescued. Scott therefore not only had to puncture Miss Blatt's "Joan of Arc" image from her battle with the "corrupt" bosses of the big city Democratic machines; he also had to present himself in a similarly "holy" light—as one of those who had worked valiantly to preserve the liberal wing of the Republican party and who must be returned to office if the American two-party system was to survive.

His repeated failure to appear on the podium at any time with candidates Barry Goldwater and William Miller on their visits to the state, and the obvious reluctance with which he was "pressured" into declaring his loyalty to the entire Republican ticket, contributed admirably to producing the second desired effect. Equally successful were his continual references to his liberal civil rights position and his strong stands against aid to Egypt and against Russian anti-Semitism. If his friendship for Israel was not the most frequent topic of his campaign speeches, it certainly came close to being at the head of the list.

Scott left no liberal cause unsuccored or furrow unsewn. When Miss Blatt criticized his role in the passage of the 1964 Civil Rights Act as being merely one of cosponsorship, Scott produced a "thank you" letter from the Democratic vice-presidential candidate, Hubert Humphrey, to attest to his active participation in the struggle. When Miss Blatt called Scott insincere in his claim to favor labor on the grounds that he had once voted for the Taft-Hartley Act, Scott came out against Section 14b—the right-to-work clause—of the same act.[47] Thus he not only got the endorsement of NAACP leaders Roy Wilkins and Clarence Mitchell,[48] but Philip Klein, prominent Philadelphia Democrat, educator, and former member of Dilworth's City Planning Commission, agreed to head his "Independents for Hugh Scott Committee";[49] Senator Javits called him a "moderate, progressive, forward-looking Republican";[50] and David J. McDonald, president of the United Steel Workers of America, upon meeting Senator Scott at the Greater Pittsburgh Airport one midnight, was seen to greet him warmly and express his hope that Scott would win.[51] A later repudiation of the incident by Mr. McDonald went barely noticed. Even the Americans for Democratic Action gave Scott a 68 percent rating in its last minute assessment of liberal members of Congress.[52] To prevent the possible alienation of regular Johnson Democrats and Clark Independents, Scott also claimed several times during the campaign that Johnson would not be "unhappy" if he were elected,[53] and that really, Joe Clark wanted him back,[54] too. At one point he also disavowed the John Birch Society.[55]

The only thing left for Scott to do now was to prove that he was a better "small-d democrat" than Genevieve Blatt. In order to destroy her crusader image he had to show that the lady in question was not as politically pure as the primary had indicated. The McCloskey issue, the Fair Campaign Practices issue, the clean elections issue, and the Musmanno bigotry issue, all combined to achieve that one remaining goal.

To tie Genevieve Blatt in with the McCloskey and Bobby Baker scandals, another favorite topic of Senator Scott, would take some doing. The senator reserved for himself the relatively mild approach that went something like this:

> She is financed by Mat McCloskey, yet she has never spoken even once against corruption. In her position on the Democratic State Committee, she has been docilely servile and humble in every respect. She was rewarded by being made Secretary of Internal Affairs.[56]

A more acid-like approach was left to others. Frank M. Matthews of the *Pittsburgh Post-Gazette*[57] labeled one such attack leveled by Mrs. Peter K. Honaman, vice-chairman of the Republican State Committee, a "guilt by association" accusation. As he reported it, Mrs. Honaman's speech began:

> "Miss Blatt is an interested party in the Bobby Baker investigation and Pennsylvania voters should not under any circumstances consider voting for her for the Senate. How did Miss Blatt get to be an interested party? Well, she is a political associate of Matthew H. McCloskey, the Philadelphia Democratic fund raiser who now is involved in the Baker investigation and she allegedly did McCloskey a favor in a state Pardons Board case. An accusation so far without substance.

> Senator Scott now serves on the investigating Rules Committee, Mrs. Honaman continued. If Miss Blatt were to defeat him she could very well be assigned to his place on that committee. . . ."[58]

Thus Miss Blatt was transformed from a "boss-fighter" into a "boss-pawn."

The Fair Campaign Practices Committee, an independent, nonpartisan, nationwide organization set up to police elections, became the central figure in the second Scott maneuver. Its chairman was a prominent Republican, Charles P. Taft, brother of the late Senator Robert A. Taft, and its executive director was Bruce L. Felknor, a former newspaperman and public relations executive. On October 1 a legislative assistant of Senator Scott, Richard Murphy, wrote to Mr. Taft charging two violations by Genevieve Blatt of the Code of Fair Campaign Practices:

> . . . smears which were specifically condemned by your Committee's Fourth Biennial State-by-State study of smear.
>
> Smear tactics are not new to Miss Blatt. Persons campaigning in her support used an outright appeal to bigotry to help her to win her party's recent primary campaign. They wanted to know how Justice Michael Musmanno spelled his name, whether he had ever changed his name, and where he was born.
>
> This is an old and sordid technique of ridiculing people whose names happen to end in A or I or O.
>
> Now Senator Scott's opponent is attempting to misinterpret and distort the legislative record of Senator Scott for partisan political purposes.
>
> On September 5 she tried to belittle Senator Scott's record by saying that she had combed Senator Scott's record and found that in 22 years he has introduced 320 bills, only 20 of which are law. And not one of them is of significance to the welfare of our country or State. . . .
>
> A further case in point is Miss Blatt's statement that Senator Scott's efforts in behalf of the Civil Rights Act of 1964 "means nothing." Senator Scott was co-sponsor of the late President Kennedy's original civil rights proposals and he was a Senate Floor Captain who helped break the filibuster and enact into law the Civil Rights Act of 1964. . . .
>
> The second violation that I respectfully call to your attention . . . concerns Miss Blatt's having grossly distorted Senator Scott's role in the issue of health care for the aged . . . she failed to say that Senator Scott offered his own legislation which he believed would provide more and better care for the aged and that Senator Scott's bill offered as an amendment was voted on by the U.S. Senate.[59]

On October 26, Senator Scott sent the Committee "full documentation of the method by which his opponent used to appeal to bigotry to win her party's primary election . . . an appeal conducted in her behalf in her presence and with her full knowledge and consent."[60] The "documentation" consisted of the Associated Press article summing up Clark's original charges against Musmanno, a *Philadelphia Bulletin* article dated April 12 which quoted from Senator Clark's release of that date, and an Associated Press article dated April 16, in which Miss Blatt declared the questions asked of Justice Musmanno by Senator Clark to have been "parenthetical and inconsequential."[61] Scott also repeated the accusation: "Despite frequent appeals from various ethnic groups that she repudiate and condemn this campaign being conducted in her behalf, she never did either."[62]

On October 16 Richard Murphy issued another release charging Miss Blatt with using "fraudulent newspaper endorsements,"[63] and reported this charge also to the Fair Campaign Practices Committee. The "endorsements" referred to was a quotation from John Calpin's January 23 article in the *Philadelphia Evening Bulletin,* claiming Miss Blatt to be the best of the Democratic primary hopefuls.[64] The quote had been used in Miss Blatt's primary literature and was also reproduced in a brochure circulated on her behalf in the present campaign.

On October 27, Miss Blatt replied to all of Scott's charges. "I believe they . . . are totally without foundation, " she wrote Taft,

> and I am confident that my letter will so illustrate. But first, please allow me to say that it is difficult to understand my opponent's contention that a critical examination of his record should be considered an unfair practice.
>
> The Fair Campaign Practices Code, to which I heartily subscribe, authorizes me to criticize his record without fear or favor. I believe the people have a right to know what he has done for 22 years in Washington. . . .
>
> I never said my opponent's effort on behalf of the Civil Rights Act meant nothing. However, I would be somewhat more objective and stop referring to it as his bill when the fact is that 46 Senators co-sponsored the legislation. . . .

And on the Calpin quote:

> When my campaign director, Michael J. Byrne, learned that Senator Scott had complained about the matter to The Bulletin, he ordered printing of the pamphlet stopped immediately. . . . This was not

done because we felt that there had been a misrepresentation of what was said in the Bulletin, but rather because we did not wish to involve the Bulletin in any dispute with my opponent. . . .

Miss Blatt then charged Scott himself with violating the Fair Campaign Practices Code "by engaging in personal vilification against me. He has implied that I am a bigot and on a television appearance October 25 in Philadelphia, he stated flatly that I was nominated with the votes of prejudiced persons."[65]

The Fair Campaign Practices Committee took both complaints under advisement and said it would investigate both, but it issued no definitive report prior to the election.

Of the entire issue, Felknor later commented:

A number of Pennsylvania ethnic associations complained at the time, declaring that this tactic [Senator Clark's questions about Musmanno] substantiated the Scott complaint, and so long as Blatt *did not specifically repudiate the incident,* Scott seemed to have her over a barrel. . . . The record-distortion accusations were in a standard setting where one candidate oversimplifies the other's position and there is ample room for charges of distortion that are technically true, and plenty of room for opposite contentions that the substance is correct. Certainly Blatt sought to make Scott's voting record look as bad as possible and his record of legislation adopted look as weak as possible, and Scott sought to make her oversimplification look as heinous as possible.

On the Bulletin's endorsement, assuming that the carry over of this column item favoring Blatt in the primary into the general election literature was inadvertent (a perfectly fair assumption), the fact remains that it did distort.[66]

Miss Blatt, in the meantime, pointed out that Charles Taft (chairman of the Fair Campaign Practices Committee) was also chairman of the Committee to Elect Moderate Republicans and had personally endorsed Senator Scott.[67] And at about the same time, Ralph McGill of the *Atlanta Constitution,* in an unrelated incident, resigned from the Fair Campaign Practices Committee because "it was cast in the light of being unfair" in its censuring of Robert Kennedy for similarly criticizing the legislative record of Senator Keating.[68]

The third method used by Scott to discredit Miss Blatt involved

Philadelphia's own nonpartisan watchdog group, the Committee of Seventy. Citing the fact that the committee would require $6,466.92 to provide "Approximately 200 impartial observers who would stop or substantially reduce the amount of vote-stealing that goes on in Philadelphia polling places,"[69] Scott challenged Miss Blatt to match his check for $3,233.45 to "help assure a clean election in Philadelphia next month."

Miss Blatt had already replied to an earlier verbal request for the money by stipulating that such a program should not be confined to Philadelphia. The *Evening Bulletin* reported:

> "If he sincerely believes that the Committee of Seventy will assure honest elections, I will be glad to join him. . . ." But she said such a program should be extended to such counties as Northumberland where she said, trustees from the county jail are used to count the votes. . . . "I'll join you in getting an honest count but let's make it everywhere. . . ."[70]

When the check for the rest of the money was not forthcoming, Senator Scott sent a telegram to Miss Blatt reminding her:

PAST DUE NOTICE STOP WHEN YOU FORWARDED MY CHECK FOR $3,233.45 TO THE COMMITTEE OF SEVENTY YOU FORGOT TO ENCLOSE YOUR OWN STOP THIS IS JUST A FRIENDLY REMINDER THAT YOU HAVE JUST AS MUCH AT STAKE IN AN HONEST PHILADELPHIA VOTE COUNT AS I DO STOP OR DO YOU QUESTION MARK COMMITTEE OF SEVENTY HOLDING CHECK PENDING RECEIPT OF YOURS STOP[71]

On October 12 Senator Scott again sent a telegram to Miss Blatt urging her to "make any contribution—even one dollar would help."[72] Finally, on October 13, at a debate before the Golden Slipper Square Club in Philadelphia, Miss Blatt tendered Scott a five-dollar bill saying, "He asked for one dollar. . . . I'm not rich but I will give him five if he will take that. I believe in clean elections although I don't believe in stunts." Senator Scott took the bill, commenting, "Now we'll just have to ask the public to do the rest of the job."[73] As Robert Kunzig, Senator Scott's administrative assistant, pointed out later: "The Committee of Seventy issue was a psychological issue—she would not contribute to a clean election — just the opposite of her position in the spring."[74] Thus was Miss Blatt characterized as reversing herself on the matter of assuring clean elections in the city of Philadelphia.

THE BIGOTRY ISSUE

Scott's employment of the bigotry charge had many facets and angles. One facet has already been outlined: the extension of his unfair campaign practices complaints to include the questions asked of Justice Musmanno by Senator Clark. Equally effective were his almost daily ethnic radio broadcasts[75] and his very frequent speeches on the subject in every part of the state.[76]

However, it was not Senator Scott, ostensibly at any rate, who initiated the bigotry issue during the fall campaign. It was a statement by Senator Clark shortly after the primary that served to rekindle the bitterness of certain spokesmen for the Italian-American community and gave them additional motivation to rally vigorously behind the candidacy of Hugh Scott.

On April 30 Senator Clark was quoted, in a long interview by Douglas Smith in the *Pittsburgh Press,* as saying that the primary was a "bad day for the bosses" but that "our task is to bind up the wounds and bring a united party behind Lyndon Johnson and Genevieve Blatt. . . . I want to let bygones be bygones." This was not a terribly unusual statement from an American politician. But Clark then proceeded to rub salt in the wounds of a "defeated" minority by saying that Justice Musmanno had received "fanatical support" from Italian-American voters, "but they are loyal Democrats and I think they will support Genevieve in the fall."

On May 1 *Unione* published an editorial clear across its eight-column front page. It was headlined, "FORCES OF BIGOTRY AND INTOLERANCE DEFEAT JUSTICE MICHAEL A. MUSMANNO — SENATOR CLARK CALLS US 'FANATICS,' SAYS WE'LL FALL IN LINE."

The editorial cited an assumption, basically accepted by Governor Lawrence,[77] that the so-called bigotry appeal had cost Musmanno all semblance of support in all counties except those with large ethnic groups. It ended with a recital of the tasks the newspaper had undertaken to follow during the campaign. In a manner that seemed bent on justifying the "fanatical" tag, the paper declared:

> . . . And we shall not forget.
>
> And we shall keep reminding our readers not to forget. We shall remind our readers of the calumny and guile of the Blatt-Clark combine through the weeks and months and years to come, if necessary.
>
> Our pride and self respect as Americans, and our future in this Commonwealth is at stake. And so that we will not be called fanatics or any other new names as a people, we will be calm, week after week.
>
> There will be no hysteria, week after week.
>
> There will be no name calling, week after week.
>
> There will be no complaining, week after week.
>
> But there will be a call to memory, the diary we all carry about with us, week after week.
>
> There will be a call to duty, week after week.
>
> There will be a reassertion of our obligations in our communities, week after week.
>
> We shall be reminding ourselves of the hurt and calumny of the past political campaign, week after week.
>
> And we shall determine that no one shall do this to us again. Never.
>
> And we hereby resolve to do all this until our ultimate objectives are achieved in proper and due and adequate form to the last full measure. And in not forgetting, we shall be asking our friends and our families and our neighbors also not to forget.
>
> All this we will be doing, week after week after week.

What the solution might be, or whether there even was one to this embittered situation, is anyone's guess. But the fact that this long and hyperemotional editorial came in a weekly newspaper *only one day after* the publication of Clark's statement on "fanaticism" in the *Pittsburgh Press,* an evening newspaper, leads one to believe that the substance of this editorial had been mapped out long in advance, and that the "fanatical" slip was merely one extra hook with which to hang the accusation of bigotry on Clark and Blatt.

In the months that followed, the *Unione* was true to its word: It never allowed its readers to forget their "persecuted" status. And its publisher, Victor Frediani, even found time later on in the campaign to put out a special four-page publication[78] for Hugh Scott, in the same tone as this editorial. This campaign paper, *Keystone Keynotes,* proclaimed the "BURNING ISSUE IN SENATE RACE: ITALO-AMERICAN SELF-RESPECT." It also asserted that "SCOTT'S OPPONENT FAILS TO CONDEMN BIGOTRY" by failing to disassociate herself from Clark's charges, as called upon to do by the *Unione.* The fact that Miss Blatt had indeed written personally to the National Secretary of the Italian Sons and Daughters of America, the parent organization of the *Unione,* on April 22, expressing just these sentiments, was unacknowledged. In contrast to Miss Blatt's intransigency, Senator Scott was lauded on the same front page for "battling bigotry in all forms." An inside box labeled "SENATOR HUGH SCOTT FAMILY TREE" then proceeded to demonstrate that:

> U.S. Senator Hugh Scott is qualified to join the Order of Italian Sons and Daughters of America, the Order Sons of Italy . . . and all other organizations which make Italian ancestry a prerequisite for joining.
>
> His maternal great-grandmother was Diana Tagliaferro, of Milan, Italy, who married the distinguished Scottish merchant John Scott, the Senator's great-grandfather. And there are many Scotts in Italy today, cousins and other relatives of the Pennsylvania Senator. Cousin Dr. Ettore Scott is a prominent resident of Florence.[79]

The meaning, of course, could not possibly have been lost on its readers. Copies were sent to as many Italian-Americans throughout the state as could be located. By all accounts, the western part of the state was blanketed with them. In the east the Italian newspapers were vocal[80] but not nearly so influential. It was in the west, not in the east, that ethnic feelings normally run so high that an annual picnic of the Italian Sons and Daughters of America could reportedly rally 50,000 to 60,000 Italian-Americans,[81] and coincidentally, it was in the normally Democratic urban counties of the west, not in the east, that Miss Blatt lost critical support.

However, Scott was not a completely passive recipient of these gifts and kudos. He was quite capable of creating such opportunities for himself. In fact, at one point, the senator demonstrated a touch of genuine genius in his handling of an especially brilliant bit of campaign "business" involving Justice Musmanno. Despite the fact that on the day after the primary election Justice Musmanno had complained bitterly, "It was that vicious slanderous campaign of Clark against me that hurt . . . and a lot of material came from Hugh Scott. . . ."[82] Scott had spies sent here to Pittsburgh, checking on my past. Oh, it was so dirty."[83]

Scott nevertheless appeared to charm the justice out of his pique. When Musmanno was called before the Senate Subcommittee on Federal Charters, Holidays, and Celebrations, of which Scott is a member, to testify on the proposal that Columbus Day be made a national holiday, Senator Scott had his photographer snap a picture of himself and the justice about to shake hands.[84] Scott then called the justice a "great Statesman-Judge,"[85] and joined Musmanno in lavishly praising the idea of a national Columbus Day holiday. As *Greater Philadelphia* magazine remarked, because this encounter took place fully two months before the justice gave up his fight for the nomination, "It didn't sound like a politician talking about a rival in an election less than three months off. It sounded more like a politician bidding for votes from supporters of a beaten man."[86]

The picture, of course, ended up in several newspapers later on in the campaign, including the *Keystone Keynotes.* On Columbus Day, Scott was able to drive home his point even more explicitly at the annual banquet of the Sons of Columbus of America, in Pittsburgh. As Hugh Flaherty of the *Philadelphia Evening Bulletin* reported it:

> Scott was the main speaker, although such Democrats as former Governor David L. Lawrence got a chance to say a few non-political words.
>
> Miss Blatt was not invited.
>
> Several leaders of the organization made it privately clear that Scott, and not Miss Blatt, was invited because Italians are still

angry about the campaign the Blatt forces conducted against
Supreme Court Judge Michael A. Musmanno. . . .

During the banquet, one of the speakers referred to Musmanno as
one of two Italians who have gained greatness in Pennsylvania.
This brought loud applause. . . .

Scott himself referred kindly to Musmanno in praising the judge's
role in trying to make Columbus Day a national holiday. He said
the judge's testimony on Scott's bill was helpful in getting it passed
in the Senate. The bill died in a House Committee. . . .

The Senator promised his audience that one of the first things he
would do if re-elected will be to revive the Columbus Day bill.[87]

After the United States Supreme Court finally handed down its
denial of certiorari on the primary contest, Justice Musmanno
was strongly urged by various state party leaders to declare his
support of the entire Democratic slate and specifically of Genevieve Blatt.[88] The justice issued a statement pledging his support for "the entire Democratic ticket in Pennsylvania"[89] but did
not mention Miss Blatt by name.[90] A week later, on October 29, a
Democratic $100-a-plate dinner was staged in Philadelphia. Pres-
ident Johnson addressed the dinner, and in a statewide television
broadcast said: "I want to ask that Judge Musmanno and every
single friend in Pennsylvania . . . come to my help again by sending
Genevieve Blatt to the Senate."[91] Musmanno still would not
endorse Miss Blatt by name, however, and Senator Scott was, by
all reports, substantially aided by his attitude.

Jack Lynch of the Associated Press commented on Scott's
continual use of the bigotry issue:

He has repeated the theme or variations of it in at least nine prepared speeches since then,[92] in extemporaneous remarks at nearly
every political appearance, and in television commercials of one
and five minute duration dealing specifically with alleged bigotry. . . .
In renewing the charge formally on an average of once a week,
Scott apparently is gaining some effect. He has been endorsed
editorially by the Pittsburgh Italian newspaper *Unione,* and he may
gain similar support from the Philadelphia Sons of Italy *Times.*[93]

Finally, on October 31, Scott ended his bigotry campaign in the small Italian-American town of Roseto, Pennsylvania. Scott told an audience of about 200:

> I have Italian blood in my veins, my great-grandmother Diana Taglia-ferro was a Milanese. He also recalled that the Roman Centurians left a fine heritage of freedom for today's world to imitate.
>
> Scott ate such Italian delicacies as chicken liver wrapped in bacon, manicotti, meatballs, pizza and imported cheeses. . . .
>
> While Scott . . . enjoyed Roseto's hospitality, local GOP leaders went about discussing the bigotry and intolerance of Genevieve Blatt . . . and *Keystone Keynotes* [was] distributed by local GOP officials.[94]

In the meantime Miss Blatt attempted, without much success, to turn the bigotry issue against Scott. She issued several statements deploring Scott's "vicious intent . . . to imply that I am a bigot."[95] But by this time it was very late in the campaign. Many people wondered why Senator Clark did not reply to Scott, since it was his statement which had set off the entire brouhaha in the first place. Bernard E. Norwitch, the senator's administrative assistant, offered this explanation:

> During the campaign the Senator did not repeat his earlier denial of the bigotry charges because Italian leaders around the state assured him and Mike Byrne it would all die down if left alone. Up until the last minute everyone was hoping Musmanno would come out in support of Gen Blatt, so why re-open old wounds by rehashing the whole thing all over again. . . .[96]

> Joe Clark had hinted that if it was a question of face or pride, he didn't care. He indicated he would do anything feasible or legitimate to get Gen Blatt elected—in so many words, he would "apologize" —but that's not the right word for it—to Musmanno. I told this to Mike Byrne. Mike called Dave Lawrence to ask him if he thought there would be any value in getting Musmanno and Clark together. Mike told him Joe Clark was willing to meet with Musmanno if it would do any good to make his own personal explanation, that he had meant no offense. Dave Lawrence did say it was worth looking into. But he called back later and said No.[97]

The question still remains, however, why Clark did not blast Scott for using such tactics.

Some Italian-Americans were already getting "fed up" with the entire issue. As one Luzerne County Republican was quoted as having said, "We voters of Italian descent resent Scott's constant reference to the bigotry issue. . . . He's making us feel like we are some group of foreigners to whom he can appeal for a bloc vote. We are Americans, not some special interest group."[98] But Luzerne County is in the northeast, not the southwest, where the *Unione* allegedly wields so much influence, and, as the statistics were later to indicate, most of the northeast's Italian-Americans went on to vote the straight party ticket.

When asked about the possible "backlash" from overuse of the bigotry issue, Senator Scott's aide Robert Kunzig replied, "For every vote we lost . . . we gained five."[99]

By election day *every major newspaper* in the state had come out in support of Hugh Scott. The reasons given ranged all the way from "he's a man of experience with a good record" to "[to] preserve the two-party system." The same papers—without exception—also urged the people to elect Lyndon Johnson. If one were not sufficiently alert to political realities, one could well have concluded that, in their opinion, it was one's patriotic duty to elect the "Johnson-Scott ticket."

NOTES

1. Interview with Robert L. Kunzig, administrative assistant to Senator Hugh Scott, March 25, 1965.

2. On one occasion he almost drew blood from Senator John F. Kennedy. "Kennedy, in a rare show of public anger, said Scott had made the most 'distorted and malign attack I have heard in my 14 years of politics.' " Warren Eisenberg, "The Affable Tiger," *Greater Philadelphia* 55 (October 1964), 71.

3. See Richard A. Doran's and Michael H. Malin's *The Two Faces of Hugh Scott,* a campaign brochure published by Milton J. Shapp, on the same theme.

4. "Press Conference," *Harrisburg Patriot,* October 11, 1964.

5. A practice which *Greater Philadelphia* labeled "Yellow Journalism"

during the Shapp-Shafer campaign. Bernard McCormick, "The Making of a Governor, 1966," *Greater Philadelphia* 57 (October 1966), 138.

6. *Philadelphia Inquirer,* October 14, 1964.

7. *Philadelphia Sunday Bulletin,* September 20, 1964.

8. Associated Press, *Harrisburg Patriot,* September 26, 1964.

9. John G. McCullough, *Philadelphia Evening Bulletin,* September 17, 1964.

10. John G. McCullough, *Philadelphia Sunday Bulletin,* September 20, 1964.

11. Interview with Miss Genevieve Blatt, Secretary of Internal Affairs, February 26, 1965.

12. Interview with Ferdinand P. Schoettle, December 3, 1964.

13. Interview with Dean Thomas M. Cooley II, University of Pittsburgh Law School, co-chairman, Southwestern Pennsylvania Volunteers for Johnson-Humphrey-Blatt, March 8, 1965.

14. Interview with State Representative Austin J. Murphy, March 9, 1965.

15. Interview with Genevieve Blatt, February 26, 1965.

16. "Quayle Poll," September 1964, p. 34.

17. *Ibid.,* p. 13.

18. "Usual" for a strictly statewide campaign.

19. "Quayle Poll," September 1964, p. 8.

20. Blatt interview, February 26, 1965.

21. The author was herself a member of the research staff at the time. This was probably the most uncoordinated and least directed effort of the campaign. Half the time we (Clifford Block, Ph.D. in psychology, Howard Bunce, M.A. candidate in political science, and myself) did not know what we were looking for. Materials supplied us by the Democratic Senatorial Campaign Committee consisted of uncondensed lists of raw, undigested, unorganized roll call votes for an eighteen-year period compiled by student interns the summer before, with no explanation of their significance beyond a House or Senate number, a title, and a symbol indicating a "key" vote. Cross reference with other sources might indicate how members of the Senate, other than Hugh Scott, may have voted on a particular issue, but a true understanding of each vote's context was just not available to us in the time we had to devote to looking for it. On several occasions when we were given specific questions to research by Ralph Widner, Miss Blatt's speech writer, we would, because of a three or five or occasionally even a twenty-four-hour time limit, telephone to various congressional committee staffs or government agencies for the information. In many instances what they gave us was either inaccurate

or so terribly oversimplified that its meaning was easily misunderstood. There was no over-all planning or even a basic decision on what types of questions we would spend our time on—beyond the injunction to "research Scott's voting record." Doran and Malin had attempted something of this sort in their brochure for Milton Shapp (see note 3 above) but we had discovered too many errors in it for us to feel free to draw very much from it. We researched each issue, therefore, as it came up, usually during the intervals between Miss Blatt's speaking engagements. The file the author had been asked to compile during the summer, largely on general non-Scott-oriented issues, was used all of two times during the campaign.

22. "Gen Blatt had the wildest schedule ever conceived by a madman." Interview with Worth Seymour, County Coordinator for Volunteers for Johnson-Humphrey-Blatt, Southwestern Pennsylvania, March 8, 1965.

23. Interview with Ralph Widner, legislative aide to Senator Joseph S. Clark, and later, Director, Appalachian Regional Commission, December 1, 1964.

24. State treasurer and auditor general.

25. He was accused by the Senate Rules Committee, of which Hugh Scott was a member, of having paid part of his profits from a government contract over to Bobby Baker as a contribution to the Democratic campaign fund for 1960.

26. Blatt interview, February 26, 1965.

27. Interview with Patrick E. Kerwin, Esq., of Bream, Kerwin, and Yoffe, Harrisburg, who served as treasurer for the Voters for Genevieve Blatt, November 19, 1964.

28. Compare this with the $1.2 million spent by Robert F. Kennedy in the Senate race in New York State. New York Times, December 8, 1964.

29. Blatt interview, February 26, 1965. Television costs in 1964 were exceptionally high in the big cities. A single twenty-second spot announcement during prime time on WCAU-TV (the CBS affiliate) in Philadelphia cost $1,250, and on WRCV-TV (NBC) $1,200. A film for that length of time, of the simplest variety and without any frills or extras, cost a minimum of $2,700. The commercial film producer in Philadelphia who supplied the latter figure wishes to remain anonymous, but the rates charged by television stations are a matter of public record and can be found in any edition of the Television Factbook, published annually by Television Digest, Inc., of Washington, D.C.

30. Kunzig interview, March 15, 1965.

31. Ibid.

32. Associated Press, *Harrisburg Patriot,* October 22, 1964.

33. Lawrence M. O'Rourke, *Philadelphia Evening Bulletin,* November 1, 1964.

34. Kunzig interview, March 15, 1965.

35. *Ibid.*

36. *Ibid.*

37. *Philadelphia Inquirer,* December 1, 1964.

38. On Sunday, December 5, 1964, the *Philadelphia Inquirer* reported that "SCOTT CAMPAIGN COSTS LEAD MISS BLATT'S, 5-1."

39. "Win With Hugh Scott," brochure provided by Eugene Cowan, press secretary to Senator Hugh Scott.

40. E. John Bucci, "Political Outlook in Pennsylvania," Swarthmore, Pa., unpublished, March 1964.

41. E. John Bucci, "Political Outlook in Pennsylvania," Swarthmore, Pa., unpublished, August 1964. The substance of these polls was kept confidential during the campaign with just the bare statistics revealed from time to time by Scott or his staff.

42. E. John Bucci, "Political Outlook in Pennsylvania," unpublished, March 1964.

43. Bucci's over-all prediction for the election was far off the mark, however. In this, his last poll conducted before the election, he held that if the voters showed any tendency to split their ballots, Scott would defeat Blatt by 56.6 percent to 43.4 percent. The actual figures were 50.7 percent to 49.3 percent, or 1.4 percent.

44. E. John Bucci, October 1964.

45. See above, pp. 123–127.

46. Duke Kaminski, *Philadelphia Evening Bulletin,* November 1, 1964. Some of Senator Clark's aides, however, thought 800,000 was a more realistic figure because of Pennsylvania's past history of ticket-splitting.

47. Duke Kaminski, *Philadelphia Evening Bulletin,* October 8, 1964.

48. Pat O'Neill, *Pittsburgh Post-Gazette,* October 17, 1964.

49. *Philadelphia Inquirer,* September 13, 1964.

50. Hugh E. Flaherty, *Philadelphia Evening Bulletin,* October 21, 1964.

51. Hugh E. Flaherty, *Philadelphia Evening Bulletin,* October 18, 1964.

52. *Philadelphia Evening Bulletin,* October 25, 1964.

53. *Pittsburgh Press,* October 4, 1964.

54. Hugh E. Flaherty, *Philadelphia Evening Bulletin,* October 20, 1964.

55. *Philadelphia Inquirer,* August 15, 1964.

56. Saul Kohler, *Philadelphia Inquirer,* October 20, 1964.

57. September 28, 1964.

58. A release for Mrs. Honaman's speech was included with the rest of Senator Scott's campaign releases provided the author by his press secretary, Eugene Cowan.

59. Release dated October 1, 1964, provided by Eugene Cowan.

60. Release dated October 26, 1964, provided by Eugene Cowan.

61. See Chapter 2, pp. 59.

62. Release dated October 26, 1964, provided by Eugene Cowan.

63. Release dated October 16, 1964, provided by Eugene Cowan.

64. See above, p. 31.

65. *Philadelphia Evening Bulletin*, October 27, 1964.

66. Letter to the author from Bruce L. Felknor, June 2, 1965. Emphasis added.

67. Duke Kaminski, *Philadelphia Evening Bulletin,* October 23, 1964.

68. R. W. Apple, Jr., *New York Times,* October 28, 1964. See Bruce L. Felknor's own description of this event in his book *Dirty Politics* (New York: W. W. Norton & Co., Inc. 1966), pp. 182-197.

69. Release dated October 1, 1964, provided by Eugene Cowan.

70. Duke Kaminski, *Philadelphia Evening Bulletin,* September 18, 1964.

71. Release dated October 8, 1964, provided by Eugene Cowan.

72. Release dated October 12, 1964, provided by Eugene Cowan.

73. Duke Kaminski, *Philadelphia Evening Bulletin,* October 14, 1964.

74. Kunzig interview, March 25, 1965.

75. About which Miss Blatt complained to the Fair Campaign Practices Committee.

76. Jack Lynch, *Harrisburg Patriot,* October 25, 1964.

77. Interview with former Governor David L. Lawrence, March 6, 1965. However, the governor held that the chief point on which the bigotry issue turned was not Musmanno's nationality, but his religion: "When Joe Clark made his attack it established that Musmanno was a Catholic. Then he announced for Blatt, therefore she must be O.K. As proof she carried York County 6 to 1."

78. *Keystone Keynotes*, November 1964.

79. *Keystone Keynotes*, November 1964, p. 3.

80. There were occasional news stories on the bigotry issue and an editorial or two, in the Italian papers in the east, but the author found no evidence of any determined and persistent effort to defeat Miss Blatt in the general election similar to that of the *Unione*.

81. Interview with the Honorable Ruggero J. Aldisert, Judge, Common Pleas Court No. 3, Allegheny County, and National President of the Italian Sons and Daughters of America, April 5, 1965.

82. A charge that Clark at first jokingly acknowledged and then just as jokingly denied.

83. Hugh E. Flaherty, *Philadelphia Evening Bulletin,* April 29, 1964.

84. Letter from Justice Musmanno to the author, March 9, 1966: "When I entered the hearing room of the Senate subcommittee, and naturally, before I testified, Senator Scott, who was sitting on the elevated platform with other Senators, came down from the platform to greet me and shake my hand. Suddenly a camera clicked. I had no idea that a picture was to be taken. Everything that was done in this connection was done by Senator Scott entirely without any knowledge on my part that he was going to do what he did. It is, therefore, not in accordance with the facts for you to say that Scott 'managed to charm the Justice out of his pique.' He didn't charm me out of anything. . . .

"I was naturally grateful for the nice things he said about me and, as a gentleman, I expressed my appreciation, but this had absolutely nothing to do with his campaign, from my side of the situation . . ."

85. Jerome S. Cahill, *Philadelphia Inquirer,* August 13, 1964.

86. Editorial, *Greater Philadelphia,* September 1964.

87. Hugh E. Flaherty, *Philadelphia Evening Bulletin,* October 12, 1964.

88. Lackawanna County Prothonotary Joseph R. Figliomeni asserts that Musmanno telephoned him at Governor Lawrence's urging to get his (Figliomeni's) reaction to the proposal. Interview, April 12, 1965.

89. *Philadelphia Evening Bulletin,* October 18, 1964.

90. The *Philadelphia Inquirer,* however, did hold that the justice's statement constituted endorsement of Miss Blatt (October 21, 1964), and the *Unione* critically took the justice to task for having done so (October 23, 1964): "In another era he would not have done it. In another era his voice would have been a shrill trumpet summoning the legions of Roman descendants to rally round a cause that was just."

91. Hugh E. Flaherty, *Philadelphia Evening Bulletin,* October 30, 1964. On this same point Michael Johnson, Director of COPE for Pennsylvania, later commented: ". . . I know Johnson was not indifferent or diffident about Gen Blatt. He did everything but seduce Musmanno twice in the same week. Had Musmanno said he wanted all his friends to vote for Gen Blatt, that would have done it." Interview, December 12, 1964.

92. Of the releases given to the author by Eugene Cowan, Senator Scott's press aide, thirteen specifically related to the subject—more than for any other topic. The author also discovered several more newspaper clippings of speeches for which there were no releases.

93. Jack Lynch, *Harrisburg Patriot,* October 25, 1964.

94. Lawrence M. O'Rourke, *Philadelphia Evening Bulletin,* November 1, 1964.

95. Signed article by Genevieve Blatt, *Philadelphia Evening Bulletin,* October 29, 1964.

96. Interview with Bernard E. Norwitch, administrative assistant to Senator Joseph S. Clark, December 1, 1964. Miss Blatt gave much the same response in explaining her own tardiness and reluctance to upset the justice by raking up what she had hoped was a dead issue.

97. Interview with Bernard E. Norwitch, March 25, 1965. Justice Musmanno asserts, however, that no one ever approached him on this subject. Letter to the author, March 7, 1966.

98. Hugh E. Flaherty, *Philadelphia Evening Bulletin,* November 1, 1964.

99. Kunzig interview, March 25, 1965.

Assessment and Aftermath

EARLY ON ELECTION night it began to look as though the people of Pennsylvania were in the process of producing another Blatt "squeaker." Genevieve Blatt maintained a very slim lead over Hugh Scott.[1] But before the night was over the paper ballots from the western part of the state began to enter the count and the truth became evident. While President Johnson was carrying Pennsylvania by a 1.4 million vote margin, the largest in its history, it was clear that Senator Scott was going to withstand the deluge.

The newspapers played with the election story for a few days while Miss Blatt delayed her concession speech to see whether or not the 100,000 absentee ballots still outstanding might be decisive. At one point the *Philadelphia Inquirer* announced that Scott's margin was only 19,458 votes — too slim for him to rest entirely at ease when something like 4.8 million votes had been cast.[2] But then, as the rural count continued to mount, all hope for the Blatt team faded and she finally did concede.[3] The margin was 70,422 — more than enough to stifle any urge to call for a recount or to have the voting machines reopened.

The results indicated one fact quite clearly: that whereas the normally Democratic counties of the southeast and northeast had fallen not far below their average for Miss Blatt, the southwest had failed her completely. Philadelphia and Lackawanna Counties, for example, had given her 142,000- and 15,000-vote pluralities respectively — only slightly less than normal in a purely statewide contest. But Allegheny County had gone for Scott by 17,000 votes, while Washington and Westmoreland Counties had turned in extremely slim Blatt leads of 6,000 and 8,000 respectively. No Democratic county gave Miss Blatt anywhere near the number of votes it produced for President Johnson—or, for that matter, for the rest of the Democratic slate. Ticket-splitting had been an almost universal phenomenon. Many factors may be legitimately suggested as causing that phenomenon, but we will examine just three: the bigotry charge, the possibility that there had been party retaliation, and the effect of Miss Blatt's sex.

THE BIGOTRY CHARGE

A considerable number of working politicians who were later interviewed by the author were sufficiently convinced of the intensity of the ethnic feelings unleashed in this campaign to testify quite strongly to its effect. Twenty-three prominent members of the state Democratic party, in addition to Justice Michael A. Musmanno, felt the bigotry issue had a great effect upon the election results. Among those interviewed were former Governor David Lawrence, Mayor Barr of Pittsburgh, Michael Johnson of COPE, and Dean Cooley of the "Southwestern Pennsylvania Volunteers for Johnson-Humphrey-Blatt." Eighteen of these twenty-three politicians were from western Pennsylvania.[4]

In the northeast, where the split was not nearly so great as in the west, one Italian-American office holder believed the bigotry issue effective enough to comment:

If it was not for the fact that I am a party man and an office holder, I'd have voted against her. I've had six terms in this job—one of the longest in the state. Nationality was never an apparent factor here for me, but there it was in the Senatorial election. . . . Scranton has appointed many Italians to state positions—three to four times more than the Democrats—and to more responsible positions. So they [the Republicans] kept the Clark thing alive— at funerals and so forth—they kept bringing it up. . . . The biggest group against Gen Blatt were the Italians. . . . A whisper campaign by the Scott people to bring out the fact that Joe Clark has no Italians on his staff and that he hates our class of people, was very effective. . . . I never saw anything like this in Pennsylvania politics before—feelings were so bitter.[5]

However, not everyone felt that bigotry had been the most important issue in the campaign. Many pointed out that Jewish voters in particular and other ethnic and socioeconomic voting groups tended to split their tickets to a greater extent than the Italian-Americans.[6] But the smallness of Scott's margin did elicit this thoughtful response from one Italian-American from western Pennsylvania:

> All professional Italians pretended—only a few were genuine—to be offended by it, but mostly it was an excuse to vent their feelings against Joe Clark. There was much bitterness among Italian office-holders . . . [but] the ethnic thing was just not that big. I wonder how much influence nationality groups have on their members. . . . [However] *maybe a stronger statement on the Italian issue might have won it for her.*[7]

In other words, since Italian-Americans were, in recent years certainly, more regularly Democratic in their voting habits than most other voting groups, fewer of them might have been induced to split for Scott than actually did if the bigotry issue had not been an issue in the campaign. And perhaps Miss Blatt might have been among those swept into victory by the circumstances of the 1964 election. At any rate, such was the thinking reflected in many of the interviews and conversations with professional politicians as well as in the newspaper comments that were available to this author.

Miss Blatt, however, was of a different opinion. "Perhaps the fact *that I'm a woman is my greatest weakness,*" she said. "It was certainly a factor—along with my Catholic religion and being a friend of Senator Clark. I don't put the blame on the bigotry issue. I believe in another week I would have turned it back on him [Senator Scott]. Many people were beginning to resent it."[8] But several points in her observation just do not coincide with those of the politicians and workers actually in the field, especially in western Pennsylvania:

> We were very much afraid of a cut here because Scott raised a totally false issue which was next to impossible to answer . . . Clark himself is not close enough to the grass roots often enough to realize how enormous a distortion was made of it, how it was

exploited . . . *Genevieve Blatt is a woman and there was some prejudice.* But had she not done so well in the primary, I might have thought this was a bigger point.[9]

Gen Blatt could not fight rumors and word of mouth criticism. The bigotry issue linked up with the civil rights issue and the national election. Money, personal appearances could not have fought it . . . Two important things beat her: the bigotry issue and the fact that the Republicans were willing to sacrifice their own candidates—even on the local level, for Hugh Scott.[10]

The heaviest percentage of the cut was due to the Italians. Joe Clark had better not run for office again—the Italians will kill him.[11]

That criminous primary campaign did indeed affect the general election. It cut down Genevieve Blatt's vote in this county considerably since the Italians are the largest single ethnic group here.[12]

The Italians were bitter. The woman factor didn't have nearly as much impact. . . . If Clark had not raised the bigotry issue, Gen Blatt would have won, *in spite of the primary split.*[13]

On this last point, however, there was much difference of opinion.

PARTY RETALIATION

Another important factor in Miss Blatt's defeat, besides her sex and the possibility that many people may have felt it necessary to vote for Scott in order to preserve the two-party system, was the effect of her having defied the party organization in the primary and the possibility of there having been an organized "cut" on the part of the leadership throughout the state to "punish " her. However, this kind of supposition is not one that can be tested by any kind of survey or study of election returns. Once again one must simply go by the testimony of the leaders themselves as to whether or not they or anyone else ordered her to be cut—or perhaps "traded off" in return for a heavy Republican vote for Johnson and Democratic state legislators.

Predictably, on the question of there having been an organized cut, the response depended upon the person being interviewed. Staunch organization supporters swore that there was not. Miss Blatt and her supporters affirmed that there was.[14] Occasionally one received word of an intraparty fight in a particular county in which each side accused the other of "dragging their feet." In one particular instance a county chairman accused a reform (hence Clark-oriented) mayor of a small city of having led the "cut Gen Blatt" movement. All throughout the general election campaign the newspapers carried stories of rumored "trade-offs" by individual state legislative or congressional candidates for Miss Blatt, and in one particular instance, this author was shown a piece of campaign literature that instructed its recipients on how to vote the entire Republican ticket except for the president and the Democratic congressional candidate from that district.[15]

But what is perhaps even more significant is the response by certain organization leaders to the question of whether or not, lacking perhaps a direct order from above, the rank-and-file precinct workers may have taken it upon themselves to urge their voters to cut Miss Blatt. In many instances the reply was affirmative.

> There were some Democrats who felt that because Dave Lawrence and Joe Barr opposed her in the primary that bad feeling existed and therefore they may have worked against her. . . . There was not the enthusiasm for her in the general as there would have been if it were not for the primary.[16]

On the question of the reaction of some ward leaders and committeemen to cut Miss Blatt because of the threats during the primary to have them prosecuted for fraud, there were these replies, "No organization can dictate enthusiasm for a candidate. . . . A committeeman . . . is not going to work to elect someone who treats him like dirt and believes he's corrupt."[17] And from a Blatt worker:

> The organization did not cut Gen Blatt in the general [election] but they did have trouble keeping . . . in line . . . those who were caught in the primary, who were exposed as having been involved in fraud. They were bitter about it.

> Others disliked Miss Blatt's "treason" against the organization, and there was also a great dislike for Joe Clark. They feel he's a "political snob" and . . . "not our kind of people."[18]

Perhaps the most interesting reply the author received about the reluctance of the local committee people to work for Miss

Blatt came from a lawyer in Westmoreland County. (He did not wish to have his name listed among those whom she had interviewed.)

There was no deliberate cut. Few people were trying to make sure committee people were working for her—and most of them weren't .... They could have felt the party didn't owe Gen Blatt hard work since she'd bucked him [Musmanno] and the party. So she was on her own. How can the same people on the precinct level go out among their friends and work *for* a candidate when earlier they had worked against her? At first they had said, *You don't want a woman, she's not qualified; Musmanno's better.* Now how are they going to reverse themselves? ... Every committeeman and committeewoman is paid, and so are the extra people brought in on election day. The county [organization] treasury pays ten to fifteen cents per vote. An army mans the polls with cars, baby-sitting, etc. You can control the vote with this kind of army—they'll just ignore certain voters and bring in certain others. They didn't cut her, but they didn't push her either. You can't tell these same people, these extra workers, to go out among their friends and neighbors, and reverse themselves. . . .

There was also some evidence of organizational disaffection with the Blatt candidacy for strictly local reasons. These reasons had little to do either with the primary or with ethnic considerations. One such instance resulted from the badly fractured condition of the Democratic organization in a southwestern county of the state.

In 1962, shortly after Senator Clark was reelected to the United States Senate, he made some rather derogatory remarks about "sleazy law enforcement" in the western counties of Pennsylvania. His comments specifically hurt those county organizations that were rumored to be "racket ridden." In particular, one Democratic county chairman who was also the county's district attorney (who for obvious reasons shall be nameless) was defeated for reelection to the district attorney's office by the active opposition of a small "Clark faction" which we shall call the Democratic Reform Force (DRF).

Since the county chairman at that time controlled the party regulars, the reform group could not defeat him in the primary when he ran for reelection as district attorney. So the DRF openly supported his Republican opponent in the general election, and thus helped to unseat him. Unfortunately, the DRF and another reform faction within the regular organization which eventually managed to capture the county commissioners' offices, were not able immediately to unseat the gentleman as county chairman as well. They needed more patronage to be able to accomplish that end. By 1964 the two reform groups had united in their opposition to the county chairman and together had managed to take most of the jobs in the county courthouse away from him, but they still were not able to eliminate him as top man in the county organization. Ostensibly, then, it was still this chairman's duty in this presidential year to lead the county campaign for the entire Democratic slate.

As one prominent member of the Democratic Reform Force expressed it:

> [The county chairman] ... was for Scott in the fall. He created a great storm about money—said there was none from Blatt "in the pot" or in the county campaign fund. There never is from a statewide candidate. Most of it comes from contributions from the payroll and the local candidates. You never find state money in a Democratic county—it all goes to the Republican counties.
>
> [The chairman] distributed money to the committee people under the eyes of the Commissioners and the ... [DRF]. He was never publicly for Hugh Scott but he was privately so. ... Of course there was a deliberate cut—of about 7,500 votes. ... [The county chairman] was for Scott because he gloated over it the next day. The fact that we [the DRF] were for Gen was enough.

Another member of the Democratic Reform Force also commented:

> Our finances went to the Volunteers for Johnson-Humphrey-Blatt because [the county chairman] was going south with the money. He spent an excessive amount ($7,000) on beautifying the campaign headquarters before any money was spent on sample ballots or workers. Therefore no one would chip in to his campaign fund, including the County Commissioners. [The chairman] therefore told the committee people there was no money—Blatt's money was not in the pot. I tried to explain that Senatorial campaign money doesn't go for precinct workers, but the impression was left. [The chairman] had accused a candidate of not cooperating,

without specifying who or what he meant. All the county candidates had put their money in the pot but not Johnson or Humphrey or Blatt. So to prevent a catastrophe, the Volunteers for Johnson-Humphrey-Blatt, which was being run by the DRF and the County Commissioners, called some of the people back and paid them out of the $2,500 they had left over from their advertising money.

A subsequent interview with the county chairman to get his reactions to these and other accusations was a fascinating one. The following are some of the key passages from the interview:

You won't get the truth from me . . . Gen Blatt was cut because of Joe Clark's support. He didn't know what conditions were like in Western Pennsylvania yet he criticized them. If she had not been tagged as his candidate, she would have won. The Italian backlash had some bearing but not enough to beat her. If word went out from the committee people to go for the straight ticket, they would have voted for her . . . I didn't say I was against her. . . .

Everything I told you is the truth except by way of dissimulation — I'm holding back certain things, not saying things which may amplify my statements . . . There'd have to be certain deals, trade-offs in the county, but I wasn't part of it myself . . . I was for the whole Democratic ticket . . .

The Gen Blatt faction used its money only for Gen Blatt. . . . The committee people resented this and cut her. The people using this money for her hurt her. Instead of putting it into the central pot, they used it only for her. So the regular committee people got sore — you can't do that . . . The Gen Blatt faction had more money than the organization — than I did. They'd have been smarter if they had turned it over to me — it would have put me on the spot. . . .

What you've written down I didn't even say . . . But this is the whole truth . . . Many times a faction goes a certain way because they don't want another faction to gain control . . . The cut was spontaneous because of the way the finances were handled. . . .

There are more rackets now than when I was the District Attorney. . . But the papers won't print it now because the DA's Republican and they're Republican. It doesn't mean there are no rackets because the papers don't say so. They deliberately print lies.

SEX

The question of sexual bias in this election campaign was strictly a quiescent one. No one made it an issue, no one referred to it publicly as a possible handicap, perhaps because no one had to. But it reared its ugly head, nevertheless, from time to time throughout the campaign: first in the count of the absentee military ballots from Philadelphia that showed Blatt to be third in a field of three, with 28 percent of the vote in contrast to Roberts' 40 percent and to Musmanno's 32 percent,[19] and with speculation that this vote reflected the attitudes of those somewhat removed from the immediate scene and not particularly conversant with the issues of the campaign; second in the Quayle poll which claimed that in fact her greatest weakness was her sex,[20] and in the Bucci polls which claimed that her sex in fact washed out any real chance she may have had to win the election; third in the expressed opinions of several prominent Democrats interviewed after the election and previously reported in this study;[21] and finally, in a survey conducted among Democratic campaign workers throughout the state. (See Appendix I.)[22]

According to this group of campaign workers three factors weighed most heavily in Genevieve Blatt's defeat in the November election: the disaffection of Italian-American voters, her sex, and the lack of enthusiastic support of her candidacy by the party organization—in that order. In addition, a straw poll conducted by the author in a single precinct in Washington, Pennsylvania, showed that while four of the ten people polled had voted for Scott because of the bigotry issue, two admitted that they had done so because they did not think a woman should be a Senator.[23] When interviewed shortly after the election, Miss Blatt believed her sex might have been her greatest weakness, not the bigotry charges.[24] But when questioned some years later her reply was a bit different:

I honestly do not know that I could suggest, much less document, any good evidence of any sexual discrimination which my candidacy may have suffered.

This is not to say, of course, that there *was* no "anti-woman" sentiment. The only person I ever heard expressing any, however, was Frank Smith, who said something to the effect that he, with a wife and several daughters, understood women and that Pennsylvania was not ready for a woman Senator. What others may have thought but never expressed to me, I have no way to know. You suggest, for example, that Governor Lawrence and Mayor Barr may not have compromised my candidacy so quickly if I had not been a woman. Perhaps not, and yet this might not have been so much because they feared a woman as candidate as it was because I did not "pound the table" and threaten reprisals, as a man might have done. You also suggest that I might have criticized Senator Clark if I had been a man; but my reluctance to criticize him probably might have been as much due to the unwillingness which a man as well as a woman would feel toward criticizing the only prominent political figure who was willing to help my candidacy. . . .

And I think you know, I was never quite "sold" on the idea of blaming my defeat in 1964 on the ethnic factor alone. I know it was important, but I have always felt that it was only one of several factors which governed the outcome. . . . They may have also included such things as anti-woman sentiment. . . .[25]

And well they may. The Bucci October poll, taken just three weeks before the election, had predicted that an over-all differential in favor of Scott resulting from the sex issue alone would be in the neighborhood of 3 percent. If correct, that would have accounted for a loss of 143,654 votes for Miss Blatt. In light of the fact that her actual loss was but by 70,422 votes, this one factor alone would more than explain Scott's victory, and all the other issues of the campaign—the bigotry issue, the party backlash, and so on—would pale to insignificance by comparison.

In 1972, speaking from the floor of the Senate at the swearing in of the newly appointed Mrs. Edwin W. Edwards, wife of the governor of Louisiana, to fill the unexpired term of the late Senator Allen J. Ellender, Senator Hugh Scott proferred this "humorous" remark: "I agree with those who argue that there should be more women in the Senate. It is fine with me as long as they do not occupy this particular seat."[26]

One would hate to think that this is the sentiment which prevails in our male-dominated political world, but one is often hard-put to believe otherwise.

CONCLUSION

The question, therefore, of why Genevieve Blatt was defeated in her bid for the United States Senate seat at the same time that the presidential candidate at the head of her ticket carried the state by the largest majority in its history is by no means a simple one. Evidence in other states—Michigan, California, Massachusetts, and Delaware—indicate that Johnson's coattails, as broad as they were, were just not broad enough to sweep into office those statewide candidates who had previously run in contested primaries or had had other serious political difficulties.[27]

But Miss Blatt's defeat included two elements not found in any other campaign—the fully developed and cleverly exploited bigotry issue, and the sex factor. Since Senator Scott won re-election by only 70,000 votes, or by the crucial deflection of 35,000 voters from the Democratic ticket, it is not altogether unreasonable to assume that one or both of these issues could have been decisive—considering the size of the Italian-American community, especially in the western part of the state, and the traditional feeling in this country that politics is a man's concern.[28]

That the bigotry issue was important to the campaign cannot be doubted; Senator Scott's actions certainly support this contention. An analysis of his campaign releases reveals that he gave this issue far more coverage than any other.[29] Politicians in the western part of the state also agreed overwhelmingly that this issue contributed to the defection of their traditionally Democratic regions to the Republicans. Scott's aides on election night expressed the opinion that it was the Italian-American voters who had provided the major ticket cuts for Senator Scott.[30] The *Unione* thereupon congratulated itself for a "job well done."[31] And by all accounts, the leaders of the Italian-American community in the western part of the state fully acknowledged their responsibility for Scott's victory. In some quarters, therefore, opinion was unanimous that Blatt's loss was due to the bigotry charge.

However, opinions do not constitute proof. And lacking a statewide post-election poll, more concrete evidence than is presented in Appendix I is not available. Bucci's poll was taken three weeks prior to the election and his over-all prediction (Scott 56.6 percent to Blatt's 43.4 percent) was sufficiently off the mark for us not to place as much confidence in it as we would in a poll taken immediately prior to or following the general election. But even had such a poll been taken, there is still some question whether or not people do in fact act upon their convictions, feelings, or attitudes. The voting statistics do not verify the assertion that a concerted Italian-American backlash far outweighed that of any other ethnic group. There was indeed large-scale ticket-splitting going on in this election. But which of the factors or combination of factors was most responsible is impossible to say.

Individual leaders respond; but do followers always necessarily do what their leaders recommend? Here too the evidence is not indisputable, for leaders are always far ahead—in one direction or another—of those they profess to lead. Party workers statewide —not necessarily those allied with either faction—listed three major factors in Genevieve Blatt's defeat. This study has attempted to explore all three causes, although one has been short-changed, necessarily, because of the almost total lack of information and the low level of consciousness about it as constituting a factor at that time.

I believe we were all somewhat vaguely aware of sexual bias existing as a negative factor then, but that awareness had not been as clearly articulated or as extensively documented as it has been since. We lived in a fool's paradise. It took the violence of the 1960s and early 1970s to make us fully aware of the North's as well as the South's discrimination against blacks. In some quarters it is still denied that such discrimination also exists against women.

Whatever the actual cause, Genevieve Blatt was defeated and the incumbent, Hugh Scott, was reelected. In any other election, this result might have been a foregone conclusion. The fact that it occurred in 1964 and that it involved the circumstances we here describe, are what justifies our asking the question with which this study began—Why? Perhaps no satisfactory reply is possible. But the events described were, and continue to be, illustrative of the politics of our times—machines still exist, ethnic voters still clamor to be heard, and the women's movement looms ever larger on the political horizon. And as far as one can see, none of these, except one might hope the machine, will disappear completely in the immediate future.

But even if political machines should disappear in the next two decades, people will still be people, and their reactions to certain political situations will not be all that different, with or without the existence of political machines. One can still recognize basic human behavior in the narrations of the battles between the Roman Optimates and Populares of 2,000 years ago, and between the Cavaliers and Roundheads of Restoration England. This narrative, although far less earthshaking in its consequences, may still be able to teach us something about human politics, and it was in that spirit that it was written.

AFTERMATH

The effects of the 1964 senatorial primary and election upon the Democratic party in Pennsylvania were not long in appearing. In the fall of the following year, the liberal branch of the Republican party made a spectacular recovery in the city of Philadelphia by running a registered Democrat and former Clark protégé, Arlen Specter,[32] for the office of district attorney against the Smith-endorsed incumbent, James C. Crumlish. Although Clark publicly broke with Specter during the campaign, he could not bring himself to back Specter's opponent. Specter, with the active support of Governor Scranton and Senator Scott, won a stunning victory against the organization. He justified his desertion of the Democratic standard by claiming that it was no longer possible for reformers to work within that party. After Specter's victory Clark reiterated his earlier comments about "bossism" within the Democratic party.

In the spring of 1966 another maverick performed the same service for the statewide Democratic organization. The party regulars once again chose a candidate "they could all agree on" — Robert P. Casey, a young and attractive state senator from Lackawanna County — to run in the gubernatorial primary. But he was challenged by Milton Shapp a Montgomery County industrialist. Shapp spent an unprecedented 1.4 million dollars,[33] rolled up a 49,000 vote victory, and further punctured the myth of the indispensability of party workers in a primary.[34]

To some observers, Milton Shapp, who had taken up the reformer's cause as "The Man Against the Machine," personified the Philadelphia suburbanite in rebellion. To others, his campaign added an interesting footnote to that other bitter primary of 1964: Milton Shapp was the first member of the Jewish faith ever to run and win in a statewide political contest in Pennsylvania. That bigotry should have been operative in the 1964 primary against Musmanno and not in 1966 against Shapp would seem, therefore, to be somewhat questionable. Shapp's victory in the primary and his subsequent dismissal of the state chairman, who had only a year before replaced Otis Morse in that position, bore witness to the increasing powerlessness of the state party organization. When former Governor Lawrence died in November, what was left of that organization seemed to die with him; the organization failed to win another major election or primary before the end of the decade.

In the fall of 1966 Shapp spent another $2.4 million dollars,[35] but lost to Raymond P. Shafer, Scranton's lieutenant governor, by 236,000 votes.[36] The amount of money Shapp had spent in that campaign became the major issue against him.

In Philadelphia the party organization also changed leaders. Frank Smith, characterized as "The Undertaker" by *Philadelphia Magazine*,[37] suffered one more primary defeat in 1967 when he opposed incumbent Mayor James Tate's bid for reelection. The mayor had been trying to accomplish what he had hoped to do in 1963 — bring the party organization under the control of his office.[38] After defeating Smith's primary choice, Philadelphia City Controller Alexander Hemphill, the mayor called for Frank Smith's resignation. No city chairman can hope to survive three primary defeats in a row and Smith, too, began to look for his own replacement. In mid-summer of 1967 he offered the position of party treasurer to Milton Shapp with the understanding that he [Smith] would stay on only until September. But Shapp turned him down. "He told Smith party unity could not be achieved as long as he remained chairman."[39]

Just prior to the election Tate tried to oust Smith through a recall vote of the ward leaders, but Smith countered with a law suit declaring the vote illegal and a momentary truce had to be called.[40] Tate's open opposition to "Boss Smith" did manage to remove the principal issue on which Arlen Specter, his Republican opponent, had chosen to run. Tate also had the good fortune to be caught in an air raid shelter in Israel during the six-day war and was present in Rome when the Roman Catholic Archbishop of Philadelphia, John J. Krol, was raised to the cardinalate; he also managed to be "right" and Specter "wrong" on two other important issues — state aid to parochial schools and Chief of Police Rizzo's tactics on keeping law and order. Thus Tate was able to beat Specter by just 11,000 votes.[41]

By election day Smith had capitulated, however, and had indicated his willingness to relinquish party control to Tate.[42] He was later appointed to an $18,700 city job[43] and was replaced by young Congressman Bill Green, Jr., in the post of city chairman. Bill Green happened to be an excellent choice for many reasons. The congressman had the name of his machine-builder father but a Kennedy-like personal image and political style. Thus neither the reformers nor the party regulars could find any reason to oppose his selection, and Mayor Tate could still manipulate the machinery from the wings.

In the 1968 presidential election, Tate's somewhat-united city organization gave Hubert Humphrey a margin of 267,000 votes with an 83 percent turnout. This, as *Bulletin* reporter Kos Semonski put it, "catapulted Tate into national prominence as a Democratic leader,"[44] and also resolved the basic weaknesses that had been plaguing the party since the death of Bill Green, Sr., in 1963. Effective control of the party machinery by the mayor continued into the term of Frank Rizzo.

In Pittsburgh, the final remnants of the Lawrence-Barr organization were not completely defeated until the fall of 1969. At that time an insurgent Democrat, Peter F. Flaherty, took the mayor's office by 45,000 votes after defeating the Barr organization candidate in the spring primary. By repeatedly rejecting all peace offers from the organization, by staffing his headquarters only with volunteers, and by refusing to endorse any of the five candidates for city council that the Barr organization had selected,[45] Flaherty deliberately made his independence from the Barr faction the major issue of the campaign and stressed his desire to bring greater participation in city matters directly to the people. His easy victory over John K. Tabor, the Republican candidate, while spending only one-fourth the money that Tabor did in his campaign,[46] demonstrated to all concerned that even in Pittsburgh it was possible for an independent to oppose the party in a primary and win handily in the general election.

On the state level Milton Shapp demonstrated the same point when he defeated Robert Casey for the gubernatorial nomination for the second time in the spring of 1970 and then went on to win the election in the fall. Thus Shapp succeeded in demonstrating, statewide, what Miss Blatt had attempted six years earlier—that machine politics are no longer acceptable to many of the voters of Pennsylvania, and that the political party and the concept of unquestioning party loyalty have undergone drastic changes over the past few decades.[47]

This particular aspect of the 1964 primary, then, has come full circle: all three machines have been defeated—again and again and again—until there can be no further doubt that the traditional political party is no longer an indispensable vehicle for either nomination or election in today's politics. What will replace the machine is still not certain. But Shapp's dependence on the mass-media and Flaherty's extensive use of volunteers and "good government" themes might indeed be indicative of the formula of the future. Not patronage but issues and the use of the media and professional campaign specialists seem to hold the key to election victory and political power. Philadelphia and other pockets of organizational control may still be far from definitively proving this trend because old habits die hard. But the state as a whole appears to have made the first leap, at any rate, away from machine politics and ward heelers and toward the "new politics" of issues and issue-oriented volunteers. With increasing affluence and education, presumably even the last bastions of party machines will eventually be infiltrated and restructured to meet the needs of the new society. The process has already begun. It is hardly likely that the years ahead will see anything but its continuation and eventual success, if the past decade and a half is any guide.

BIGOTRY FINALE

As for that other aspect of the 1964 primary — the bigotry issue and the presumed Italian "backlash" in the general election — this too had its repercussions in the years that followed particularly in the lives of the two "culprits."

In 1966 Miss Blatt decided to stand for reelection to a third term as Secretary of Internal Affairs. Ordinarily this office is not a controversial one, but Miss Blatt's role in the earlier campaign had insured the presence of the spotlight for her and whomever the Republican party might choose to run against her. It was perhaps only to be expected that the major weapon to be used against her did indeed turn out to be the bigotry charge.

Shortly after her defeat in the senatorial election two years earlier, the *Philadelphia Inquirer* had put out an editorial reeking with moral condemnation and disgust for Miss Blatt's "sickening performance" during a press conference in which she had conceded her defeat. In answer to questions on the bigotry issue put to her by some reporters, Miss Blatt had indicated that the entire argument between Senator Clark and Justice Musmanno had stemmed from some campaign brochures put out for the justice which had not been quite factual:

> That campaign material in the primary campaign had indicated, for example, a certain period of World War I service [,] indicated that he had been [sic] combat service overseas and came out with the rank of captain. Actually, that was not quite the facts, and I think Senator Clark wanted to have the facts brought out.[48]

Indignantly the *Inquirer* retorted:

> She apparently could not leave this issue alone. Musmanno brochures during the primary campaign, she declared, indicated that he had served overseas and left with the rank of captain. This, she insisted, was not true.
>
> Justice Musmanno must be tired knocking down this and other insinuations of the Blatt-Clark brand, but he answered the latest attack by pointing out again that he served overseas for five years, was twice wounded and came out with the rank of captain. . . .[49]

Actually the *Inquirer* was wrong on two points: Miss Blatt was referring to the justice's World War I record when he had served for six months in the army as a private in a Virginia training camp; it was in World War II that the justice had served overseas and was twice wounded. Also he retired from the navy with the rank of rear admiral, not captain.

Miss Blatt replied to this charge with a letter to Walter Annenberg on November 24 pointing out the discrepancies in the editorial, but no retraction or even recognition of the errors was ever made. In fact this letter was ignored, as her earlier letter to the *Unione* had been. But this accusation and this particular editorial were to serve as the basis for similar charges used to defeat her in 1966.

In two pieces of campaign literature widely circulated that fall the same accusation, quoting from the *Inquirer,* was again made — but the condemnation was even more bluntly expressed: "Miss Blatt's statement, as here recorded, was an outright falsehood. And she could not help but know that it was a fabricated untruth."[50] The headline on this flyer was titled, "DOES GENEVIEVE BLATT'S PAST PERFORMANCE ENTITLE HER TO BE ELECTED?" and was reprinted from an October issue of the *Unione*. Later, John B. DiGiorno, national secretary of the Italian Sons and Daughters of America, indicated that 200,000 copies of this piece had been circulated.[51]

The second piece, an advertisement from the Erie *Morning News* of October 31, 1966,[52] also made the same accusation, urging the voters to WIPE OUT INTOLERANCE IN PENNSYLVANIA." It was signed "Committee for John K. Tabor, John B. DiGiorno."

Shortly thereafter Mr. Tabor won the election by 67,000 votes and served as the Commonwealth's Secretary of Internal Affairs until that office was eliminated through constitutional revision a few years later.[53]

The bigotry issue returned to haunt Senator Clark as well; shortly after Miss Blatt's second defeat the senator made a statement demanding the ouster of Frank Smith as the Philadelphia city chairman.[54] He then left on a three-week tour of Eastern Europe.

Three days later Smith replied with a "scathing denunciation . . . contained in a five-page statement given exclusively to *The Inquirer*" which was headlined, "SMITH CALLS CLARK BIGOT, FOE OF PARTY."[55]

In addition to raking up the old charge of Clark's anti-Italian bigotry against Musmanno, Smith also portrayed him as anti-Negro, anti-Semitic, and anti-Catholic, deriving these charges from the fact that Clark had on several occasions opposed Democratic candidates who happened to be of these persuasions. One particularly vicious charge, however, was phrased in this way: "I was not particularly surprised when I first heard mention of the shortening of Milton Shapp's name from Shapiro," the Democratic chairman said. "It was from the lips of Senator Clark himself in Philadelphia's Warwick Hotel, when he angrily shouted it out."

If this charge were true, it would indeed make Clark out to be a bigot. He would, in fact, have been using the same tactics in 1966 that the Musmanno-Smith forces allege he used in 1964. The author, therefore, personally scoured all the editions of the *Philadelphia Inquirer* for ten of the twelve months of 1966, paying particular attention to the primary months, in the belief that if anyone had covered such a story, this newspaper certainly would have. But nothing was found having to do with Clark. The only prominent allusion to Shapp's family name that was mentioned during the primary came at the bottom of a page in the May 19 issue in a short article entitled, "SHAPP TO SEE ILL MOTHER" in which it was revealed that his mother's name was Shapiro. Several of Senator Clark's aides were then questioned on the matter. According to them this comment had indeed been made at the Warwick Hotel at a meeting of Democratic leaders in January of 1965, a full year before Shapp announced his candidacy for the governorship—but not by Senator Clark. They would not reveal the name of the individual who made the remark for the record, but there supposedly were eight or nine other persons in the room who also heard it and who could have denied the accusation for the Senator. None, however, had volunteered to do so.

Joseph Napolitan, who was Shapp's campaign manager as well as his pollster in this election, referred only to the *Inquirer's* persistent and repeated publicity on this name-change in his un-published report to the candidate on the full campaign.[56] Had Clark's alleged statement been given any circulation prior to or during that time, Napolitan would surely have had to mention it.

At this point Justice Musmanno joined with Smith and accused Clark of McCarthyism and once again of bigotry:

Senator Clark will deny that he is intolerant, but the people will determine for themselves how much tolerance there is in his system, Musmanno said.

The Justice said that Clark went to Pittsburgh in April, 1964, to oppose the nomination of a candidate of Polish extraction who at the time was hospitalized.

In speaking in a Jewish synagogue for [the candidate's] opponent, Clark referred to his own candidate as a "white, Anglo-Saxon Pro-testant," emphasizing the words "white" and "Protestant," Musman-no said.[57]

Interestingly enough, this accusation was found to be partially true. In an article entitled "MOLLY YARD [GARRETT] HAILED 'BOSS-ISM' FOE" the incident was recorded in these words:

[Senator Clark] turned to Mrs. Garrett and noted that she is a White Anglo-Saxon Protestant. . . . But I don't believe you people here care whether she's Armenian, Greek, Argentine or Watusi.

I think you realize she's a competent candidate who knows what she's talking about regardless of race, creed or national origin.[58]

Q.E.D.

Within a month's time an announcement was made that an organization had been formed called "ABC": Alliance to Beat Clark, and that it had already signed up about 500 members.[59] Joseph G. Feldman, chairman of the group was a registered Dem-ocrat, a member of the Philadelphia board of education, and a successful attorney who frequently practiced before the state supreme court.[60] Feldman's attacks on Clark, in substance, followed those of Chairman Smith and Justice Musmanno, and they were equally virulent. His stated purpose was to see to it that Clark was not elected to a third term in the United States Senate, and asserted that Justice Musmanno should be selected to replace him. Since the senator was not due for reelection until 1968 this organization would have to sustain the tempo of its activities over the next year and a half.

In fact, the justice and Mr. Feldman did just that. They managed to keep a steady stream of accusations and denunciations flowing against the senator in an almost unending fashion. The major thrust of their campaign soon became not so much the bigotry charge, however, but the senator's position on Vietnam. Characterizing him as a "stained dove," Justice Musmanno condemned the senator for "recommending that we stop shooting in Vietnam while allowing the Communists to kill and mangle American soldiers."[61] When Clark announced his candidacy for reelection during the last week of June in 1967, the justice issued a statement saying he was giving serious consideration to the possibility of running for the seat himself. But this was the year of Smith's defeat and Musmanno's candidacy was not heard of again.

In the meantime Justice Musmanno continued to draw the spotlight both for his political and nonpolitical activities.[62] When Yale University published the Vinland Map indicating that the Norsemen had discovered America before Columbus the justice took a trip to New Haven, examined the map, and called it a "piscatorial prevarication."[63] When Luigi Barzini's book The Italians was issued, Musmanno denounced it as a "defamation of the Italians" and published a rebuttal.[64] And when Pope Paul and the Second Vatican Council first contemplated the abolition of meatless Fridays the justice pleaded with them to reconsider.[65] At one point he even defended Santa Claus in a mock trial on television.

The image he projected was that of a scrappy and indefatigable old fighter with much "moxie" and a flair for the fantastic. Sympathy for him as a personality continued to build up, and as a result, the ire of the Italian-Americans against Clark was kept alive and smoldering, just waiting for the moment for it to burst into flames. That moment came in the spring of 1968.

By then the justice was indeed too old to run for the Senate and his major organizational support, Frank Smith, was no longer on the scene. Another Italian-American, Congressman John Dent, from a small town in western Pennsylvania where there was a large Italian population in both the town and the county (Jeannette, Westmoreland County), came forward to oppose Clark in the primary. For several weeks he pounded hard on the Vietnam issue, criticizing Clark's hesitation to endorse President Johnson for reelection, and even attempting to get the state party's policy committee to rescind its endorsement of the Senator—an action taken by the committee before Dent himself entered the race. From all accounts Dent was making considerable headway when President Johnson's announcement of his retirement put a complete halt to this particular strategy. For the last three weeks of the campaign the entire matter fizzled and Clark appeared to be a "shoo-in."[66] Nevertheless, Senator Clark lost heavily in western Pennsylvania and won the primary by a bare 55,000 vote margin while Senator Eugene McCarthy, another dove, was carrying the state by nine to one.[67]

In the fall Clark's Republican opponent, Congressman Richard S. Schweiker, defeated Senator Clark handily by 260,000 votes while the rest of the Democratic slate from Humphrey on down carried the state. Clark indeed was the only statewide Democrat who failed to be elected. Philadelphia, in fine style, presented him with a 188,000 vote plurality,[68] but it was not enough to counter the combined reaction of the suburbanites who favored the liberal Republican, riflemen who resented his support for strong gun-control legislation, and the angry Italians of western Pennsylvania. Thus Clark lost not only suburban Philadelphia counties like Montgomery (Schweiker's home) and Delaware, but Allegheny and Erie as well, while only barely carrying the traditionally Democratic but heavily Italian counties of Westmoreland, Washington, and Fayette. Indeed a "top campaign aide" was quoted as "muttering darkly" against "hunters and Italians" as the cause of the senator's defeat.[69]

Senator Clark, it seems, had accumulated too many enemies throughout the course of his career—with the Italians of western Pennsylvania as perhaps the most bitter. Justice Musmanno who had died during the campaign, on Columbus Day, had been laid to rest with much ceremony and many sympathetic reminiscences on the part of most of the newspapers throughout the state. Of course the articles all recalled his battle with Miss Blatt and her chief supporter and did so just prior to the election. One would have been hard-put to be an Italian and not to regret his passing, in votes as well as in sentiment.

The dramatic finale to Scenario II was perhaps just a bit too predictable, too opéra bouffe—Senator Clark's political career destroyed by the Justice's death and the sentiment surrounding it. All that was needed was a chorus singing in grand and glorious harmony, something on the order of: *"Sic semper tyrannis!"*

NOTES

1. Joseph H. Miller, *Philadelphia Inquirer*, November 4, 1964.

2. Joseph H. Miller, *Philadelphia Inquirer*, November 5, 1964.

3. But only long after Senator Scott had already claimed the victory as his own. *Philadelphia Inquirer*, November 20, 1964.

4. For additional statistics, consult Appendix I.

5. Emphasis added.

6. This finding is in complete harmony with that of many previous studies of Jewish electoral behavior, for example, Lawrence Fuchs, *The Political Behavior of American Jews* (Glencoe, Ill.: Free Press, 1956), and Glazer and Moynihan, *Beyond the Melting Pot* (Cambridge: Massachusetts Institute of Technology Press, 1963).

7. Emphasis added.

8. Interview with Miss Genevieve Blatt, February 25, 1965. Emphasis added.

9. Interview with Dean Thomas M. Cooley II, co-chairman, Southwestern Pennsylvania Volunteers for Johnson-Humphrey-Blatt, March 8, 1965. Emphasis added.

10. Interview with F. William Kittridge, purchasing officer for Washington County, March 8, 1965.

11. Interview with Hugo Parente, mayor of Monessen, Westmoreland County, March 9, 1965.

12. Interview with Anthony Cavalcante, chairman, Fayette County Board of Commissioners, March 10, 1965.

13. Interview with George R. Sweeny, chairman, Democratic party of Westmoreland County, March 8, 1965.

14. Said Miss Blatt on this point: "Yes, I have evidence of a cut in the southwest, southeast, and northeast. It happened and I know it did. I can't prove anyone ordered it to happen. Yet I know from association with lower echelon political people that they take great pride in the ticket. They are more anxious to punish deviates than Frank Smith or Dave Lawrence. I don't hold it against them."

15. On the question of an "organized" cut, Michael Johnson, Director

of COPE, commented (during our interview): "If the Democratic organization is going to take credit for the landslide for Lyndon Johnson they
must take some responsibility for Gen Blatt's defeat. You have to work at
defeat under these circumstances. . . . I am convinced many people did
not vote because they thought the Presidential result was a foregone
conclusion. Therefore, more Democrats than Republicans did not vote.
The Democratic Party is responsible for this. They should have worked
harder." (December 12, 1964).

16. Interview with Aldo Colautti, executive secretary to Mayor Joseph
Barr, Pittsburgh, March 2, 1965.

17. Interview with Eugene Armeo, publicity director, Philadelphia
County Democratic committee, February 23, 1965.

18. The gentleman did not wish to be identified with this particular
quote. Emphasis added.

19. See above, p. 76.

20. See above. p. 109 and p. 114.

21. See above, p. 137 and p. 139.

22. See below, pp. 165–166.

23. See Appendix I, p. 167.

24. See above, p. 136.

25. Letter to the author, January 30, 1978.

26. Quoted by Hope Chamberlin, *A Minority of Members: Women in
the U.S. Congress* (New York: New American Library, 1972), p. 360.

27. On this point Miss Blatt's letter of January 30, 1978 suggests that
there was

> . . . a feeling on the part of too many people that Senator Scott had
> supported President Johnson fairly well on the international
> issues and that it was a good idea to have a strong Republican
> like him in the Senate who could help the President when nec-
> essary but hold him back when that was appropriate. One of my
> very best Republican friends told me after the election that he had
> gone into the voting booth all set to split his ticket for me then, as he
> frequently had done in the past, but when he simply "could not
> vote for Goldwater" and consequently "had to" split his ticket for
> Johnson, he "just could not see having Johnson in the presidency
> without a good Republican watchdog in the Senate." In view of
> what happened to Salinger in California that year—and he was
> much better known and better financed than I was—I am inclined
> to think that many people shared my friend's point of view and
> wanted someone "in there" to check on the President.

28. The evidence on this point is well-nigh overwhelming: from public
opinion polls to scientific studies of political socialization and recruitment as well as attitudinal research in this country and around the world.
The literature is so extensive, in fact, that it would be useless to try to
summarize it in one footnote. Mary Cornelia Porter has recently put

together a bibliography on this and related issues in a book edited by Jane S. Jaquette, *Women in Politics* (New York: John Wiley & Sons, 1974), pp. 343-359, as has Wilma Rule Krauss, "Political Implications of Gender Roles: A Review of the Literature," *American Political Science Revue* 68 (Dec. 1974), 1706-1723. See also, the bibliography.

29. Thirteen releases, as compared with four directed to Negroes and five to Jews; whereas Miss Blatt directed twelve to women, three to Jews, one to Negroes, and only one to Italians. Of the two, therefore, Scott waged by far the more comprehensive ethnic campaign.

30. *Philadelphia Evening Bulletin,* November 4, 1964.

31. November 6, 1964.

32. Formerly an assistant counsel to the Warren Commission during its investigation of the assassination of President Kennedy and author of the "single bullet" theory.

33. *New York Times,* June 17, 1966.

34. *Philadelphia Evening Bulletin,* May 19, 1966. "Milton Shapp got a lot of mileage out of characterizing the primary battle as the 'Man against the Machine.' His victory once again makes it quite clear that the Democratic machine is more like a 1905 Singer than a 1966 Mustang." *Greater Philadelphia Magazine* 57 (June 1966), 29-30.

35. *The New York Times,* December 9, 1966.

36. *The New York Times,* December 11, 1966.

37. Stuart Brown, "The Undertaker," *Philadelphia Magazine* 58 (May 1967), 47. (*Greater Philadelphia Magazine* changed its name to *Philadelphia Magazine* in February 1967.)

38. See below, p. 28.

39. *Philadelphia Evening Bulletin,* June 30, 1967.

40. Harmon Y. Gordon, *Philadelphia Evening Bulletin,* October 25, 1967.

41. Paul F. Levy, *Philadelphia Evening Bulletin,* November 8, 1967.

42. Joseph F. Lowry, *Philadelphia Evening Bulletin,* October 27, 1967.

43. *Philadelphia Evening Bulletin,* December 12, 1967.

44. *Philadelphia Evening Bulletin,* November 6, 1968.

45. Donald Janson, "Pittsburgh Elects a Democratic Mayor," *The New York Times,* November 5, 1969.

46. *Ibid.*

47. It is somewhat ironic that, while Milton Shapp did indeed gain political prominence as "The Man Against the Machine" in 1966, his present gubernatorial administration of Pennsylvania was recently reported as being "the most corrupt in modern history" in an article by Wendell Rawls, Jr., in the Sunday, January 22, 1978, edition of *The New York Times* "The Week in Review" section, entitled, "Marston Upsets Pennsylvania's Way of Life, But Briefly," p. E.3.

48. Unpublished transcript of the press conference, November 19, 1964. Provided by Miss Blatt.

49. "A Sickening Performance," *Philadelphia Inquirer,* November 22, 1964.

50. Both of which were sent to me anonymously from Pittsburgh.

51. Interview, July 7, 1967.

52. Erie is another city known to have a heavy concentration of Italian-Americans.

53. He later ran for Mayor of Pittsburgh on the Republican ticket but was defeated by Peter Flaherty.

54. *Philadelphia Evening Bulletin,* November 10, 1966.

55. *Philadelphia Inquirer,* November 13, 1966.

56. Joseph Napolitan, "An Analysis of the 1966 Campaign for Governor of Pennsylvania" (Philadelphia: unpublished, n.d.).

57. *Philadelphia Inquirer,* Novemver 15, 1966.

58. Sherly Uhl, *Pittsburgh Press,* April 7, 1964.

59. *New York Times,* December 9, 1966.

60. Greg Walter, " 'It is Necessary for a Politician not to Get so Far Ahead of his Troops That he Gets Shot in the Ass,' " *Philadelphia Magazine* 58 (June 1967), 59.

61. *Philadelphia Inquirer,* April 28, 1967.

62. "Judges and Politics," editorial, *Philadelphia Evening Bulletin,* July 5, 1967.

63. He later commented that Yalemen "have gone into the moss-covered kitchen of rumor and, on the broke-down stove of wild speculation, fueled by ethnic prejudices, have warmed over the stale cabbage of Lief's discovery of America." *Time,* October 22, 1965, p. 25B.

64. Michael A. Musmanno, *An American Replies to a Defamation of the Italians* (Firenze: Il Campo Editore, 1965).

65. *Pittsburgh Press,* February 28, 1966.

66. Ben A. Franklin, "Clark Given Edge in Pennsylvania," *The New York Times,* April 21, 1968.

67. Ben A. Franklin, "McCarthy Lead 9-1 in Pennsylvania," *The New York Times,* April 25, 1968.

68. George R. Packard III, *Philadelphia Evening Bulletin,* November 6, 1968.

69. *Ibid.*

Vote Analysis

THE FINAL VOTE in the 1964 sen-
atorial election was: Blatt, 2,359,026; Scott, 2,429,448. In Philadelphia County Miss Blatt received 523,870 votes to Hugh Scott's
381,546, giving her a plurality of 142,324. By contrast, President
Johnson's plurality in Philadelphia was 430,912. But since this
was an atypical presidential election, it might be fairer to compare Miss Blatt's figures with those of Grace Sloan, candidate for
auditor general, who led in the row-office count on the statewide
level. Her plurality in Philadelphia was 317,059—still more than
twice that of Miss Blatt. Therefore, that a cut against Miss Blatt
was operative in the city is highly probable. The next question is,
where in the city did it take place?

At first glance the figures indicate that the cut was universal.
But on closer inspection, some areas appear to have cut her
more than others. According to a study conducted by the city
Democratic organization, the highest proportion of vote-cutting
appeared in the Jewish wards of the city where Hugh Scott had
always had a considerable following.[1] In the 50th ward the gap
between President Johnson and Genevieve Blatt was almost 11,000
votes, or 24 percent. The other Jewish wards averaged between
3,000 and 4,000 votes less for Blatt than for Johnson.

The second area showing a heavy vote cut was that of the
independent, upper-income "fringe wards" bordering the suburbs.
They too averaged a drop of about 3,000 to 4,000 votes each. The
black wards of the city showed an average drop of only 2,000
votes, or between 13 percent and 14 percent, while the South

Philadelphia Italian-American wards ranged from a drop of 1,000 votes, or 12 percent in the 48th ward, to one of 2,000 votes, or 11 percent in the 26th. Therefore, the greatest percentage of straight Democratic votes came from the Italian wards of South Philadelphia.

When these figures were reported to other Democratic politicians, they tended to cite the work done among the Italian-American community by independent union organizers. The unions do not generally wield the influence in Philadelphia that they do elsewhere,[2] but the Amalgamated Clothing Workers of America is by far the city's most powerful labor group since most of the workers in the city's vast men's clothing industry are members, and the greatest number of these, at that time, were Italian-American. Three individual sources — Michael Johnson, Director of COPE in Pennsylvania, Genevieve Blatt, and Bernard E. Norwitch, Senator Clark's administrative assistant — each identified one man as having been most responsible for the low rate of ticket-splitting in South Philadelphia — Thomas DiLauro,[3] who heads the local there. According to them, Mr. DiLauro was "furious"[4] about the bigotry charge and spent a "great deal of money"[5] to counteract the Scott campaign. The results seem to indicate that he had had some success — if they are correct in their analysis of the bigotry charge.

On the basis of the Philadelphia statistics alone, therefore, one would not have much evidence to back up the belief that the bigotry issue had had much of an impact upon the voters of Pennsylvania. Instead, other factors would have to be considered of far greater importance: Senator Scott's long-standing appeal to Jews because of his amity for Israel, his independent Republican image among the upper-income voters, and his wooing of the NAACP, especially in the last few weeks of the campaign.[6] Similar results would be indicated for Lackawanna County also, except for the almost total lack of black voters there. Strong party loyalty among Italian-American officeholders counteracted, to a great extent, whatever tendency there might have been to split for ethnic reasons in their county.[7]

But Western Pennsylvania, by some indications, was another matter entirely. Allegheny County voters have always been highly unpredictable. In a study made of their behavior in statewide elections from 1958 to 1964, it was discovered that whereas Philadelphia has always gone Democratic despite the eventual outcome of the election, Allegheny County has not gone consistently for either party. In fact, whenever a Democratic candidate lost Allegheny County he or she also lost the election. This generalization held true for George Leader in his battle against Hugh Scott in the 1958 senatorial election, for Richardson Dilworth in his fight for the governorship with William Scranton in 1962, and for Genevieve Blatt in 1964. Whenever a Democrat won Allegheny County, he or she also won the election — despite a landslide vote the other way for the rest of the ticket.[8] Thus Clark and Blatt both won Allegheny County in 1962 when Scranton won the governorship, as did Blatt and Lawrence in 1958 when Scott first won his seat in the Senate.

In 1964 Hugh Scott defeated Genevieve Blatt by 17,115 votes in Allegheny County; President Johnson took the county by 233,500 while Grace Sloan won her election as auditor general by 158,537. The latter figure is fully 175,652 votes greater than those for Genevieve Blatt in the county, or 1,000 votes more than Sloan's margin over Miss Blatt in Philadelphia. Considering the fact that there were almost 200,000 more registered voters in Philadelphia than in Allegheny County, those figures are pertinent indeed. In other words, whatever the cut against Miss Blatt may have been in Philadelphia County, it was considerably greater, proportionately, in the city of Pittsburgh and its environs.[9]

Unfortunately for political analysts, Pittsburgh is far less compartmentalized ethnically (except for blacks) than Philadelphia. Therefore it is far more difficult to identify the wards as specifically Italian, Jewish, black, and so on. An attempt was made to do so by the use of census data, but to no avail. Wherever there were large concentrations of first and second generation Italian-Americans, there were also considerable numbers of first and second generation Russians, Poles, Germans, and Czechs. It was virtually impossible to separate out the purely Italian wards from those of other ethnic groups. A similar attempt based on "educated guesses on the part of the ward chairmen"[10] was also made by Mrs. Rosemary Plesset, information director of the Allegheny

County Democratic Committee. According to her figures only two wards could be properly described as Italian, having more than a 50 percent Italian-American population; only one ward was predominately white Anglo-Saxon Protestant, two were Polish, five were black, and none was predominately Jewish (although the population of two were over 33 percent Jewish).

Even so, there was no regularity among any of the so-identified wards that would indicate a single-minded purpose on the part of any ethnic group per se to cut Genevieve Blatt. The two Italian wards differed considerably in the degree of the cut; the first ward cut her by 6 percent; the eighth by 14 percent. In other words, the percentage of the cut in one of the two Italian wards was more than twice that of the other ward. The same holds true for the black wards (7 percent to 16 percent) and the Polish wards (5 percent and 10 percent). Only in the two wards where over 33 percent of the population was Jewish was the cut consistently higher than in the rest of the city. Those wards cut Genevieve Blatt by 16 percent and 29 percent respectively. But because of Scott's long-standing record of support for Israel, this was not totally unexpected.

Despite the difficulty in positively identifying Pittsburgh's wards ethnically, an attempt was made to survey results in the six statewide elections previous to 1964 to determine if the 1964 senatorial results showed any difference in voting pattern.[11] For this purpose, the 26th ward in Philadelphia and the 8th ward in Pittsburg were chosen to represent the Italian-American population on the basis of the 1950 and 1960 censuses. To provide a measure of comparison the 32d ward of Philadelphia and the 5th ward of Pittsburgh were selected as indicators of black reactions. No wards were chosen to represent the different Jewish populations because of the exceptional problem of identification of such wards in Pittsburgh and because of the heavy migration of Philadelphia's Jewish population from the center city into the outlying northern wards during the 1950s.

Aside from the fact that the 1960 presidential election was the highwater mark of Italian-American political participation and that the 1964 presidential election marked the highpoint of black participation, there seems to be little difference in the reactions of Italians and blacks over the years studied. When the Italian-Americans split their tickets in favor of one candidate over another, so did blacks. The only difference was one of degree. Although Italian-Americans have not been as active politically as members of other ethnic and socioeconomic groups, blacks traditionally have been even less so, and the figures reflect this fact.

The 1964 election, however, is an exception to this trend. Here the pressure was on blacks to demonstrate their solidarity behind Johnson and against Barry Goldwater. The civil rights movement made it even more imperative that blacks alert the political powers that be to their growth in independence and political awareness. As indicated earlier, Scott made several very strong bids for black support, and Cecil Moore, among others, expended considerable energy to supply him with it. This unusual degree of activity among the black voting population was visably demonstrated in the election results. In every instance the black wards cut Genevieve Blatt to a greater degree than did the Italian wards. In all instances studied the 1964 cut was several percentage points higher than that of any previous election. The data is there, but its interpretation is necessarily inconclusive.[12]

It is impossible, on the basis of these figures, to determine the exact effect that the bigotry issue may have had on the Italian-American population or on any other ethnic group. Similar studies of the suburban townships and cities around Pittsburgh have yielded the same inconclusiveness, as did studies of Washington and Westmoreland Counties. The figures alone do not enable one to gauge the effectiveness of a specific campaign tactic.

The only method that has a hope of approximating accuracy in making such a determination — at least in this particular instance — is to ask the people themselves. Unfortunately, however, no funds were available to this investigator for an extensive postelection survey to discover the actual response of the voters to the different campaign issues. Substitute measures had to be taken to fill in the gap.[13] The chief device was to ask the politicians themselves, and then the most active of the campaign volunteers, what they thought the reactions of the voters had been.

To obtain as broad a sampling of the politicians and of politically involved "amateurs" as possible, a questionnaire was sent to seventy-one Democrats who had been active in the campaign throughout the state, asking their opinion of, among other things, the effect of the bigotry issue in their own counties. Of these seventy-one asked, twenty-eight, or 39.4 percent, returned the questionnaire. Three were county chairmen, eleven had worked in the campaign under the aegis of the Volunteers for Johnson-Humphrey-Blatt, ten were Blatt coordinators in the primary and general elections, and three had served in other capacities. In all they represented twenty-three of the sixty-seven counties, or 34 percent of the state, and were fairly evenly distributed geographically.

To the question of whether or not Senator Clark's statements on Musmanno had had any effect in the primary, twelve felt it had a great effect in their counties, ten felt it had little effect, and six said it had none at all. Of those who said it had a great effect, positively or negatively, eight were from the western part of the state, three from the east, one from the center.

In reply to the question as to whether or not Clark's statements had had a greater effect in the general election than in the primary, ten felt that it had, thirteen felt the effect to be the same, four thought it had no effect; one did not reply to that part of the questionnaire.

As to whether or not it was possible to gauge or document the extent of the Italian-American backlash, twelve felt that it was not possible, seven that there was definite evidence of it, and four that it might be possible to do so, but could offer no definite proof of it.

When they were asked to list the factors in Genevieve Blatt's defeat: fourteen referred to the disaffection of Italian-American voters, thirteen to her sex, and eleven to her lack of enthusiastic support by the party organization in their counties.

In conducting personal interviews with the sixty-one politicians listed in Appendix II, the author did not ask exactly the same questions of each, since these were in-depth interviews with questions devised to elicit the most pertinent information from each respondent and were usually composed on the spot. But of those active politicians to whom the author did speak of the subject, and whose reactions she was able to gauge throughout each conversation (forty-three in all), forty-one felt there definitely had been an Italian-American backlash against Miss Blatt. Of these forty-one, twenty-three felt there was to a great extent, four only slightly, and thirteen to a moderate extent. Of those twenty-three who felt the backlash was extensive, eighteen were from the western part of the state and three of these felt that it was the most important factor in her loss.[14] To make some attempt to test the validity of their reactions, and despite the fact that the author was fully aware that anything short of an extensive random survey would be inadequate, she nevertheless went to the county which her informants indicated had experienced the greatest degree of Italian-American backlash, and to that city in the county considered to have felt it most pronouncedly — the city of Washington in Washington County.[15] There, she obtained a street list of one heavily Italian-American precinct and spoke to ten registered Democrats who had Italian last names. Of this number, two refused to tell her how they voted, one voted the straight Democratic ticket, two voted for Scott because they did not think a woman should be a Senator, one voted for Scott because she "just didn't like Genevieve Blatt," and *four* voted for him because of Clark's statements on Musmanno. In other words, seven out of ten Italian-American registered Democrats in a Democratic city voted for Scott, and four of those seven attributed their decision to do so to their disaffection over the Musmanno incident. Of course one cannot conclude from these ten voters that the entire Italian-American community in the western part of the state felt the same way about the bigotry issue. But the intensity of their reactions was evident.

At one point in her canvassing, the author encountered one man, a small businessman, so angry over the Musmanno incident that he exploded a stream of epithets against Senator Clark, and it was all she could do to make a safe retreat from his office. The author is inclined to believe that had she been able to continue her canvassing, she would probably have turned up many others just like him.

The sex issue is another matter requiring a statewide poll for verification. Although our survey of campaign workers indicated it was the second most important factor in the campaign, only twenty of those whom I personally interviewed mentioned it in their lists of reasons for Miss Blatt's loss. The one difference for this issue, as far as verification is concerned, is the fact that E. John Bucci did attempt to predict its impact on the election three weeks ahead of time. According to his calculations 8 percent of the voters would vote against a woman candidate. As we indicated earlier, this works out to a 3 percent differential in Scott's favor when tahe "pro-women" sentiment is factored in. If this prediction was correct, the possible loss of more than 144,000 votes would account for *more than twice* the actual number of votes by which Scott won the election. However, Bucci's overall election prediction was off by more than 5.9 percent — perhaps because of the time between when the poll was taken and the actual election (three weeks). This matter only serves to emphasize how difficult it has been to determine the actual effects of any one issue on this campaign. The figures are there, but the interpretation must necessarily remain ambiguous.

NOTES

1. Interview with Francis R. Smith, Chairman, Philadelphia County Democratic Committee, April 21, 1965. The identification of wards upon an ethnic basis was accomplished strictly by the extimate of "old pols" who were intimately familiar with their wards.

2. At least not before the 1967 spring primary in which they actively intervened on behalf of Mayor Tate and against his organization-backed opponent, Alexander Hemphill.

3. Mr. DiLauro, however, denied any responsibility in the matter and refused to be interviewed about it.

4. Interview with Michael Johnson, Executive Vice-President of the Pennsylvania AFL-CIO and Director of COPE, December 12, 1964.

5. Interview with Bernard E. Norwitch, December 1, 1964.

6. Cecil Moore, Local Director of the NAACP, admitted to having paid workers in about 165 divisions to "Vote only for Scott. . . . We're interested in making Negroes conscious of their ability to split votes. . . . As long as the Democrats have us, they'll only give us crumbs. The Re-

publicans don't have enough of us to matter so they can ignore us. We have to get the Negro politically sophisticated so he'll be able to split tickets so neither party can disregard us." *Philadelphia Evening Bulletin*, November 13, 1964.

7. Interview with Joseph R. Figliomeni, Prothonotary of Lackawanna County, April 12, 1965. At the instigation of some officeholders Miss Blatt was invited to an Italian-American League dinner held in Scranton just prior to the election; the audience of 900 people gave her a standing ovation.

8. This generalization did not hold true for Milton Shapp in 1966, however. Shapp won both Philadelphia and Allegheny counties and still managed to lose by over 200,000 votes.

9. Two percent greater, to be exact. Whereas Philadelphia County cut Miss Blatt by 16 percent, the Allegheny County vote for Miss Blatt was 18 percent less than its vote for Lyndon Johnson. The differences between Mrs. Sloan and Miss Blatt in Philadelphia and Allegheny Counties were 12 percent and 13 percent respectively. The statewide difference between the Johnson and Blatt totals was 16 percent whereas that between Sloan and Blatt was 8 percent.

10. Letter to the author, March 15, 1965.

11. 1952, 1954, 1956, 1958, 1960, and 1962.

12. Compare these figures for the above-mentioned wards in the 1962 senatorial contest between Clark and Van Zandt and the 1964 Blatt-Scott election. In 1962, Philadelphia and Pittsburgh Italian-Americans split in favor of Senator Clark and against his Democratic gubernatorial running-mate, Richardson Dilworth, by 2 percent and 4 percent respectively, while blacks did the same by 1 percent and 2 percent. In 1964 the split in favor of President Johnson and against Miss Blatt in the two Italian wards was 5 percent and 7 percent respectively, and in the two black wards, 6 percent and 8 percent.

If we arbitrarily select the 50th ward of Philadelphia and the 14th ward of Pittsburgh as indicators of Jewish voters are much more inclined two elections we get results somewhat consistent with those above, differing primarily in the fact that Jewish voters are much more inclined to ticket-splitting than average. In 1962 these two wards of Philadelphia and Pittsburgh cut Dilworth by 6 percent and 16 percent respectively, and in 1964 they cut Miss Blatt by 24 percent and 29 percent. However, there are too many imponderables in these figures for us to be at all confident of their meaning.

13. An attempt was made to analyze the Survey Research Center's data from the Michigan Consortium, but not enough Italian-American

voters from Pennsylvania had been included in their sample to make the results meaningful—fewer than ten, in fact. A similar request for data from the Roper Public Opinion Research Center at William College in Massachusetts produced the same result.

14. Several thought the issue clearly affected other ethnic groups as well—Slavs especially.

15. According to the 1960 census, Washington City had a total population of 26,028 with 4,296 residents of "foreign stock." 1,462 of these were listed as having come from Italy. In the 1964 election 4,766 persons voted for Scott while only 4,456 cast their votes for the Democratic candidate— by all accounts a truly unusual departure from their traditional voting patterns.

APPENDIX II

Persons Interviewed

The names of those persons who granted the author interviews, which constituted the bulk of the material used for this book, are listed here alphabetically:

The Honorable Ruggero J. Aldisert, Judge, Common Pleas Court No. 3, Allegheny County. Judge, U.S. Circuit Court, Pittsburgh, Pennsylvania.

Miss Isabel Allias, Staff, Voters for Genevieve Blatt.

Mr. Eugene Armeo, Publicity Director, Philadelphia County Democratic Committee.

The Honorable Joseph A. Barr, Mayor, The City of Pittsburgh.

Mr. John Bevec, County Commissioner, Washington County.

Mr. Raymond A. Berens, Staff, Voters for Genevieve Blatt.

Miss Genevieve Blatt, Secretary of Internal Affairs, The Commonwealth of Pennsylvania. Judge Commonwealth Court, Harrisburg, Pennsylvania.

Mr. Michael J. Bryne, Executive Assistant to Senator Joseph S. Clark.

Mr. E. John Bucci, Political and Market Pollster, Swarthmore, Pennsylvania.

Mr. Anthony Cavalcante, Chairman, Board of Commissioners, Fayette County.

Mr. Robert Ceisler, Attorney-at-Law, Washington County.

Mr. Aldo Colautti, Executive Secretary to Mayor Joseph A. Barr.

Dean Thomas M. Cooley II, Professor, University of Pittsburgh Law School. Co-Chairman, Southwest Pennsylvania Volunteers for Johnson-Humphrey-Blatt.

Mr. Eugene Cowan, Press Secretary to Senator Hugh Scott.

Mr. John B. DiGiorno, National Secretary, Order Italian Sons and Daughters of America.

Mr. Richard Doran, Executive Director, Southeast Pennsylvania Volunteers for Johnson-Humphrey-Blatt.

Mr. Paul D'Ortona, President, Philadelphia City Council.

Mr. William Duffield, Solicitor, Fayette County.

Mr. Bruce Felknor, Executive Director, Fair Campaign Practices Committee. Publishing Company Executive, Chicago, Illinois.

The Honorable Andrew T. Fenrich, State Representative, Allegheny County.

Mr. Joseph R. Figliomeni, Prothonotary, Lackawanna County.

Mr. Nicholas J. Fisfis, Staff, Voters for Genevieve Blatt.

Abraham E. Freedman, Esq., Freedman, Borowsky and Lorry, Philadelphia.

Mr. Raymond E. Gardlock, Director, Redevelopment Authority, Westmoreland County.

Miss Libby Goldstein, Staff, Southeast Pennsylvania Volunteers for Johnson-Humphrey-Blatt.

Mr. Michael A. Hanna, Chairman, Washington County Democratic Committee.

Gregory M. Harvey, Esq., Morgan, Lewis and Bockius, Philadelphia.

Mr. Michael Johnson, Executive Vice President, Pennsylvania AFL-CIO.

Philip Kalodner, Esq., Schapiro, Stalberg, Cook, Murphy and Kalodner, Philadelphia.

Patrick E. Kerwin, Esq., Bream, Kerwin and Yoffe, Harrisburg.

Mr. F. William Kittridge, Purchasing Officer, Washington County.

Mr. James Knox, County Controller and Chairman, Allegheny County Democratic Committee.

Mr. Robert L. Kunzig, Administrative Assistant to Senator Hugh Scott. Judge, U.S. Court of Claims, Washington, D.C.

The Honorable David L. Lawrence, Former Governor, Commonwealth of Pennsylvania.

Mr. Joseph Lockard, Administrative Assistant to Frank Smith, Chairman, Philadelphia County Democratic Committee.

Miss Ann Lowell, Staff, Pennsylvania State Democratic Committee.

Dr. William McClelland, Chairman, County Commissioners, Allegheny County.

Mr. Joseph Marzzacco, Assistant County Solicitor, Lackawanna County.

Mr. Patrick J. Mellody, Chairman, Lackawanna County Democratic Committee.

Mr. Otis Morse, Chairman, Democratic State Committee.

Mr. Robert W. Munley, Assistant District Attorney, Lackawanna County.

The Honorable Austin J. Murphy, State Representative, Washington County.

The Honorable Michael Angelo Musmanno, Associate Justice, The Supreme Court of Pennsylvania.

Mr. Bernard E. Norwitch, Administrative Assistant to Senator Joseph S. Clark.

Mr. Michael O'Pake, Staff, Pennsylvania Democratic State Committee.

The Honorable Hugo Parente, Mayor, The City of Monessen, Westmoreland County.

Mrs. Rosemary Plesset, Director, Information Service, Allegheny County Democratic Committee.

Mrs. Iris Richey, Staff, Voters for Genevieve Blatt.

Mr. Stephen Richman, Chairman, Win with Hugh Scott Committee, Washington County.

Mr. David B. Roberts, Prothonotary, Allegheny County.

Miss Dolores Rozzi, Justice of the Peace, Stockdale, Washington County.

Mr. Robert Sabbato, Deputy Chairman of Public Relations, Pennsylvania Democratic State Committee.

Ferdinand P. Schoettle, Esq., Morgan, Lewis and Bockius, Philadelphia.

Professor Timothy Scully, University of Scranton.

Dr. William C. Seyler, Deputy Secretary of Internal Affairs, Commonwealth of Pennsylvania. Assistant Vice President and Secretary, Temple University.

Mr. Worth Seymour, County Coordinator, Southwest Pennsylvania Volunteers for Johnson-Humphrey-Blatt.

Mr. Francis R. Smith, Chairman, Philadelphia County Democratic Committee.

Mr. George R. Sweeny, Chairman, Westmoreland County Democratic Committee.

The Honorable Charles B. Sweet, President Judge, Court of Common Pleas, Washington County.

Martin Vigderman, Esq., Freedman, Borowsky and Lorry, Philadelphia.

Mr. Ralph Widner, Legislative Assistant to Senator Joseph S. Clark. Planning Executive, Publishing Administrator, Columbus, Ohio.

. . . And one Westmoreland County Attorney who preferred to remain anonynous.

These titles, with a few exceptions, were those current during the time of the 1964 senatorial campaign in Pennsylvania.

Chronology
of Events

1949   Democratic reform elements headed by Richardson Dilworth and Joseph S. Clark defeat the Republican "machine" in Philadelphia by capturing the office of City Treasurer and City Controller.

1950   Dilworth runs for Governor of Pennsylvania with Judge Michael A. Musmanno of the Court of Common Pleas as his running-mate for Lieutenant Governor; both lose but Musmanno is censured by the American Bar Association for not resigning his judgeship while campaigning for political office.

1951   Musmanno runs against the Democratic incumbent for Justice of the Pennsylvania Supreme Court and wins.

1952   Clark becomes Mayor of Philadelphia.

1954   George Leader is elected Governor of Pennsylvania—the second Democrat in this century to acquire the office. Genevieve Blatt is elected Secretary of Internal Affairs. Congressman William Green succeeds James A. Finnegan as Chairman of the Philadelphia Democratic City Committee.

1956   Dilworth succeeds Clark as Mayor of Philadelphia. Clark is elected to the United States Senate.

1958   Hugh Scott defeats George Leader for the position of United States Senator. David L. Lawrence succeeds Leader as Governor of Pennsylvania; Blatt is reelected Secretary of Internal Affairs.

1960   John F. Kennedy is elected President of the United States, receiving a 300,000 vote *plurality* from the city of Philadelphia, while his nationwide margin is 118,000.

1962   William W. Scranton defeats Dilworth for Governor of Pennsylvania while Blatt is reelected Secretary of Internal Affairs and Clark is reelected to the Senate. James H. J. Tate succeeds Dilworth as Mayor of Philadelphia.

1963   Tate runs and wins election on his own as Mayor of Philadelphia; John F. Kennedy is assassinated; William Green dies; Frank Smith succeeds Green as Chairman of the Philadelphia Democratic City Committee.

1964   January   Tate tells reporter that Blatt is likely to be the Democratic Party candidate for the United States Senate. Paul D'Ortona asks Musmanno if he would like to run for the Senate.

The State Democratic Policy Committee meets and endorses Musmanno before the primary.

February   Blatt files in the Democratic primary for the United States Senate; Clark supports Blatt.

April   Clark asks questions about Musmanno's name, age, and birthplace. Blatt appears to defeat Musmanno by a slight margin.

August   The Democratic National Convention meets in Atlantic City to nominate Lyndon Johnson and Hubert Humphrey for President and Vice President.

September   Blatt is certified the primary winner by the State Elections Bureau.

October 12   The U.S. Supreme Court refuses to hear Musmanno's appeal.

November   Scott defeats Blatt by 70,000 votes while Johnson carries the state by 1.4 million.

1966   Blatt is defeated for Secretary of Internal Affairs by John K. Tabor.

1968   Musmanno dies on Columbus Day. Clark is defeated for United States Senate by Richard S. Schweiker.

1969   Peter Flaherty defeats the Lawrence-Barr organization in Pittsburgh in the mayoralty election.

Bibliography and Related Readings

While the following list of publications is not intended to be exhaustive, it is meant to be representative of the professional literature in those fields of political science touched upon in this book—especially political parties, machine politics, ethnic and sexual politics, and participation and voting.

This bibliography was originally intended to be annotated. However, the list of books and articles that have come to be considered the most important in these fields in recent years, grew to such a length that annotation proved to be out of the question: far more pages would have been added to the text of this book than had been originally planned or budgeted for. The expediency of simply listing the major sources by category was then decided upon, with the following result.

POLITICAL PARTIES

General

Abbott, David W., and Edward T. Rogowsky, eds., *Political Parties*, 2nd ed. (Chicago: Rand McNally College Publishing Co., 1978).

Broder, David, *The Party's Over: The Failure of Politics in America* (New York: Harper and Row, 1972).

Burns, James MacGregor, *The Deadlock of Democracy* (Englewood Cliffs, N.J. : Prentice-Hall, 1963).

Chambers, William Nesbit, and Walter Dean Burnham, eds., *The American Party Systems: Stages of Political Development,* 2nd ed. (New York: Oxford University Press, 1975).

Eldersveld, Samuel J., *Political Parties: A Behavioral Analysis* (Chicago: Rand McNally, 1964).

Greenstein, Fred I., *The American Party System and the American People* (Englewood Cliffs, N.J. : Prentice-Hall, 1963).

James, Judson, *American Political Parties in Transition* (New York: Harper and Row, 1974).

Ladd, Everett Carll, Jr., *American Political Parties: Social Change and Political Response* (New York: W. W. Norton, 1970).

Ladd, Everett Carll, Jr. with Charles D. Hadley, *Transformations of the American Party System: Political Coalitions from the New Deal to the 1970's*, rev. ed. (New York: W. W. Norton, 1978).

Leiserson, Avery, *Parties and Politics: An Institutional and Behavioral Approach* (New York: Alfred A. Knopf, 1958).

Lipset, Seymour Martin, and Stein Rokkan, eds., *Party Systems and Voter Alignments* (New York: Free Press, 1967).

Lubell, Samuel, *The Future of American Politics* (Garden City, N.J. : Doubleday, Anchor, 1956).

Maisel, Louis, and Paul M. Sacks, eds., *The Future of Political Parties,* Sage Electoral Studies Yearbook, vol. 1 (Beverly Hills, California: Sage Publications, 1975).

Merelman, Richard M., "Electoral Instability and the American Party System," *Journal of Politics* 32 (February 1970), 115-139.

Ranney, Austin, *Curing the Mischiefs of Faction: Party Reform in America (Berkeley and Los Angeles: University of California Press, 1975, 1976).*

Rubin, Richard L., *Party Dynamics: The Democratic Coalition and the Politics of Change* (New York: Oxford University Press, 1978).

Sundquist, James L., *The Dynamics of the Party System: Alignment and Realignment of Political Parties in the United States* (Washington, D.C. The Brookings Institution, 1973).

———, "Whither the American Party System?" *Political Science Quarterly* 88 (December 1973), 559-581.

Divisive Primaries

Bernstein, Robert A., "Divisive Primaries Do Hurt: U. S. Senate Races, 1956-1972" *American Political Science Review* 71 (June 1977), 540-545.

Hacker, Andrew, "Does a 'Divisive' Primary Harm a Candidate's Election Chances?" *American Political Science Review* 59 (March 1965), 105-110.

Johnson, Donald and James Gibson, "The Divisive Primary Revisited: Party Activists in Iowa," *American Political Science Review* 68 (March 1974), 67-77.

Election Campaigns

Adamany, David, "Money, Politics and Democracy: A Review Essay," *American Political Science Review* 71 (March 1977), 289-304.

Agranoff, Robert, *The New Style in Election Campaigns* (Boston: Holbrook Press, 1972).

Alexander, Herbert E., ed., *Campaign Money: Reform and Reality in the States* (New York: Free Press, 1976).

_____, *Financing Politics: Money, Elections and Political Reform* (Washington, D.C. : Congressional Quarterly, Inc., 1976).

Cummings, Milton C., Jr., ed., *The National Election of 1964* (Washington, D.C. : Brookings Institution, 1966).

Kelley, Stanley, Jr., *Political Campaigning* (Washington, D.C.: Brookings Institution, 1960).

Kraus, Sidney, ed., *The Great Debates* (Bloomington: Indiana University Press, 1962).

Mendelsohn, Harold, and Irving Crespi, *Polls, Television, and the New Politics* (Scranton, Pa. : Chandler, 1970).

Napolitan, Joseph, *The Election Game and How to Win It* (Garden City, N.Y. : Doubleday, 1972).

Rubin, Bernard, *Political Television* (Belmont, California: Wadsworth, 1967).

Shadegg, Stephen C., *The New How to Win an Election* (New York: Taplinger, 1972).

Incumbency

Erikson, Robert S., "The Advantage of Incumbency in Congressional Elections," *Polity* 3 (Spring 1971), 395-405.

Ferejohn, John A., "On the Decline of Competition in Congressional Elections," *American Political Science Review* 71 (March 1977), 166-175.

Kostroski, Warren Lee, "Party and Incumbency in Post-War Senate Elections," *American Political Science Review* 67 (December 1973), 1213-1234.

Issues and Ideologies

American Political Science Association, Committee on Political Parties, "Toward a More Responsible Two-Party System," *American Political Science Review* 44 (September 1950), Supplement.

Apter, David E., ed., *Ideology and Discontent* (New York: Free Press, 1964).

Burnham, Walter Dean, "American Politics in the 1970's: Beyond Party?" in William Nesbit Chambers and Walter Dean Burnham, eds., *The American Party Systems: Stages of Political Development*, 2nd ed. (New York: Oxford University Press, 1975), pp. 308-357.

———, "American Voting Behavior and the 1964 Elections," *Midwest Journal of Political Science* 12 (June 1968), 1-40.

———, "The Changing Shape of the American Political Universe," *American Political Science Review* 61 (March 1965), 7-28.

Congressional Quarterly, Inc., "The Democratic Left Faces a Dilemma," *Congressional Quarterly Weekly Report* 36 (December 16, 1978), 3431-3433.

Converse, Philip E., "Information Flow and the Stability of Partisan Attitudes," in Angus Campbell et al., eds., *Elections and the Political Order* (New York: John Wiley & Sons, 1966), pp. 136-157.

———, "The Nature of Belief Systems in Mass Politics," in David E. Apter, ed., *Ideology and Discontent* (New York: Free Press, 1964), pp. 206-261.

Converse, Philip E., Warren E. Miller, Jerrold G. Rusk, and Arthur G. Wolfe, "Continuities and Change in American Politics: Parties and Issues in the 1968 Election," *American Political Science Review* 58 (December 1969), 1083-1105.

Free, Lloyd and Hadley Cantril, *The Political Beliefs of Americans: A Study of Public Opinion* (New York: Simon and Shuster, Clarion Book, 1968).

Gallup, George H., *Gallup Poll Public Opinion: 1935-1971*, 3 vols. (New York: Random House, 1972).

Kessel, John, "Comment: The Issues in Issue Voting," *American Political Science Review* 66 (June 1972), 459-465.

Key, V. O., Jr., *The Responsible Electorate: Rationality in Presidential Voting, 1936-1960* (Cambridge, Mass.: Harvard University Press, Belknap Press, 1966).

Ladd, Everett C., Jr., "The New Lines Are Drawn: Class and Ideology in America," *Public Opinion* 1 (July-August 1978), 48-53.

Ladd, Everett C., Jr. and Charles D. Hadley, *Political Parties and Political Issues: Patterns in Differentiation Since the New Deal* (Beverly Hills, California: Sage Publications, 1973).

Margolis, Michael, "From Confusion to Confusion: Issues and the American Voter (1956-1972)," *American Political Science Review* 71 (March 1977), 31-43.

Miller, Arthur H., Warren E. Miller, Alden S. Raine, and Thad A. Brown, "A Majority Party in Disarray: Policy Polarization in the 1972 Election," *American Political Science Review* 70 (September 1976), 75-558.

Nie, Norman H. (with Kristi Andersen), "Mass Belief Systems Revisited: Political Change and Attitude Structure," *Journal of Politics* 36 (August 1974), 540-591.

Pomper, Gerald M., "From Confusion to Clarity: Issues and American Voters, 1956-1958," *American Political Science Review* 66 (June 1972), 415-428.

_____, "Toward a More Responsible Two-Party System? What, Again?" *Journal of Politics* 33 (November 1971), 916-940.

Ranney, Austin, *The Doctrine of Responsible Party Government: Its Origins and Present State* (Urbana: University of Illinois Press, 1962).

RePass, David E., "Issue Salience and Party Choice," *American Political Science Review* 65 (June 1971), 389-400.

Saloma, John S. III and Frederick H. Sontag, *Parties: The Real Opportunity for Effective Citizen Politics* (New York: Vintage Books, 1972, 1973).

Segal, David, "Partisan Realignment in the United States: The Lesson of the 1964 Election," *Public Opinion Quarterly* 3 (Fall 1968), 441-444.

PARTICIPATION AND VOTING

Political Participation

Lane, Robert E., *Political Life: Why People Get Involved in Politics* (Glencoe, Illinois: Free Press, 1959).

Milbrath, Lester W., *Political Participation: How and Why People Get Involved in Politics,* 2nd ed. (Chicago: Rand McNally, 1977).

Nie, Norman H. and Sidney Verba, "Political Participation," in Fred I. Greenstein and Nelson W. Polsby, eds., *Handbook of Political Science,* vol. 4 (Reading, Mass.: Addison-Wesley, 1975), pp. 1-74.

Nie, Norman H., Sidney Verba, and John R. Petrocik, *The Changing American Voter* (Cambridge, Mass,: Harvard University Press, 1976).

Verba, Sidney and Norman H. Nie, *Participation in America: Political Democracy and Social Equality* (New York: Harper and Row, 1972).

Voting Behavior

Abramson, Paul R., "Generational Change in American Electoral Behavior," *American Political Science Review* 68 (March 1974), 93-105.

Axelrod, Robert, "Where the Votes Come From: An Analysis of Electoral Coalitions: 1952-1968," *American Political Science Review* 66 (March 1972), 11-20.

Barber, James A., Jr., *Social Mobility and Voting Behavior* (Chicago: Rand McNally, 1970).

Berelson, Bernard, Paul Lazarsfeld, and William McPhee, *Voting* (Chicago: University of Chicago Press, 1954).

Burdick, Eugene and Arthur Brodbeck, *American Voting Behavior* (New York: The Free Press, 1959).

Burnham, Walter Dean, *Critical Elections and the Mainsprings of American Politics* (New York: W. W. Norton, 1970).

_____, "Theory and Voting Research: Some Reflections on Converse's 'Change in the American Electorate'," *American Political Science Review* 68 (September 1974), 1002-1023.

Campbell, Angus, "Surge and Decline: A Study of Electoral Change," in Angus Campbell et al., eds., *Elections and The Political Order* (New York: John Wiley and Sons, 1966), pp. 40-62.

Campbell, Angus, and Philip E. Converse, *The Human Meaning of Social Change* (New York: Russell Sage Foundation, 1972).

Campbell, Angus, Philip E. Converse, Warren E. Miller, and Donald E. Stokes, *The American Voter* (New York: John Wiley and Sons, 1960).

_____, *Elections and the Political Order* (New York: John Wiley and Sons, 1966).

Converse, Philip E., "Public Opinion and Voting Behavior," in Fred I. Greenstein and Nelson W. Polsby, eds., *Handbook of Political Science,* vol. 4 (Reading, Mass.: Addison-Wesley, 1975), pp. 75-169.

Flanigan, William H., *Political Behavior of the American Electorate,* 2nd. ed. (Boston: Allyn and Bacon, 1972).

Froman, Lewis A., Jr., *Congressmen and Their Constituencies* (Chicago: Rand McNally, 1963).

Frost, Richard T., "Stability and Change in Local Politics," *Public Opinion Quarterly* 25 (Summer 1961).

Greeley, Andrew M., *Building Coalitions* (New York: New Viewpoints, 1974).

Hamilton, Richard, *Class and Politics in the United States* (New York: John Wiley and Sons, 1972).

Kelley, Stanley, Jr., and Thad W. Mirer, "The Simple Act of Voting," *American Political Science Review* 67 (June 1974), 572-591.

Key, V.O., Jr., "A Theory of Critical Elections," *Journal of Politics* 17 (February 1955), 3-18.

Kirkpatrick, Samuel, ed., *American Electoral Behavior: Change and Stability* (Beverly Hills, California: Sage Publications, 1976).

Mayhew, David, "Congressional Elections: The Case of the Vanishing Marginals, "*Polity* 6 (Spring 1974), 295-317.

Philips, Kevin P., *The Emerging Republican Majority* (New York: Doubleday, 1969).

Polsby, Nelson W., "The Institutionalization of the House of Representatives, "*American Political Science Review* 62 (March 1968), 144-168.

Pomper, Gerald, *Elections in America* (New York: Dodd, Mead, 1968).

_____, *Voters' Choice: Varieties of American Electoral Behavior* (New York: Harper and Row, 1975).

Scammon, Richard M., and Ben J. Wattenberg, *The Real Majority* (New York: Coward, McCann and Geoghegan, 1970).

Wallace, David, *First Tuesday* (Garden City, N.Y. : Doubleday, 1964).

URBAN AND MACHINE POLITICS

General

Banfield, Edward C., *Big City Politics* (New York: Random House, 1965).

_____, *Political Influence: A New Theory of Urban Politics* (New York: Free Press, 1961)

_____, *The Unheavenly City: The Nature and Future of Our Urban Crisis* (Boston: Little, Brown, 1968, 1970).

Banfield, Edward C. and James Q. Wilson, *City Politics* (New York: Vintage Books, 1963).

Bonjean, Charles M., Terry N. Clark, and Robert L. Lineberry, eds., *Community Politics: A Behavioral Approach* (New York: Free Press, 1971).

Cooke, Edward F. and G. Edward Janosik, *Guide to Pennsylvania Politics* (New York: Henry Holt, 1957).

Cornwall, Elmer E., "Bosses, Machines and Ethnic Groups, " *The Annals* 353 (May 1964), 27-39.

Dahl, Robert, *Who Governs?* (New Haven: Yale University Press, 1961).

Fainstein, Norman I. and Susan S. Fainstein, *Urban Political Movements* (Englewood Cliffs, N.J.: Prentice-Hall, 1974).

Flynn, Edward J., *You're the Boss: The Practice of American Politics,* Viking Press, 1947. Reprint, New York: Collier Books, 1962.

Gosnell, Harold, *Machine Politics: Chicago Model* (Chicago: University of Chicago Press, 1937).

Hahn, Harlan, ed., *People and Politics in Urban Society* (Beverly Hills, California: Sage Publications, 1972).

Katz, Daniel and Samuel J. Eldersveld, "The Impact of Local Party Activity on the Electorate, "*Public Opinion Quarterly* 25 (Spring 1961), 16-17.

Lamb, Curt, *Political Power in Poor Neighborhoods* (New York: Halstead, 1975).

Levin, Murray, *The Alienated Voter: Politics in Boston* (New York: Holt, Rinehart and Winston, 1962).

Manso, Peter, ed., *Running Against the Machine: The Mailer-Breslin Campaign* (Garden City, N.Y.: Doubleday, 1969).

Martin, Roscoe C. et al., *Decisions in Syracuse: A Metropolitan Action Study* (Garden City, New York: Doubleday, 1965).

Petshek, Kirk R., *The Challenge of Urban Reform: Politics and Programs in Philadelphia* (Philadelphia, Pa.: Temple University Press, 1973).

Presthus, Robert, *Men at the Top: A Study in Community Power* (New York: Oxford University Press, 1964).

Rakove, Milton, *Don't Make No Waves . . . Dont Back No Losers: An Insider's Analysis of the Daley Machine* (Bloomington: Indiana University Press, 1975).

Reichley, James, *The Art of Government: Reform and Organization Politics in Philadelphia* (New York: The Fund for the Republic, 1959).

Rossi, Peter and Phillip Cutwright, "The Impact of Party Organization in an Industrial Setting," in Morris Janowitz, ed., *Community Political Systems* (Glencoe, Ill.: Free Press, 1961).

Royko, Mike, *Boss: Richard J. Daley of Chicago* (New York: New American Library, 1971).

Sayre, Wallace S., and Herbert Kaufman, *Governing New York City: Politics in the Metropolis* (New York: W. W. Norton, 1960, 1965).

Sheftor, Martin, "The Emergence of the Political Machine: An Alternative View, " in Willis D. Hawley et al., *Theoretical Perspectives on Urban Politics* (Englewood Cliffs, N.J.: Prentice-Hall, 1976).

Stave, Bruce M., *The New Deal and the Last Hurrah: Pittsburgh Machine Politics* (Pittsburgh: University of Pittsburgh Press, 1970).

Tolchin, Martin and Susan Tolchin, *To the Victor. . . : Political Patronage from the Clubhouse to the White House* (New York: Random House, 1971).

Warner, Samuel, *The Private City* (Philadelphia: University of Pennsylvania Press, 1968).

Williams, Oliver P. and Charles Press, eds., *Democracy in Urban America: Readings on Government and Politics* (Chicago: Rand McNally, 1961).

Wolfinger, Raymond E., "Why Political Machines Have Not Withered Away and Other Revisionist Thoughts," *Journal of Politics* 34 (May 1972), 365-398.

ETHNIC POLITICS

General

Bailey, Harry A., Jr., and Ellis Katz, eds., *Ethnic Group Politics* (Columbus, Ohio: Charles E. Merrill, 1969).

Cornwell, Elmer E., Jr., "Party Absorption of Ethnic Groups: The Case of

Providence, Rhode Island," *Social Forces* 38 (March 1960), 205-210.

Fuchs, Lawrence H., ed., *American Ethnic Politics* (New York: Harper and Row, 1968).

Glazer, Nathan and Daniel Patrick Moynihan, *Beyond the Melting Pot: The Negroes, Puerto Ricans, Jews, Italians and Irish of New York City,* 2nd ed. (Cambridge, Mass.: M.I.T. Press, 1970).

_____, eds., *Ethnicity: Theory and Experience* (Cambridge, Mass.: Harvard University Press, 1975).

Handlin, Oscar, "The Immigrant in American Politics," in David Frederick Bowers, ed., *Foreign Influences in American Life* (Princeton, N.J.: Princeton University Press, 1944), 88-98.

Hawkins, Brett W. and Robert Lorinskas, *The Ethnic Factor in American Politics* (Columbus, Ohio: Charles E. Merrill, 1970).

Kleppner, Paul, *The Cross of Culture* (New York: Free Press, 1970).

Lenski, Gerhard, *The Religious Factor* (Garden City, N.Y. : Doubleday, 1961).

Levy, Mark R. and Michael S. Kramer, *The Ethnic Factor: How America's Minorities Decide Elections* (New York: Simon and Schuster, 1973).

Litt, Edgar, *Beyond Pluralism: Ethnic Politics in America* (Glenview, Ill.: Scott, Foresman, 1970).

Makielski, Stanislaw J., *Beleaguered Minorities: Politics in America* (San Francisco: W.H. Freeman, 1973).

Miller, Abraham Hirsh, *Ethnicity and Political Behavior: An Investigation of Partisanship and Efficacy,* Ph.D. dissertation (Ann Arbor, Michigan: University of Michigan Microfilms, 1968).

Nie, Norman H., Barbara Currie, and Andrew M. Greeley, "Political Attitudes Among American Ethnics: A Study of Perceptual Distortion," *Ethnicity* 1 (December 1974), 317-343.

Novak, Michael, *The Rise of the Unmeltable Ethnics: Politics and Culture in the Seventies* (New York: Macmillan, 1972).

Parenti, Michael J., "Ethnic Politics and the Persistence of Ethnic Identification," *American Political Science Review* 61 (September 1967), 717-726.

Pavlak, Thomas J., "Social Class, Ethnicity and Racial Prejudice, " *Public Opinion Quarterly* 37 (Summer 1975), 225-231.

Schnall, David J., *Ethnicity and Suburban Local Politics* (New York: Praeger, 1975).

Wolfinger, Raymond E., "The Development and Persistence of Ethnic Group Voting, " *American Political Science Review* 59 (December 1965), 896-900.

White Ethnic Groups

Clark, Terry Nichols, "The Irish Ethnic and the Spirit of Patronage," *Ethnicity* 2 (December 1975), 305-359.

Gabriel, Richard A., *Ethnic Voting in Primary Elections: The Irish and Italians of Providence, Rhode Island* (Kingston, Rhode Island: Bureau of Government Research, 1969).

Gallo, Patrick J., *Ethnic Alienation: The Italian Americans* (Cranbury, N.J. : Fairleigh Dickenson University Press, 1974).

Gans, Herbert J., *The Urban Villagers: Group and Class in the Life of Italian Americans* (New York: Free Press, 1962).

Isaacs, Stephen D., *Jews and American Politics* (Garden City, N.Y. : Doubleday, 1974)

Kantowicz, Edward R., *Polish-American Politics in Chicago* (Chicago: University of Chicago Press, 1975).

Krickus, Richard, *Pursuing the American Dream: White Ethnics and the New Populism* (Bloomington: Indiana University Press, 1976).

LaGumina, Salvatore J., *Ethnicity in American Political Life: The Italian-American Experience* (New York: American Italian Historical Association, 1968).

McCaffrey, Lawrence J., "The Conservative Image of Irish America," *Ethnicity* 2 (September 1975), 271-280.

Schneider, William, Michael D. Berman, and Mark Schultz, "Bloc Voting Reconsidered: Is There a Jewish Vote?" *Ethnicity* 1 (December 1974), 345-392.

Whyte, William Foote, *Street Corner Society: The Social Structure of an Italian Slum*, 2nd ed. (Chicago: Univeristy of Chicago Press, 1955).

The Black Voter

Aberbach, Joel D., and Jack L. Walker, "The Meanings of Black Power: A Comparison of White and Black Interpretations of a Political Slogan," *American Political Science Review* 64 (June 1970), 367-388.

_____, *Race in the City* (Boston: Little, Brown, 1973).

Abramson, Paul R., *The Political Socialization of Black Americans: A Critical Evaluation of Research on Efficacy and Trust* (New York: Free Press, 1977).

Aikin, Charles, ed., *The Negro Votes* (San Francisco: Chandler, 1962).

Bailey, Harry A., Jr., ed., *Negro Politics in America* (Columbus, Ohio: Charles E. Merrill, 1967).

Bellush, Jewel and Steven M. David, *Race and Politics in New York City: Five Studies in Policy-Making* (New York: Praeger, 1971).

Bond, Julian, *Black Candidates: Southern Campaign Experiences* (Atlanta, Georgia: Southern Regional Council, 1969).

Bullock, Charles S. III, and Harrell Rodgers, Jr., *Black Political Attitudes* (Chicago: Markham, 1972).

Carmichael, Stokely and Charles Hamilton, *Black Power* (New York: Random House, 1967).

Clubok, Alfred B., John M. De Grove, and Charles D. Farris, "The Manipulated Negro Vote: Some Pre-Conditions and Consequences," *Journal of Politics* 26 (February 1964), 112-129.

Cole, Leonard A., *Blacks in Power: A Comparative Study of Black and White Elected Officials* (Princeton, N.J.: Princeton University Press, 1976).

Daniel, Johnnie, "Negro Political Behavior and Community Political and Socioeconomic Structural Factors," *Social Forces* 47 (March 1969), 275-288.

Ershowitz, Miriam and Joseph Zikmund, eds., *Black Politics in Philadelphia* (New York: Basic Books, 1973).

Glantz, Oscar, "The Negro Vote in Northern Industrial Cities," *Western Political Quarterly* 13 (December 1960), 999-1010.

Greenstone, J. David and Paul E. Peterson, *Race and Authority in Urban Politics* (New York: Basic Books, 1974).

Keech, William R., *The Impact of Negro Voting: The Role of the Vote in the Quest for Equality* (Chicago: Rand McNally, 1968).

Marvick, Dwaine, "The Political Socialization of the American Negro," *The Annals* 361 (September 1965), 112-127.

Matthews, Donald R. and James W. Prothro, *Negroes and the New Southern Politics* (New York: Harcourt, Brace and World, 1962).

Meier, August and Elliot Rudwick, *CORE: A Study in the Civil Rights Movement, 1942-1968* (New York: Oxford University Press, 1973).

Morris, Milton D., *The Politics of Black America: An Annotated Bibliography* (Carbondale, Ill.: Public Affairs Research Bureau, Southern Illinois University, 1971).

———, *The Politics of Black America* (New York: Harper and Row, 1975).

Parsons, Talcott and Kenneth B. Clark, eds., *The Negro American* (Boston: Beacon Press, 1965, 1966).

Peeks, Edward, *The Long Struggle for Black Power* (New York: Scribner's Sons, 1971).

Pomper, Gerald, "Black and White Asunder," in Gerald Pomper, *Voters Choice: Varieties of American Electoral Behavior* (New York: Harper and Row, 1975), pp. 117-141.

Rainwater, Lee, and William L. Yancy, eds., *The Moynihan Report and the Politics of Controversy* (Cambridge, Mass.: M.I.T. Press, 1967).

Segal, David R., and Richard Schaffner, "Status, Party and Negro Americans," *Phylon* 29 (Fall 1968), 224-230.

Sindler, Allen P., "Negroes, Ethnic Groups and American Politics," *Current History* 55 (October 1968), 207-212.

Storing, Herbert J., ed., *What Country Have I? Political Writings by Black Americans* (New York: St. Martin's Press, 1970).

Van der Slik, Jack R., ed., *Black Conflict with White America: A Reader in Social and Political Analysis* (Columbus, Ohio: Charles E. Merrill, 1970).

Walton, Hanes, Jr., *Black Political Parties: An Historical and Political Analysis* (New York: Free Press, 1972).

_____, *Black Politics: A Theoretical and Structural Analysis* (Philadelphia: J. B. Lippincott, 1972).

Weisbrod, Robert J., and Arthur Stein, *Bittersweet Encounter: The Afro-American and the American Jew* (Westport, Conn.: Negro Universities Press, 1970).

Willie, Charles V., ed., *Black/Brown/White Relations: Race Relations in the 1970's* (New Brunswick, N.J.: Transaction Books, 1977).

Wilson, James Q., *Negro Politics: The Search for Leadership* (New York: Free Press, 1960).

WOMEN AND POLITICS

General

Amundsen, Kirsten, *A New Look at The Silenced Majority: Women and American Democracy*, rev. ed. (Englewood Cliffs, N.J.: Prentice-Hall, 1977.

Andreas, Carol, *Sex and Caste in America* (Englewood Cliffs, N.J.: Prentice-Hall, 1971).

Bennett, Edward M. and Harriet M. Goodwin, "Emotional Aspects of Political Behavior: The Woman Voter," *Genetic Psychological Monographs* 58 (August 1958), 3-53.

Boals, Kay, "On Getting Feminine Qualities into the Power Structure," *University* (Fall 1972), 6-12.

Boyd, Rosamonde Ramsay, "Women and Politics in the United States and Canada," *The Annals* 375 (January 1968), 52-57.

Bullough, Vern L. and Bonnie Bullough, *The Subordinate Sex: A History of Attitudes Toward Women* (Urbana: University of Illinois Press, 1973).

Cade, Toni, ed., *The Black Woman: An Anthology* (New York: New American Library, 1970).

Chafe, William Henry, *The American Woman: Her Changing Social, Economic and Political Roles, 1920-1970* (New York: Oxford University Press, 1972).

Degler, Carl N., "Revolution Without Ideology: The Changing Place of Women in America," *Daedalus* 93 (Spring 1964), 653-670.

Duverger, Maurice, *The Political Role of Women* (Paris: UNESCO, 1955).

Erskine, Hazel, "The Polls: Women's Role," *Public Opinion Quarterly* 35 (Summer 1971), 275-290.

Fyes, Eva, *Patriarchal Attitudes* (New York: Stein and Day, 1970).

Githens, Marianne and Jewel L. Prestage, eds., *A Portrait of Marginality* (New York: David McKay Co., 1977).

Gornick, Vivian, and Barbara K. Moran, eds., *Women in Sexist Society: Studies in Power and Powerlessness* (New York: Basic Books, 1971).

Greenstein, Fred I., "Sex Related Political Differences in Childhood," *Journal of Politics* 23 (May 1961), 353-371.

Gruberg, Martin, *Women in American Politics* (Oshkosh, Wisconsin: Academia Press, 1968).

Harris, Louis and Associates, *The 1972 Virginia Slims American Women's Public Opinion Poll* (New York: Louis Harris Associates, n.d.).

Iglitzen, Lynn B., "The Making of the Apolitical Woman: Femininity and Sex-Stereotyping in Girls," in Jane S. Jaquette, ed., *Women in Politics* (New York: John Wiley, 1974), pp. 25-36.

————, "Political Education and Sexual Liberation," *Politics and Society* 2 (Winter 1972), 241-254.

Jaquette, Jane S., ed., *Women in Politics* (New York: John Wiley, 1974).

Krauss, Wilma Rule, "Political Implications of Gender Roles: A Review of the Literature," *American Political Science Review* 68 (December 1974), 1706-1723.

Lansing, Marjorie, "The American Woman: Voter and Activist," in Jane S. Jaquette, ed., *Women in Politics* (New York: John Wiley, 1974), pp. 5-24.

Lynn, Naomi B., "Women in American Politics: An Overview," in Jo Freeman, ed., *Women: A Feminist Perspective* (Palo Alto, California: Mayfield, 1975).

Lynn, Naomi B., Ann Matasar, and Marie Rosenberg, *Research Guide in Women's Studies* (Morristown, N.J. : General Learning Press, 1974).

Mead, Margaret and Frances B. Kaplan, eds., *American Women: Report of the President's Commission on the Status of Women and Other Publications of the Commission* (New York: Charles Scribners', 1965).

Mezey, Susan Glick, "Does Sex Make a Difference? A Case Study of Women in Politics," *Western Political Quarterly* 31 (December 1978), 492-501.

Millett, Kate, *Sexual Politics,* New York: Doubleday, 1970. Reprint New York: Avon Books, 1971.

Orun, Anthony, et al., "Sex, Socialization and Politics," *American Sociological Review* 39 (April 1974), 197-209.

Pierce, John C. et al., "Sex Differences in Black Political Beliefs and

Behavior," *American Journal of Political Science* 17 (May 1973), 422-430.

Potter, David, "American Women and American Character," in J. Hogue, ed., *American Character and Culture* (De Land, Florida: Everett, 1964).

Rossi, Alice, "Equality Between the Sexes: An Immodest Proposal," *Daedalus* 93 (Spring 1964), 607-652.

Steinem, Gloria, "Women Voters Can't Be Trusted," *Ms.* 1 (June 1972), 47-51.

Women in Politics

Allen, Florence E., "Participation of Women in Government," *The Annals* 251 (May 1947), 94-103.

Bullock, Charles S. III, and Patricia Lee Findley Heys, "Recruitment of Women for Congress: A Research Note," *Western Political Quarterly* 25 (September 1972), 416-423.

Chamberlin, Hope, *A Minority of Members: Women in the United States Congress* (New York: New American Library, Mentor, 1973).

Chisholm, Shirley, *Unbought and Unbossed* (Boston: Houghton-Mifflin, 1970).

Colon, Frank T., "The Elected Woman," *Social Studies* 58 (November 1967), 256-261.

Conference for Women State Legislators, *Women State Legislators: Report from a Conference for Women in Political Life,* Pocono Manor, Pa., 1972. Sponsored by the Center for the American Woman and Politics (New Brunswick, N.J.: Eagleton Institute of Politics, Rutgers, The State University, 1973).

Costantini, Edmond, and Kenneth A. Craik, "Women as Politicians: The Social Background, Personality and Political Careers of Female Party Leaders," *Journal of Social Issues* 28, no. 2 (1972), 217-236.

Dreifus, Claudia, "Women in Politics: An Interview with Edith Green," *Social Policy* (January/February 1972), 16-22.

Fisher, Marguerite J., "Women in Political Parties," *The Annals* 251 (May 1947), 87-93.

Jennings, M. Kent and Norman Thomas, "Men and Women in Party Elites: Social Roles and Political Resources," *Midwest Journal of Political Science* 4 (November 1968), 469-492.

Kelly, Reta May, and Mary Boutilier, *The Making of Political Women: A Study of Socialization and Role Conflict* (Chicago: Nelson-Hall, 1978).

Kirkpatrick, Jeane, *Political Woman* (New York: Basic Books, 1974).

Lamson, Peggy, *Few Are Chosen: American Women in Political Life Today* (Boston: Houghton-Mifflin, 1968).

Lash, Joseph, *Eleanor and Franklin* (New York: New American Library, 1971).

Lee, Marcia Manning, "Why So Few Women Hold Public Office: Democracy and Sexual Roles," *Political Science Quarterly* 91 (Summer 1976), 297-314.

Patrick, Catherine, "Attitudes About Women Executives in Government Positions," *Journal of Psychology* 19 (February 1944), 3-34.

Wells, Audrey Seiss, and Eleanor Cutri Smeal, "Women's Attitudes Toward Women in Politics: A Survey of Urban Registered Voters and Party Committeewomen," in Jane S. Jaquette, ed., *Women in Politics* (New York: John Wiley, 1974), pp. 54-72.

The Women's Movement

Deckard, Barbara, *The Women's Movement: Political, Sociological and Psychological Issues* (New York: Harper and Row, 1975).

Freeman, Jo, *The Politics of Women's Liberation* (New York: David McKay, 1975).

Kraditor, Aileen S., ed., *Up From the Pedestal: Selected Writings From the History of American Feminism* (New York: Quadrangle Books, 1968).

Lewis, Helen Matthews, *The Woman's Movement and the Negro Movement: Parallel Struggle for Rights* (Charlottesville: University of Virginia Press, 1949).

O'Neill, William L., *Everyone Was Brave: A History of Feminism in America* (New York: Quadrangle Books, 1969, 1971).

Rossi, Alice, "Sex Equality: The Beginning of Ideology," in Mary Lou Thompson, ed., *Voices of the New Feminism* (Boston: Beacon Press, 1971).

Thompson, Mary Lou, ed., *Voices of the New Feminism* (Boston: Beacon Press, 1971).

Whiteleather, Melvin K., ed., "Seven Polarizing Issues in America Today: ... Women's Liberation," *The Annals* 317 (September 1971), 118-139.

WOMEN IN POLITICAL THEORY

Butler, Melissa, "Early Liberal Roots of Feminism: John Locke and the Attack on Patriarchy," *American Political Science Review* 72 (March 1978), 135-150.

Christenson, Ron, "Political Theory of Male Chauvinism: J. J. Rousseau's Paradigm," *Midwest Quarterly* 13 (April 1972), 291-299.

Marx, Karl, Fredrich Engels et al., *The Woman Question* (New York: International Publishers, 1951).

Mill, John Stuart, *The Subjection of Women* (Cambridge, Mass.: Massachusetts Institute of Technology Press, 1970).

Tanenbaum, Susan, "Montesquieu and Mme. de Stael: The Woman as a Factor in Political Analysis," *Political Theory* 1 (February 1973), 92-103.

Wollstonecraft, Mary, *A Vindication of the Rights of Women,* 1792. Reprint, New York: W. W. Norton, 1967.

RELATED READINGS

Hispanics and American Indians

Brown, Dee, *Bury My Heart at Wounded Knee* (New York: Holt, Rinehart and Winston, 1970).

Castro, Tony, *Chicano Power: The Emergence of Mexican America* (New York: Saturday Review Press, 1974).

Deloria, Vine, Jr., *Behind the Trail of Broken Treaties* (New York: Delta, 1974).

De Shepro, Theresa Aragon, *Chicanismo and Mexican-American Politics* (Seattle: Centro de Estudios Chicanos, University of Washington, 1971).

Garcia, F. Chris, *Political Socialization of Chicano Children: A Comparative Study with Anglos in California Schools* (New York: Praeger, 1973).

Josephy, Alvin M., Jr., *Red Power* (New York: American Heritage Press, 1971).

May, Herbert L., *The American Indian: A Rising Ethnic Force* (New York: H. W. Wilson, 1973).

Mencarelli, James and Steve Severin, *Protest: Red, Black, Brown Experience in America* (Grand Rapids, Mich.: Eerdmans, 1975).

Pino, Frank, *Mexican Americans: A Research Bibliography* (East Lansing: Latin American Studies Center, Michigan State University, 1974).

Salteim, P. M., and R. C. Mings, "The Projected Impact of Cuban Settlement in Voting Patterns in Miami," *The Professional Geographer* 24 (May 1972), 123-131.

Schockley, John Staples, *Chicano Revolt in a Texas Town* (Notre Dame, Ind.: University of Notre Dame Press, 1974).

Steiner, Stanley, *La Raza: The Mexican Americans* (New York: Harper and Row, 1970).

Svensson, Francis, *The Ethnics in American Politics: American Indians* (Minneapolis: Burgess, 1973).

Taylor, Theodore W., *The States and Their Indian Citizens* (Washington, D.C.: U.S. Department of the Interior, Bureau of Indian Affairs, 1972).

United States Commission on Civil Rights, California Advisory Committee, *Political Participation of Mexican Americans in California: A Report to the U.S. Commission on Civil Rights* (Washington, D.C.: U.S. Government Printing Office, 1971).

Index

ABOUT THE AUTHOR

MARIA J. FALCO is Dean of the College of Arts and Sciences, Loyola University, New Orleans. She is the author of *Truth and Meaning in Political Science: An Introduction to Political Inquiry,* and editor of *Through the Looking-Glass: Epistemology and the Conduct of Political Inquiry: An Anthology.*

DATE DUE

GAYLORD · PRINTED IN U.S.A.

Library of Congress Cataloging in Publication Data

Falco, Maria J
   "Bigotry!"

   (Contributions in political science ; no. 34
   ISSN 0147-1066)
   Bibliography: p.
   Includes index.
   1. Elections — Pennsylvania — Case studies.
   2. United States. Congress. Senate — Elections —
   Case studies. 3. Sexism — United States — Case studies.
   I. Title. II. Series.
   JK1184.P4F34   329'.023'74804   79-7468
   ISBN 0-313-20726-7

Library of Congress Catalog Card Number: 79-7468
ISBN: 0-313-20726-7
ISSN: 0147-1066

First published in 1980

Greenwood Press
A division of Congressional Information Service, Inc.
51 Riverside Avenue, Westport, Connecticut 06880

Printed in the United States of America

10 9 8 7 6 5 4 3 2 1

"BIGOTRY!"

ETHNIC, MACHINE, AND SEXUAL POLITICS IN A SENATORIAL ELECTION

MARIA J. FALCO

Contributions in Political Science, Number 34

Greenwood Press
Westport, Connecticut • London, England